FOOD SECURITY
FACTS AND ISSUES

FOOD SECURITY
FACTS AND ISSUES

Edited by

N. Mukundan

M.A., M.Phil, Post-graduate
Assistant Professor
Department of Economics
Government Arts College
Karur, (Tamil Nadu)
(INDIA)

DPH

DISCOVERY PUBLISHING HOUSE PVT. LTD.
NEW DELHI-110 002

Published by:
Tilak Wasan

DISCOVERY PUBLISHING HOUSE PVT. LTD.
4383/4B, Ansari Road, Darya Ganj
New Delhi-110 002 (India)
Phone : +91-11-23279245, 43596064-65
Fax : +91-11-23253475
E-mail : discoverypublishinghouse@gmail.com
sales@discoverypublishinggroup.com
parul.wasan@gmail.com
web : www.discoverypublishinggroup.com

***First Edition:* 2014**

ISBN: 978-93-5056-419-6

Food Security: ***Facts and Issues***

Printed at:
Dynamic Printers
Delhi

THE GANDHIGRAM RURAL INSTITUTE – DEEMED UNIVERSITY
RE-ACCREDITED BY NAAC WITH 'A'GRADE
GANDHIGRAM – 624 302

Dr.N.NARAYANASAMY
REGISTRAR

Phone : (0451)2452323
E.Mail : gricc@ruraluniv.ac.in

15.11.2012

Foreword

Food security is defined as tire status of the people who have secured access to food and live without hunger, fear of hunger or starvation. In other words no one should suffer from hunger and poverty. However, inspite of increasing food productivity and production over a period of time, a sizeable segment of the population in our country are not assured of sufficient food in their day-to-day life. It is a matter of serious concern. And, if need to be viewed very seriously as it has very discernible geographic, economic and political implication both in developing and developed countries.

The data on availability of essential food items have clearly indicated that net availability of food item have declined over a period of time. For instance, the net availability cereals increased from 398.9 gram per day in 1962 to 458.7 gram in 2002; however it declined to 442.8 gram in 2007. Similarly the per capita net availability of pulses was 62.2 gram per day in 1962; it came down to 35.5 gram per day in 2007 recording a sharp decline of 45 per cent. The pattern in the availability of food grains indicates that the six decades of planned development has not yielded the desired result of ensuring sustainable food grains availability either through its production and pricing policy or through its initiative launched towards fair distribution of food grains to the vulnerable section of the population in the country. If therefore, obviously implies that a large section of the population is exposed to hunger and malnutrition. It is against this backdrop the Post-graduate Department of Economics, Government Arts College, an autonomous college in Karur in Tamil Nadu has organized a Seminar on *"Food Security: Facts and Issues"* sponsored by University Grants Commission, New Delhi. The seminar is quit timely and meaningful.

The outcome of the seminar has been edited and brought out as a book under the title *"Food Security: Facts and Issues"*. The book has opened up various issues for discussion among the researcher, policy-makers, development catalysts and other concerned and would definitely help in providing pragmatic solution to the issues related to food security.

I appreciate the sincere efforts made by Sri. N. Mukundan, Assistant Professor of Economics and his colleagues in the Department of Economics, Government Arts College in Karur in organizing the seminar and in bringing out a valuable volume on Food Security.

I sincerely believe that this edited volume will be of immense use to the students, researchers, teachers, policy-makers and other concerned with the theme of food security.

N. N 15.11.12

(N.NARAYANASAMY)

Acknowledgements

The first State Level UGC seminar on "Food Security in Tamil Nadu: Issues and Challenges" organized by the P.G. Department of Economics of our college is a historical occasion. It provides an opportunity and paves way for thought provoking discussions and intellectual interaction of the researchers, social scientists, rural development experts, economists and NGOs, on a single platform to exchange their knowledge and ideas. The main objective of the seminar is to activate the thinking process of the academicians about the current burning issues of food security. In this connection, a seminar on food security can provide an opportunity to create a forum to deliberate and discuss among researchers, social scientists, rural development experts, economists and NGOs, on a single platform to highlight the significance of food security from national point of view. Therefore, it is felt important to identify and delineate areas for further research which would strengthen the public distribution system.

I express my thanks profusely to Dr. S. Neelakantan, former Director, Madras Institute of Development Studies, Chennai, and Prof. and Head (Retd.) Department of Economics, Bharathidasan University, Tiruchy, for delivering the inaugural address and Prof. G. Gnanasekaran, Head, Department of Economics, St. Joseph College (Autonomous) Tiruchy, for delivering the valedictory address.

I express my deep sense of gratitude to Dr. N. Narayanasamy, Registrar, Gandhigram Rural Institute (Deemed University) for writing a foreword to this book.

I take this opportunity and privilege to thank Prof. M. Sellamuthu, Principal in-charge, Government Arts College (Autonomous), Karur who has been a constant source of inspiration for me. I am also much thankful to Heads of the various departments, staff members and non-teaching staff for making the seminar an enviable one.

At this juncture, I wish to thank the strong moral support rendered by the Executive Chairman, office bearers and beloved member friends of the Association of Economists of Tamil Nadu for the benefit of the seminar.

My heartfelt thanks are also due to Smt. N. Indirani, my beloved mother for her blessings and Mrs. M. Vijayalakshmi, my beloved wife for her understanding and for freeing me from all household responsibilities in order to concentrate successfully on this book and give a good completion to it. I also thank my daughters M. Krubashini and M. Thanushini who allowed me to work and also refreshed me at regular intervals with playfulness without getting tired. This safe home scaffolding has enabled me to complete the stupendous task without tiredness. The list is too long to be paraded here, although I wish to spell out some names only. In no way it detracts my grateful thanks to others whom I elect to keep anonymous.

Finally, on behalf of the Department of Economics, I would like to place on record our sincere gratitude to the University Grants Commission, New Delhi which sponsored the seminar. My sincere thanks to Messers Discovery Publishing House Pvt. Ltd., New Delhi for accepting to publish the book in time.

Above all, I thank God for his unmerited grace and genuine guidance all through the embryo, development and delivery stages of this intellectual work.

N. Mukundan

Contents

List of Contributors

Dr. N. Radhakrishnan, Assistant Professor, PG and Research Department of Economics, Muthurangam Government Arts College (Autonomous) Vellore, Tamil Nadu.

Dr. M. Soundara Pandian, Professor, Department of Rural Industries and Management, Gandigram, Rural Institute, Gandhigram, Tamil Nadu.

Dr. C. Dhandapani, Associate Professor and Head i\c Department of Economics Thiruvalluvar University, Searkad, Vellore, Tamil Nadu.

Dr. K. Joseph Raj, Assistant Professor of Economics, S.T. Hindu College, Nagercoil, Tamil Nadu.

Dr. Indhumathi, Associate Professor and Head, PG Department of Economics, Government Arts College, (Autonomous) Karur, Tamil Nadu.

Dr. S.Lourdu Initha, Associate Professor, Department of Commerce, S.I.V.E.T College, Chennai, Tamil Nadu.

Dr. (Mrs) S. Muthunagai, Assistant Professor, Department of Geography, Queen Mary's College (Autonomous), Chennai, Tamil Nadu.

Dr. K. Manikandan, Assistant Professor, Department of Economics, Gandhigram Rural, Institute, Gandhigram, Tamil Nadu.

Dr. P. Veerasamy, Assistant Professor, Department of Economics, Annamalai University, Annamalai Nagar, TN.

Dr. S. Ponnarasu, Assistant Professor, PG and Research Department of Economics, Gobi Arts And Science College, (Autonomous) Gobichettipalayam, Tamil Nadu.

Dr. S. Thamilarasan, Assistant Professor, Department of Economics, Annamalai University, Economics Wing DDE, Annamalai University, Annamalai Nagar, Tamil Nadu.

Dr. R. Velu Raj, Assistant Professor and Head, Department of Co-operative Management, Rajiv Gandhi Arts and Science College, Puducherry.

Dr. A.M. Ayyothi, Assistant Professor, Department of Economics, Government Arts College, Tiruvannamalai.

Dr. Velu Suresh Kumar, Assistant Professor, PG and Research Department of Economics, H.H. The Rajah's College (Autonomous), Pudukkottai, Tamil Nadu.

Dr. V.J.R. Emerlson Moses, Assistant Professor, PG and Research Department of Economics, Muthurangam Government Arts College (Autonomous), Vellore, Tamil Nadu.

Dr. A. Joseph Xavier, Assistant Professor, Department of Commerce, Ayya Nadar Janaki Ammal College, Sivakasi, Tamil Nadu.

Dr. A. Kalaiselvi, Assistant Professor, Department of Economics, Government Arts College for Women (Autonomous) Pudukkottai, Tamil Nadu.

Dr. R.Kunjammal, Assistant Professor, Department of Economics, Government Arts College for Women (Autonomous) Pudukkottai, Tamil Nadu.

T. Thamizhvanan, Assistant Professor, PG and Research Department of Economics, Government Arts College (Autonomous), Kumbakonam, Tamil Nadu.

S. Sivasankaran, Assistant Professor, PG Department of History, Government Arts College (Autonomous), Karur, Tamil Nadu.

M. Samithurai, Assistant Professor, PG and Research Department of Economics, AVC College (Autonomous), Mannampandal. Tamil Nadu.

R. Geetha, Assistant Professor, Department of Geography, Queen Mary's College (Autonomous), Chennai, Tamil Nadu.

C. Sivakozhundu, Assistant Professor, Department of Economics, Thiruvalluvar University, Serkkadu, Vellore, Tamil Nadu.

R. Poorani, Assistant Professor, Department of Economics Government Arts College for Women (Autonomous) Pudukkottai, Tamil Nadu.

G. Kumar, Assistant Professor, Department of Economics, Annamalai University, Economics Wing DDE, Annamalai University, Annamalai Nagar, Tamil Nadu.

G. Mallika, Assistant Professor, Department of Commerce, Arulmigu Kalasalingam College of Arts and Science, Krishnakoil, Tamil Nadu.

P. Srinivasan, Assistant Professor and Head, Department of Hotel Management and Catering Science, Sri Kaliswari College, Sivakasi, Tamil Nadu.

S.Vijayalalitha, Assistant Professor, Department of Geography, Queen Mary's College (Autonomous), Chennai, Tamil Nadu.

G. Geetha, Assistant Professor, Department of Geography, Queen Mary's College (Autonomous), Chennai, Tamil Nadu.

A. Sulthan Mohideen, Assistant Professor, Department of Commerce, H.K.R.H. College, Uthamapalayam, Tamil Nadu.

S. Govindan, Ph.D Research Scholar Department of Economics, Thiruvalluvar University Searkad, Vellore, Tamil Nadu.

S. Suganthi, Research Scholar, Department of Economics, Gandhigram Rural, Institute, Gandhigram, Tamil Nadu.

A. Saltheen, Full-time Ph.D Research Scholar, Department of Rural Industries and Management, Gandhigram Rural, Institute, Gandhigram, Tamil Nadu.

S. Mahima, Full-time Ph.D Research Scholar, Department of Economics, Avinashilingam-Deemed University for Women, Coimbatore, Tamil Nadu.

M. Nandhakumar, M.Phil Research Scholar, Department of Economics, Bharathiar University, Coimbatore, Tamil Nadu.

P. Matheswaran, M.Phil Scholar, PG and Research Department of Economics, Gobi Arts And Science College, (Autonomous) Gobichettipalayam, Tamil Nadu.

D. Ramachandran, M.Phil Scholar, PG and Research Department of Economics, Muthurangam Government Arts College (Autonomous), Vellore Tamil Nadu.

K. Nagendiran, M.Phil Research Scholar, Department of Economics, Thiruvaliuvar University, Serkkadu, Vellore 612106.

M. Vadivel, PhD Scholar, Department of Economics, Gobi Arts and Science College, Gobichettipalayam, Tamil Nadu.

Dr. S. Ponnarasu, Assistant Professor, Department of Economics, Gobi Arts and Science College, Gobichettipalayam, Tamil Nadu.

1

Food Security
An Approach Paper

N. Mukundan

INTRODUCTION

The concern of food-vulnerable society relationship is very important a prerequisite for a hunger-free India. India is still home to the largest number of under-nourished and malnourished children and women. In spite of various social interventions the situations have not improved. Food security is undoubtedly a major concern and top priority for the government today. Over the various Five-year Plan periods we have been working towards increasing agricultural production on one hand, and developing an efficient mechanism for reaching food to every needy person in the most inaccessible of conditions, on the other. Therefore, the elimination of hunger improved food production is the cornerstone of food security. World Bank Development Report (1986) defined food security as "access by all people at all time to enough food for an active, healthy life". Food Agriculture Organization (FAO 1983) defined food security as "ensuring that all people at all time have both physical and economic access to basic food they need". Once India being labeled as a nation surviving on a ship-to-mouth basis But at present the situation is overcome. The record production of wheat and rice in 2011-12. It is touch to high 250.42 million tonnes, surpassing last year's best of 244.78 million tonnes.

Despite of the availability of food grains for meeting the requirements of the entire population we are still far from generation the necessary purchasing power or effective demand from the poor to satisfy their needs. Since, effective food security implies achievement of both physical and economic access to food, a large sector of our population can still be considered to be suffering from food insecurity despite the bulging stocks of food grains with food corporation of India.

Facts and Issues of Food Security

Malnutrition

"The concept of 'food security implies' a situation that exists when all people, at all time, have physical, social and economic access to sufficient, sage and nutrition's food that meets their dietary needs and food preferences for an active and healthy line" (FAO 2002). Food and Agricultural Organization statistical picture clearly stated that there are 22 countries, 16 of which are in Africa, in which the undernourishment prevalence rate is over 35 per cent. The World Summit on Food Security took place in Rome, Itlay (2009) pointed out that 60 per cent of the world's under nourished people live in Asia and a quarter in Africa. 48 per cent of our children undernourished (Hunger and Malnutrition Report, 2012). The statement of Prime Minister Manmohan Singh that it was national shame. India is still home to the largest number of under-nourished and malnourished children and women. The above survey stated that the prevalence of malnutrition is significantly higher among children from low-income families. Birth weight is an important risk-factor for child malnutrition. The prevalence of under-weight in children born with a weight below 2.5 kg is 50 per cent. While that among children born with a weight above 2.5 kg is 34 per cent. Between 1990-91 and 1991-97, the annual rate of growth of food grains was only 1.7 per cent which is lower than the current population growth of 1.9 per cent. The availability of food grains is only 182 kg per year as against the nutritional norm of 300 kg per year on per capita basis. Moreover, availability of pulses is only 34 grams per day against the norm of 47 grams fixed by the Indian Council of Medical Research and much below the 80 grams per day fixed by the World Health Organization compounding the fragile food situation in the country. There fore the need of the hour to the tackling large scale malnutrition.

The Right to Food

To make food-for-all a legal right. It is not only a basic human right, it is also a basic human need. It is the right of every man, woman or child to have physical and economic access at all time to adequate food or means for its procurement in ways consistent with human dignity and honour. Gandhiji rightly pointed out that the elimination of hunger free India should involve opportunities for everyone to earn their daily bread, since the process of ending hunger should not lead to the erosion of human dignity. To fulfil the right to food means that the government must facilitate the right to food by providing the environment for the people to be able to feed themselves and or provide the needed support where people cannot feed themselves for reasons beyond their control through various social safety net programmes, food for education programme, food for work, community grain banks, etc). Collaboration between public and private sectors is also important for achieving durable food security, poverty alleviation and the right to food. Ensuring that every man, woman or child gets adequate food, health care and education is not only a moral imperative but is a national investment with high economic returns with which the country stands to benefit in the long range. A noted agriculture scientist rightly pointed out that the brightest jewel in the crown of Indian democracy will be the conferment of the right to food through the National Food Security Bill, (it was recently introduced in Parliament) when it is implemented, Gandhiji 's dream of a hunger-free India into reality. It is stature of social protection programmed against hunger in human history. The National Food Security Bill, 2001 provides the last chances to launch a frontal attack on poverty-induced hunger and to realize Mahatma Gandhi's desire that the God of Bread should be present in every home and hut in India (M.S. Swaminathan, 2011).

Poverty

A good economics that concentrates on the even distribution of economic opportunities and benefits is essential. Further, the economic success depends on the hunger-free India. The Millennium Goals call for halving of hunger–poverty between 1990 and 2015 it is well documented that most poor families in the world spend 80 per cent of their total income on food grains. Further, people often fail to eat enough food only because they do not have sufficient purchasing power. In a poor developing country, the incidence of poverty is very closely linked to the availability of food, in which the staple food grains still remain predominant, accounting for two-thirds of the daily energy intake of the population. The measurement of poverty in India has traditionally adopted a nutritional norm specified in terms of an average daily energy intake measured in calories. According to recent estimates, approximately 36 per cent of the Indian population lives below the poverty line. This means their income is not sufficient to buy enough food. About 70 per cent of these poor people live in rural areas. Though both central and state governments have formulated and implemented various schemes to alleviate poverty or improve the social security of the most deprived sections. The World Commission on Environment and Development (WCED) stated that the major problems of human society is population, food supply, energy, industry and urban agglomerations. Further, the report clearly reveals that security cannot merely political and military but it must be ecological, economic and social as well as food security *i.e.,* the ability of obtain sufficient food to meet the needs of all citizens. The Committee on World Food Security views it as the physical and economic access to adequate food for all household members without undue risk of losing such access. Planning Commission views it as the eradication of hunger and starvation by ensuring availability, accessibility and affordability of balanced food and nutrition to all people of the country specially the underprivileged. India today has over 65 million tonnes of wheat and rice in government stocks;

downs; yet poverty induced hunger affects over 200 million persons. Schemes Such as *Antyodaya Anna Yojana, Annapoorna,* and *Sampoorna Gram Rozgar Yojana* are good in concept but weak in implementation. So, the future crisis on the food front is likely emanate not only from not being able to meet the increased demand; but also on the distribution front, in terms of equitable distribution of food grains production from economic growth. The starvation deaths staring in some parts of India, therefore, are not entirely the outcome of the short fall in production, but more a result of inefficient distribution and inaccessibility or what Amartya Sen calls it "entitlement failure".

Agriculture Crisis

At present the prospects of agriculture turning hopeless situation in Cauvery delta region. The research study clearly shows that the kuruvai cropping area has come down to 67.63 per cent and the yield by 24.19 per cent . In addition the agriculture has projected the figure for Samba and Thaladi crops. The area sown for Samba had come down by 14.25 per cent and Thaladi by 64.50 per cent respectively. The expected yield will also come down by 65.79 per cent and 31.96 per cent respectively. This will affect the total food production of the State of Tamil Nadu and the individual farm household. Studies by and large have confirmed that the present agrarian crisis has started after the introduction of economic reforms in India. As it is evident that decline in public investment in agriculture would also affect the private sector investment in agriculture, which would finally affect growth in agriculture (Vaidyanathan, 2006).

Changing Food Consumption Pattern in India

The dietary mix, and its flavour, is rapidly changing in the Indian consumes. The sustained economic growth (over 8% per annum) and rise in per capita income (3.5% 4% per annum) have gradually diversified the basket in favour of high-value foods, such as fruits, vegetables, milk, meat, eggs, etc., and as per the estimates of the National Sample Survey data, the per capita consumption of cereals for the people below poverty line declined by 10 per cent over the period 1983 to 1999-2000. But their consumption of milk increased by 30 per cent vegetables by 5 per cent of fruits by 63 per cent, and of meat, eggs and fish by 10 per cent the same period. This change is also reflected in the rapidly rising exports of high value agriculture, during the last two decades. Despite coming up from a low base, these percentages reflect a surge towards increased consumption and export of high value agro-products.

To achieve food security, emphasis is to be laid on improved agricultural production but it is a multifaceted problem, therefore multi-pronged strategies is need of the hour. Gandhiji started way back in 1929 that sever our village is to establish *Swaraj*, everything else is but an idle dream. Since, India opened up its agricultural sector to trade. There has been a market reduction in the growth of food grains output. It could be noted that food grains output in the year 2000-02 was about 196 million tonnes, it rose to 211 million tonnes in 2002-03. But unfortunately in India about 200 millions do not have access to regular and adequate quantities of food. Hunger, malnutrition and under nourishment are widespread. It could be noted that many parts of rural India death due to starvation is still prevalent. In this situation how can India ensure sustainable food security for a billion. Unless more sustainable food security is introduced none will succeed in the long-term.

Policy Suggestions

- High growth in rural employment in rural areas *i.e.,* implementation of food for work programmes effectively.
- Need for Public investment in agriculture research.
- Effective implementation of targeted distribution of food grains.
- To motivate the farmers diversification of cropping pattern.

REFERENCES

Anton Son-Ogle, Brita, Olle Gustafson, Lef Holmgre and Thorkild Tylleskar, '*Nutrition, Agriculture and Health When Resources are Scare*'. Swedish University of Agricultural Sciences, Uppsala University, 1996.

James, Philip., '*Ending Malnutrition by 2020 An Agenda for Change in the Millennium*', Final Report to the ACC/SCN by the Commission on the Nutrition Challenges of the 21st Century, 2000.

Jaysheela and Vishwanatha, 'Food Security in India: Issues and Challenges' in Falendra K. Sudan (Ed.,) *India Economic Development*, Serials Publication, New Delhi, 2006.

King, Elizabeth M. and Andrew D, Mason, '*Engendering Development through Gender Equality in Rights, Resources and Voice*', A World Bank Policy Research Report. New York: Oxford University Press, 2001.

Narayan, Deepa, Robert Chambers, Meera Kaul Shah and Patti Petesch '*Voices of the Poor Crying out for Change*'. New York: Oxford University Press for the World Bank, 2000.

Ramesh Babu., 'Rur*al Women And Environmental Development*' Kisan World No. 7, Vol. 21, July, 1994.

Rai, D.K. and B. Rai, 'Food Security: Challenges and Opportunities'; *Kisan World*, Vol. 34, No. 7, July 2007.

Rai, B, 'Food Security and the Right to Food' *Kisan World*, Vol. 35 No. 6, June 2008.

Sundar. I, 'Food Security and Sustainable Livelihood'; *Kisan World*, Vol. 31, August 2004.

Swaminathan, M.S., *To the Hungry, God is Bread*, The Hindu, Oct. 1 2011.

Shivay, Yashbir Singh and Dinesh Kumar, 'Crop Diversification and Change in Food Habits of Rural India'; *Kurukshetra* Vol. 55, No. 12, Oct. 2007.

Tripathy. K.K, 'Food Security and Food Management in India: A Review'; *Kurukshetra* Vol. 58, No. 8, June 2008.

Vaidyanathan., 'Has Agrarian Crisis Made any Impact on Agricultural Wages and Employment'. *Journal of Labour Economics* Vol. 49, No. 4, Oct. Dec. 2006.

2

Globalisation and Food Security in India
Issues and Challenges

N. Radhakrishnan

INTRODUCTION

The performance of agriculture is important for availability and a access to food as more than 55 per cent people in the country are dependent on this sector. The performance of the overall agriculture sector and the factors responsible for the slowdown provide an explanation for the decline in the growth of food production. It may be noted that food grains, pulses, oilseeds, sugar fruits and vegetables, poultry, dairy, meat, fish, etc., constitute the bulk of the output in the agriculture sector.

Ensuring food security ought to be an issue of great importance for a country like India where more than one-third of the population is estimated to be absolutely poor and one-half of all children malnourished in one way or another. There have been many emerging issues in the context of food security in India in the last two decades. These are:

(i) economic liberalization in the 1990s and its impact on agriculture and food security;

(ii) establishment of WTO, particularly the Agreement on Agriculture (AoA) under it;

(iii) challenges of climate change; crisis of the three Fs, *viz.*, food prices, fuel prices, and financial crisis;

(*iv*) the phenomenon of hunger amidst plenty, *i.e.*, accumulation of stocks in the early years of this decade and in 2008-09 along with high levels of poverty;

(*v*) introduction of targeting in the Public Distribution System (PDS) for the first time in the 1990s;

(*vi*) 'Right to Food' campaign for improving food security in the country and the Supreme Court Orders on mid-day meal schemes;

(*vii*) proposal for National Food Security Law (Right to Food); and

(*viii*) monitorable targets under the Tenth and Eleventh Five-year Plans similar to the Millennium Development Goals (MDGs) on poverty and women and child nutrition.

These developments in the past two decades have provided both opportunities and challenges for food and nutrition security of the country.

Health and economic development are inter-related. India is home for 19 per cent of world's children has the largest number of children in the world. India has 414 million children under three years of age in malnourished. Nearly 1.8 million infants die each year. Thirty-four per cent of the children are under-weight.

In spite of the best effort taken by the government to help the poor children, the nutritional status is very poor, the reason being the socio-economic environment in which they live. The parents of the poor children living in poor conditions could not afford to provide them with good food. They were also in the habit of sending them for labour work in hostels, household activities, etc.

Food availability is a necessary condition for food security. India is more or less self sufficient in cereals but deficit in pulses and oilseeds. Due to changes in consumption patterns, demand for fruits, vegetables, dairy, meat, poultry, and fisheries has been increasing. There is need to increase crop diversification and improve allied activities. It may be noted that the slowdown in agriculture growth could be attributed to structural factors on the supply side, such as public investment, credit, technology, land and water management, etc., rather than globalisation and trade reforms per se. Access to food can be increased through employment due to growth in labour intensive sectors and/or through social protection programmes. The malnutrition problem is much broader than that of access to food.

This chapter examines the issues and challenges of food security in the context of globalisation.

Concept of Food Security

The United Nations defines food security as all people at all times having both physical and economic access to the basic food they need. For approximately two billion people throughout the world, this security is anything but guaranteed. Food security is a complicated issue that is susceptible to many forces.

World Development Report (1986) defined food security "access by all people at all times to enough food for an active, healthy life". Food and Agriculture Organization (FAO, 1983) defined food security as "ensuring that all people at all times have both physical and economic access to basic food they need.

Staatz (1990) defined food security as "the ability to assure, on a long-term basis, that the food system provides the total population access to a timely, reliable and nutritionally adequate supply of food.

Problems of Food Security in India

The problem of food security in India is currently one of acquiescence, as a sizable share of the population lacks economic and physical access to sufficient food. Poverty in India is falling but concerns over food security are increasing. With a network of more than 4.62 lakh fair price shops, Public Distribution System (PDS) is perhaps the largest distribution machinery of its type in the world through which Government of India ensures food security at the micro-level. Each year PDS is said to distribute commodities worth more than Rs. 30,000 crore to about 160 million families. However, doubts have been raised about the efficacy and cost-effectiveness of the PDS, especially in the light of the growing food inflation, food subsidy, food stocks and food insecurity. The problem facing the country today is not one of shortage of food grains but of managing the surplus. Therefore, there is a need to explore the possibility of introducing innovative ideas to eliminate hunger and make food available to the poor at an affordable and sustainable basis.

India has witnessed high economic growth in the past one decade, but the problem of food and nutrition insecurity still remains a great threat to a large number of poor and vulnerable people in the country. According to the FAO report the stark reality is that India has 29 per cent of the 872.9 million under-nourished people in the world. WHO reports that 49 per cent of the world's underweight children, 34 per cent of the world's stunted children and over 46 per cent of world's under-nourished children live in India. Further, 456 million people (about 42%) of the population in India are below the new international poverty line (*i.e.*, earning less than $1.25 per day) and India is ranked at 67, way below neighbouring countries like China (Ranked 9) and Pakistan (Ranked 52), in 2010 Global Hunger Index prepared by International Food Policy and Research institute (IFPRI). So what it all means is that achievement of food security at the national level has not percolated down to the level of individual household and thus has not resulted in food and nutritional security.

Economists and agricultural specialists have predicted that even if with the intervention of technology and policy measures the food security situation in India is expected to be worse in the coming years. The food demand will be driven by income, population growth, urbanization, and income distribution at a faster rate. But supply will lag behind the increased demand and there will be supply demand gap of food grains in the upcoming years particularly 2025 to 2050 which will worsen the scenario of food grain availability and food security in India.

A large percentage of households in the country are not in a position to raise its food expenditure to neutralize the effect of inflation. This is surely going to aggravate food and nutrition deficiency in the country. This indicates concern over food insecurity and ineffectiveness of Targeted Public Distribution System [TPDS].

Globalisation and Indian Agriculture

The issues of farmer's suicide become global issue and concern despite that different governments across the globe denied the farmers suicide but slowly accepted the deaths and started to understand the stress of farmers. Globalisation is pushing the farmers to the final edge and there exists sufficient powerful evidence across the globe that suicides are the consequences of indebtedness. Despite occurrence of good monsoons during the last couple of years, the farmers suicide continue to take place in one or the other State in India after globalisation.

The living styles of agricultures in America and Europe is quite astonishable. Their agricultural practice generally goes not involve heavy application of latest technology and do not follow even modern agriculture. Economic Co-operation and Development Association (ECDA) is taking care of agriculturists. The Governments declare subsidy and direct income assistance to all agriculturists. The comparison of Indian agriculturist with either America or Europe reveals shocking trends which are model to follow even in all developing countries including India. The agriculturists in India are worst suffers and constantly different ideological.

Suicide is the new technique followed by the farmers. In the last 14 years 1997-2010 there have been nearly unimaginable whopping of 2 lakhs farmers commit suicide in the country and a disturbing 67 per cent of those belongs to just 5 States, Karnataka, Andhra Pradesh, Maharashtra, Madhya Pradesh and Chattisgarh, which are popularly termed as "suicidal belt" areas. The crisis now is not only manifested in the increasing suicide but also in other forms such as throwing the produce on the roads, demand to delink from the global market, demand to come out of WTO etc. Before the farming community is pushed to final edge their worry, concern should be properly addressed in the interest of farming community in particular and agriculture in general.

Challenges in Indian Agriculture Sector

Focusing on the challenges of agriculture in the context of the WTO, it is said that Trade liberalization, was anticipated to provide very attractive growth avenues for growth of agricultural exports. Those who strongly favored liberalization and free trade argue that increase in imports should not be a cause for concern as exports fetch much higher gain than what is paid through imports. This argument is further used to make a case for achieving food security through self reliance rather than self sufficiency. This is based on the premise that liberalization of trade would help in much higher increase in exports than in imports and also help in improving efficiency in allocation of resources. Based on this logic, net trade is an indicator of self reliance. Thus, agriculture is passing through many challenges and the following are some of the important issues:

1. Rising cost of agricultural production couple with declining total factor productivity.
2. Low, oscillating and more or less stagnated yield levels of major commodities couple with high yield gaps.
3. Widening disparities among irrigated and un-irrigated tracts.
4. Regional imbalances in agricultural production.
5. Decline or stagnation in public capital formation.
6. Low competitiveness of Indian agriculture in the context of globalisation and the WTO.
7. Sluggish, imbalanced and eroded agricultural research, education, extension and training.

Agricultural Production in India

Attainment of self-sufficiency in food grains at the national level is one of the country's major achievements in the post-independence period. After remaining a food deficit country for about two decades after independence, India became largely self-sufficient in food grain production at the macro level. There have hardly been any food grain imports after the mid-1970s. Food grain production in the country increased from about 50 million tonnes in 1950-51 to around 233.9 million tonnes in 2008-09. The growth rate of food grains has been around 2.5 per cent per annum between 1951 and 2006-07. The production of oilseeds, cotton, sugarcane, fruits, vegetables, and milk has also increased appreciably.

Table 2.1: Trend and Growth Rates of Agricultural Production in India

(% per annum)

Crop Groups/ crops	Production		Yields	
	1986-87 to 1996-97	1996-97 to 2007-08	1986-87 to 1996-97	1996-97 to 2007-08
Foodgrains	2.93	0.93	3.21	1.04
Cereals	3.06	0.97	3.36	1.19
Coarse Cereals	1.19	1.53	3.66	2.25
Pulses	1.32	0.36	1.49	-0.02
Oilseeds	6.72	1.99	3.32	1.49
Rice	3.06	1.02	2.37	1.22
Wheat	4.09	0.65	2.93	0.34

Source: CAC, Ministry of Agriculture (2009).

The experience of the past two decades shows that growth rates of production and yield have declined for crop groups/crops during the period 1996-2008 as compared to the period 1986-97 (Table 2.1). The growth rate of food grain production declined from 2.93 per cent to 0.93 per cent during the same period. The growth rate of production was much lower than that of population in the latter period. Similarly, growth rate of yields of food grains declined from 3.21 per cent to 1.04 per cent. There was also a decline in growth rates of production and yields for cereals, pulses, rice and wheat.

Per Capita Availability of Food Grains in India

The net availability of food grains is estimated at 87.5 per cent of gross production. In order to obtain the figure for net availability of foodgrains, figures for requirement for seeds, farm animal feed, and waste are deducted from gross production and net imports are added, apart from adjustments for changes in government stocks. Here we are assuming that there is no net change in private stocks.

Table 2.2: Net Availability of Cereals and Pulses

Year	Per Capita net Availability per day (grams)			Edible Oil (kg.)	Vanaspati (kg.)	Sugar (Nov-Oct.) (kg.)
	Cereals	Pulses	Total Food Grains			
1951	334.2	60.7	394.9	2.5	0.7	5.0
1961	399.7	69.0	468.7	3.2	0.8	4.8
1971	417.6	51.2	468.8	3.5	1.0	7.4
1981	417.3	37.5	454.8	3.8	1.2	7.3
1990	435.3	41.1	476.4	5.3	1.1	12.3
1991	468.5	41.6	510.1	5.5	1.0	12.7
1992	435.5	34.3	468.8	5.4	1.0	13.0
1993	427.9	36.2	464.1	5.8	1.0	13.7
1994	434.0	37.2	471.2	6.1	1.0	12.5
1995	457.6	37.8	495.4	6.3	1.0	13.2
1996	442.5	32.7	475.2	7.0	1.0	14.1
1997	466.0	37.1	503.1	8.0	1.0	14.6
1998	414.2	32.8	447.0	6.2	1.0	14.5
1999	429.2	36.5	465.7	8.5	1.3	14.9
2000	422.7	31.8	454.4	9.0	1.4	15.6
2001	386.2	30.0	416.2	8.2	1.3	15.8
2002	458.1	35.4	494.1	8.8	1.4	16.0
2003	408.5	29.1	437.6	7.2	1.4	16.3
2004	426.9	35.8	162.7	N.A.	N.A.	N.A.
2005	390.9	31.5	422.4	N.A.	N.A.	N.A.
2006	412.8	32.5	445.3	N.A.	N.A.	N.A.
2007	407.4	35.5	442.8	N.A.	N.A.	N.A.

Source: Economic Survey 2008-2009, Government of India.

Per capita net availability of foodgrains increased by about 10 per cent over the last 56 years, between 1951 and 2007 (Table 2.2). However, net availability declined if we compare 1961 (469 grams per day) with 2007 (443 grams). In other words, significant increase in foodgrains has not been able to keep pace with the increase in population. In the year 2007, per capita availability of foodgrains was only 443 grams, much lower than 501 grams in 1991. During the period 1951 to 2007, per capita availability of pulses has declined.

Demand and Supply Projections of Food up to 2020

There have been many studies on demand and supply projections. Mittal (2006) projected demand for rice at 84.2 million tones for 2011, 96.4 million tones for 2021, and 101.5 million tonnes for 2026. The corresponding supply projections are 95.7, 105.8, and 111.2 million tonnes respectively, envisaging a surplus of 11.46, 9.38, and 9.73 million tones respectively. Mittal's projections for wheat demand are 59.8, 66.1, and 68.1 million tonnes for the above mentioned years as compared to the supply projections of 80.2, 91.6, and 97.9 million tonnes indicating surpluses of 20.41, 25.53, and 29.84 million tonnes for 2011, 2021, and 2026 respectively. For total cereals, the projected surpluses are 27.59, 12.76, and 4.63 million tonnes.

In the case of pulses and oilseeds, the country would have to depend on imports, even by 2020. According to some projections, the household demand for milk and milk products would increase from 64 million tonnes in 2000 to 166 million in 2020, and fruits and vegetables from 48 million tonnes to 113 million tonnes.

Given the shifts in consumption patterns, towards non-cereal food, and even to non-food, we feel that the demand projections of the Ministry of Agriculture on food grains of around 250 million tonnes for 2020 are reasonable. There would be enough supply to meet the demand for food grains by 2020.

Table 2.3: Estimated Production and Projected Demand of Food Grains

Crop	2008-09			2011-12			2020
	Projected Demand	Estimated Production	Surplus/ Shortfall	Projected Demand	Projected Production	Surplus/ Shortfall	Projected Demand
Rice	92.87	99.15	6.28	98.79	104.21	5.42	111.9
Wheat	72.72	80.58	7.86	77.36	83.61	6.25	79.9
Coarse Cereals	35.9	39.48	3.58	38.19	35.75	-2.44	37.3
Pulses	17.51	14.66	-2.85	19.91	15.73	-4.18	23.8
Foodgrains	219.0	233.88	14.88	234.26	239.3	5.04	252.8
Sugarcane	275.9	271.25	-4.66	322.54	305.51	-17.03	—
Oilseeds	47.4	28.16	-19.27	53.39	27.53	-25.86	—

Source: Ministry of Agriculture (2009).

The implementation of National Food Security Act (2010) will provide a statutory basis for a framework which assures food security for all. According to this proposed law, every family below the poverty line in rural as well as urban will be entitled by law, to 25 kg of rice or wheat per month at Rs. 3 per kg. It is felt that the statutory guarantee to food with fixed entitlements to the poor would be an important step in the direction of ensuring food and nutritional security of the country.

Policy Suggestions

1. Future growth of agriculture has to be based on yield gains. In the present context, more food has to be produced from less land with shrinking natural resources, which is really a tough task for the farmers.
2. Agricultural research extension and training have been sluggish, despite the India Vision 2020 and greater role attached to the Indian Council of Agricultural Research. Possibilities of demand-driven (for export purposes) and location – specific research and developmental programmes may be explored vigorously.
3. All possible efforts should be taken up to bridge the gap between actual yields and the potential and if possible to the level of competing countries yields of all products to avail the opportunities.
4. Creation of an extensive network of rural infrastructure for establishing an appropriate interface of product and factor markets. This calls for increased public investment in agriculture.
5. Poverty and food insecurity is greater in rainfed and dry land areas. Small farms can be helped in increasing productivity by having access to extension services and better water management. Sustainable agriculture should be the focus of interventions.

Conclusion

India has many policies and programmes. However, food insecurity and malnutrition continue to be high. The problem is with both design and implementation of the programmes. The focus of reforms can now be shifted to more efficient delivery systems of public services. It has been recognized that better governance is very important for effective functioning of food-based programmes. Social mobilization, community participation and decentralized approach are necessary in this context. It may, however, to be noted that governance has to be contextualized in relation to the socio-economic environment. Appropriate institutions are needed for better implementation of policies and programmes. For example, rural institutions in areas like land, water, marketing of agricultural and non-agricultural products, credit, technology, and infrastructure are needed for better governance. Similarly, people-centric programmes and institutions are needed for better implementation of social protection schemes.

The consequence of the globalisation process, as far as agriculture is concerned, is that economic globalisation can be expected to encourage agricultural specialization. It may therefore eliminate mixed or environmentally balanced types of agricultural systems, as were common in Asia. It tends to encourage monocultures, for instance. Globalisation reduces diversity of genetic material used commercially in agriculture, encourages the supply of standardized produces and increases uniformity of methods used in agricultural production. In longer terms, these trends may be inimical to agricultural sustainability.

REFERENCES

Chopra and Surabhi (2009), Holding the State Accountable for Hunger, *Economic and Political Weekly*, Vol. 44, No. 33, August 15.

CLEM TISDELL (2005), Globalisation and World Economic Policy, Serials Publications, New Delhi.

Datt, Ruddar and Sundharam K.P.M. (2007), *Indian Economy*, S. Chand and Company Ltd., New Delhi.

Mahendra Dev, S. and Alakh N. Sharma (2010), *Food Security in India: Performance, Challenges and Policies*, Oxfam India Working Papers Series, New Delhi.

Radhakrishna, R. and Parikh K. (2002), *Food and Nutrition Security*, India Development Report, Oxford University Press, New Delhi.

Sukale, Vikas Vinayakro (2003), Implementation of GATT and Indian Agriculture, *Southern Economist*, Vol. 42, No. 2, May 15.

Thakur, Anil Kumar (2010), Globalisation and Its Implications for Indian Agriculture, *Southern Economist*, Vol. 49, No. 1, May 1.

The Hindu, Sunday July 3, 2011.

www.womenhealth.com

3

Food Security in India
An Overview

T. Thamizhvanan

INTRODUCTION

Ensuring food security ought to be an issue of great importance for a country like India where more than one-third of the population is estimated to be absolutely poor and one-half of all children malnourished in one way or another. There have been many emerging issues in the context of food security in India in the last two decades. These are:

(i) economic liberalization in the 1990s and its impact on agriculture and food security;

(ii) establishment of WTO, particularly the Agreement on Agriculture (AOA) under it;

(iii) challenges of climate change; crisis of the three Fs, *viz.*, food prices, fuel prices, and financial crisis;

(iv) the phenomenon of hunger amidst plenty, *i.e.*, accumulation of stocks in the early years of this decade and in 2008-09 along with high levels of poverty;

(v) introduction of targeting in the Public Distribution System (PDS) for the first time in the 1990s;

(vi) 'Right to Food' campaign for improving food security in the country and the Supreme Court Orders on mid-day meal schemes;

(vii) proposal for National Food Security Law (Right to Food); and

(viii) monitorable targets under the Tenth and Eleventh Five-year Plans similar to the Millennium Development Goals (MDGs) on poverty and women and child nutrition.

These developments in the past two decades have provided both opportunities and challenges for food and nutrition security of the country are briefly discussed.

Review of Literature

Number of studies have been done in food security in India. Important studies are detailed discussion in below. The per capita energy consumption of the lowest three details has been show to be much below the recommended norms in all states, the situation being exaggerated in the chronically food deficit states and having deteriorated over time between 1961 of 1983, reported by NSSO utilisation of the PDS shows that 44 per cent of population depend on PDS for.

The poorest states account for the smallest shares of PDS food supplies from the central government, while a disproportionately large share is allocated to relatively prospectors urban areas (Sarvekshana, 1990), (Subbarao, 1989). They have criticized to the PDS in Andhra Predesh is the loose to getting. Deposited shortages in PDS supply so that present coverage of the poorest groups in relatively small. Another problems in the fact that the scheme is socially regressive since rice is disbursed twice a month while the poor subsist from day to day (Radhakrishna and Indrakant, 1987), have show the beneficial effects of the PDS on welfare levels of the poor while also illustrating that this beneficial effect could have been much greater if targeting had been limited to the lowest 40 per cent. This level of targeting would also ensure great sustainability and cost effectiveness. Haries (1991) noted that the contained availability of food grains through the system the major factor governing access to supplies and insensitivity of the system to the needs of large households with the largest dependency ratios. Further in times of shortage, the poorest households were also the most likely to lose access to PDS supplies through the mortgage of their entitlement cards (Ravi Srivastaava, 2000). The study was carried among 2250 households across 120 villages found that multiplicities of agencies, poor coordination and low administrative accountability have combined to cripple the delivery and partial drawing of quota was substantially contributed for leakage.

According to the International Food Policy Research Institute's 2011 Global Hunger Index, the upshot of this perennial problem is that about 60 million children in India are underweight and malnourished, while 21 per cent of the population as a whole general is malnourished. Unfortunately, this problem is unlikely to change anytime soon, with the recent introduction of the National Food Security Bill threatening to continue market inefficiencies in food supply and extend the problem of malnutrition far into the future. The developmental repercussions of this situation are dramatic, not only for individuals who suffer numerous health issues resulting from malnutrition but also for the economy at large. Malnutrition results in a loss of productivity , indirect losses from impaired cognitive development, and losses from increased long-term health care costs.

According to a report by the World Bank, productivity losses in India due to stunted growth, iodine deficiencies, and iron deficiencies are equivalent to almost 3 per cent of GDP. While during the colonial era famine was the primary result of 'food insecurity,' malnutrition has replaced it as the chief concern of legislators and economists. He showed that famine was rarely the result of a lack of food, but rather the result of intervening economic factors, such as unemployment, declining wages, and, as is often the case in India, poor food distribution systems. The current problem in India is of that nature: it's not so much a lack of nutrient – rich food, but rather a weakness in the food supply chain. High prices for the consumer, as well as limited quantity and quality, all resulting from supply chain inefficiency, are sustaining increased malnutrition amongst the poor population. In developing countries, often 70 per cent or more of the population lives in rural areas. In that context, agricultural development among smallholder farmers and landless people provides a livelihood for people allowing them the opportunity to stay in their communities. In many areas of the world. Land ownership is not available, thus people who want or need to farm to make a living have little incentive to improve the land.

The number of studies has been discussed on PDS, related to food security has not been studied and measured quantitatively, present study will remove this gap and will show how for the rural population have been benefited in PDS terms of the objective of PDs.

Objectives

The objectives of the present study are:

1. To analyse the performance and challenges of food security in India,
2. To study the food security policies India, and
3. To find out the availability of food access, absorption and nutrition.

Methodology

The present Chapter is organised as policies regarding availability of food, assess to food and nutrition indicators. It is attempt to performance of challenges of food security in India based on various review of literatures. This paper are focus on secondary data in regarding to various books, reviews, Journals, Newspapers, Magazine, Reports Internet and also is used by statistical tools in the average method.

Results And Discussion

Availability of Food

Food grain production in the country increased from about 50 million tones in 1950-51 to around 233.9 million tones in 2008-09. The growth rate of food grains has been around 2.5 per cent per annum between 1951 and 2006-07. The production of oilseeds, cotton, sugarcane, fruits, vegetables, and milk has also increased appreciably. The experience of the past two decades shows that growth rates of production and yield have declined for crop groups/crops during the period 1996-2008 as compared to the period 1986-97. Table 3.1 shows that the growth rate of food grain production declined from 2.93 per cent to 0.93 per cent during the same period. The growth rate of production was much lower than that of population in the latter period. Similarly, growth rate of yields of food grains declined from 3.21 per cent to 1.04 per cent. There was also a decline in growth rates of production and yields for cereals, pulses, oilseeds, rice, and wheat.

Table 3.1: Trend Growth Rates in Production and Yields of Food Grains and Oilseeds

(% per annum)

Crop groups/ crops	Production		Yields	
	1986-87 to 1996-97	1996-97 to 2007-08	1986-87 to 1996-97	1996-97 to 2007-08
Food grains	2.93	0.93	3.21	1.04
Cereals	3.06	0.97	3.36	1.19
Coarse Cereals	1.19	1.53	3.66	2.25
Pulses	1.32	0.36	1.49	-0.02
Oilseeds	6.72	1.99	3.32	1.49
Rice	3.06	1.02	2.37	1.22
Wheat	4.09	0.65	2.93	0.34

Source: Ministry of Agriculture, 2009.

Reasons for Decline in Food Production

The performance of the overall agriculture sector and the factors responsible for the slowdown provide an explanation for the decline in the growth of food production. There are both short run and long run problems in Agriculture. Farmers' suicides continue unabated, even increasing in some states, as growth rate in yield is on the decline. Farming is fast becoming a non-viable activity. Further scope for increase in net sown area is limited. Land degradation in the form of depletion of soil fertility, erosion, and water logging has increased. There has been decline in the surface irrigation expansion rate and a fall in the level of the ground water table. Exposure of domestic agriculture to international competition has resulted in a high order of volatility in prices. Disparities in productivity across regions and crops, and between rain fed and irrigated areas has increased. Long term factors like steeper decline in per capita land availability and shrinking of farm size are also responsible for the agrarian crisis. Land issues such as SEZs, land going to non-agriculture, alienation of tribal land etc. are becoming important. Table 3.2 shows that progress on all these fronts has slowed down since the mid-1990s. Expansion has taken place only in the case of agricultural credit. There has, however, been some revival in agriculture in recent years, wherein agricultural growth of more than 4 per cent was recorded between 2003-04 and 2007-08.

Table 3.2: Trend Growth Rate in Area, Input use, Credit and Capital Stock in Agriculture (1980-81 to 2005-06)

	1980-81 to 1990-91	1990-91 to 1996-97	1996-97 to 2005-06
Technology	3.3	2.8	0.0
Public Invest	3.9	1.9	1.4
Private Invest	0.6	2.2	1.2
Irrigated Area	2.3	2.6	0.6
Area under Fruits and Veg.	5.6	5.6	2.7
NPK Use	8.2	2.5	2.3
Credit	3.7	7.5	14.4

Source: *Economic Survey* 2007.

Per Capita Availability of Food Grains

The net availability of food grains is estimated at 87.5 per cent of gross production. In order to obtain the figure for net availability of food grains, figures for requirement for seeds, farm animal feed, and waste are deducted from gross production and net imports are added, apart from adjustments for changes in government stocks. There is no net change in

Table 3.3: Net Availability of Cereals and Pulses

Year	Per capita net Availability per day (grams)			Edible Oil (kg.)	Vanaspati (kg.)	Sugar (Nov.-Oct.) (kg.)
	Cereals	Pulses	Total Food Grains			
1951	334.2	60.7	394.9	2.5*	0.7*	5.0*
1961	399.7	69.0	468.7	3.2	0.8	4.8
1971	417.6	51.2	468.8	3.5	1.0	7.4
1981	417.3	37.5	454.8	3.8	1.2	7.3
1990	435.3	41.1	476.4	5.3	1.1	12.3
1991	468.5	41.6	510.1	5.5	1.0	12.7
1992	434.5	34.3	468.8	5.4	1.0	13.0
1993	427.9	36.2	464.1	5.8	1.0	13.7
1994	434.0	37.2	471.2	6.1	1.0	12.5
1995	457.6	37.8	495.4	6.3	1.0	13.2
1996	442.5	32.7	475.2	7.0	1.0	14.1
1997	466.0	37.1	503.1	8.0	1.0	14.6
1998	414.2	32.8	447.0	6.2	1.0	14.5
1999	429.2	36.5	465.7	8.5	1.3	14.9
2000	422.7	31.8	454.4	9.0	1.4	15.6
2001	386.2	30.0	416.2	8.2	1.3	15.8
2002	458.1	35.4	494.1	8.8	1.4	16.0
2003	408.5	29.1	437.6	7.2	1.4	16.3
2004	426.9	35.8	462.7	N.A.	N.A.	N.A.
2005	390.9	31.5	422.4	N.A.	N.A.	N.A.
2006	412.8	32.5	445.3	N.A.	N.A.	N.A.
2007	407.4	35.5	442.8	N.A.	N.A.	N.A.

Source: *Economic Survey*, 2008-09.

private stocks. Per capita net availability of food grains increased by about 10 per cent over the last 56 years, between 1951 and 2007 However, net availability declined if we compare 1961 (469 grams per day) with 2007 (443 grams). In other words, significant increase in food grains has not been able to keep pace with the increase in population. In the year 2007, per capita availability of food grains was only 443 grams much lower than 501 grams in 1991. During the period 1951 to 2007, per capita availability of pulses has declined significantly. On the other hand, per capita availability of sugar and edible oils has increased over time. As show in the Table 3.3.

Changes in Consumption Patterns and Demand for Non-cereal Food

In spite of, increase in per capita real expenditure during the period 1972-73 to 2004-05, the per capita cereal intake declined in both rural and urban areas. However, the fall in cereal consumption was offset by increase in the consumption of non-cereal food. It is now widely recognized that the food basket is more diversified and dramatic changes in food consumption patterns have taken place in India in the post-Green Revolution period. As shown in Table 3.4, the share of cereals in total consumption declined significantly even for the bottom 30 per cent of the population in both rural and urban areas. The reduction in average cereal consumption may not be of concern because the decline is mostly driven by reduced consumption among the middle and top deciles. Substitution away from cereals to other foods is expected when income increases. In recent years, however, there has been decline in the cereal consumption of the poor.

Performance in Access to Food and Nutrition

At the individual level, food security means that all members of the society have access to the food they need, either from their own production, from the market and/or from the government's transfer mechanism. In order to achieve food security it is also important that the poor have sufficient means to purchase food. Poor people cannot afford to purchase the food they need at market prices, and therefore, social protection programmes are needed. Adequate purchasing power for the poor to buy food can be ensured in two ways.

Table 3.4: Percentage Share of Cereals by Population

Year	Rural				Urban			
	Bottom 30%	Middle 40%	Top 30%	All 30%	Bottom 40%	Middle 30%	Top	All
1970-71	53.65	43.65	29.49	38.15	38.85	28.19	13.37	21.58
1990-91	39.37	30.68	18.22	25.93	27.55	19.13	9.49	15.12
1993-94	35.68	27.87	15.72	22.95	25.59	17.14	8.18	13.32
2004-05	29.34	22.04	12.49	18.28	20.59	13.29	6.29	10.21

Source: Ministry of Agriculture 2006.

One is to have an employment intensive pattern of growth which can provide remunerative work to the poor and enhance their power to purchase food. Another way is to increase incomes and subsidize food through social protection programmes like PDS and employment programmes. Even if there is availability as well as access to food, there is no guarantee of adequate absorption or nutrition, especially since, nutrition depends on many other factors such as the condition of pregnant women, breast feeding, health factors, hygiene, drinking water, sanitation, etc. The performance of both are access to food and nutritional indicators.

Conclusion

In the present research paper have examined the performance, challenges, and policies in food security in terms of availability, access, food availability is a necessary condition for food security. India is more or less self sufficient in cereals but deficit in pulses and oil seeds. Due to changes in consumption patterns, demand for fruits, vegetables, dairy, meat, poultry, and fishery products has been increasing. There is a need to increase crop diversification and improve allied activities. It may be noted that the slowdown in agriculture growth could be attributed to structural factors on the supply side, such as public investment, credit, technology, land and water management, etc., rather than globalization and trade reforms To conclude, there are many policy challenges being faced by Indian agriculture. Both price and non-price factors are important.

REFERENCES

Dev, S. Mahendra (2008), *Inclusive Growth in India: Agriculture, Poverty and Human Development*, Oxford University Press, Delhi.

Dreze, J. (2004), "Democracy and Right to Food", *Economic and Political Weekly*, April 24, Vol. 39.

Gaiha, R. (2003), "Does Right to Food Matter?", *Economic and Political Weekly*, October 4, 2003 Vol. 38, No. 40.

GoI (2007), "Report of Steering Committee on Agriculture for the XIth Plan", Planning Commission, Government of India.

GoI (2008), "Draft 11th Five-year Plan", Planning Commission, Government of India.

Gulati, Ashok (2009), "Emerging Trends in Indian Agriculture: What can we Learn from These?" Second Prof. Dayanath Jha Memorial Lecture, National Centre for Agricultural Economics and Policy Research, New Delhi.

Joshi P. K. and A. Gulati (2003), *From Plate to Plough: Agricultural Diversification in India*, Paper Presented at the Dragon and Elephant: A Comparative Study of Economic and Agricultural Reforms in China and India, New Delhi, India, March 25-26.

Rao, C.H.H. (2005), *Agriculture, Food Security, Poverty and Environment*, Oxford University Press, New Delhi.

Swaminathan, M.S. (2000), *Weakening Welfare: The Public Distribution of Food in India*, Left Word Books, New Delhi.

APPENDIX-I

Table 3.1: Food Security

Food Security	2007	2010
Calorie Supply Per Capita	2,352	—
Population undernourished	21.00%	—
Children Undernourished	—	48.00%
Under 5 Mortality Rate (per 1,000)	—	63.00

Source: *Economic Survey*, 2008-09.

Table 3.2: Agriculture Production

Agriculture Production	2006	2007	2008	2009
Rice Production	139,137,000 MT	144,570,000 MT	148,260,000 MT	131,274,000 MT
Wheat Production	69,354,500 MT	75,806,700 MT	78,570,200 MT	80,680,000 MT
Maize Production	15,097,000 MT	18,955,400 MT	19,730,000 MT	16,680,000 MT
Soybean Production	8,857,000 MT	10,968,000 MT	9,905,000 MT	10,217,000 MT

Source: Economic Survey, 2008-09.

Table 3.3: Agriculture Exports

Agriculture Exports	2006	2007	2008	2009
Rice Exports	4,747,929 MT	6,469,258 MT	2,488,289 MT	2,156,409 MT
Wheat Exports	46,633 MT	237.00 MT	1,121 MT	29.00 MT
Maize Exports	637,411 MT	2,727,720 MT	3,537,300 MT	2,600,820 MT
Soybean Exports	3,528 MT	7,460 MT	44,838 MT	24,699 MT

Source: Economic Survey, 2008-09.

Table 3.4: Agriculture Importer

Agriculture Importer	2005	2006	2007	2008
Rice Imports	260.00 MT	162.00 MT	145.00 MT	85.00 MT
Wheat Imports	37,760 MT	6,079,560 MT	2,677,830 MT	20.00 MT
Maize Imports	1,632 MT	2,000 MT	4,273 MT	7,280 MT
Soybean Imports	2.00 MT	336.00 MT	29.00 MT	38.00 MT

Source: Economic Survey, 2008-09.

4

Issues of Food Security in India

Velu Suresh Kumar

INTRODUCTION

The concept of food security has undergone considerable changes in recent years. Food availability and stability were considered good measures of food security till the seventies and the achievement of self-sufficiency was accorded high priority in the food policies of developing countries. Though India has made substantial progress in terms of overcoming transient food insecurity by achieving self-sufficiency in food production, it could not solve the problem of chronic food insecurity. This necessitated a change in approach and as a result, food energy intake at household level is now given prominence in assessing food security. Food energy intake depends on many factors, most importantly on purchasing power and availability of food of appropriate quantity and quality at affordable prices.

In policy design, a distinction is made between transient and chronic food security. Transitory food insecurity is associated with the risks related to either access or the availability of food during the off-season, drought and inflationary years and so forth. Policies such as those relating to price stabilization, credit, crop-insurance and temporary employment creation are initiated for stabilizing the consumption of the vulnerable groups. In contrast, the problem of chronic food insecurity is primarily associated with poverty and arises due to continuously inadequate diet. The strategy to overcome this problem includes intervention (agricultural production programmes, infrastructure, human resource development, etc.) to raise the purchasing power of the poor through the endowments of land and non-land assets and by generating employment opportunities, as well as long-term growth-mediated interventions to improve food availability and incomes of the poor. India is one of the few countries which have experimented with a broad spectrum of programmes for improving food security. It has already made substantial progress in terms of overcoming transient food insecurity by giving priority to self-sufficiency in food grains and through procurement and public distribution of food grains, employment programmes, etc. However, despite a significant reduction in the incidence of poverty chronic food insecurity persists in a large proportion of India's population. At the national level, we have solved the problem of food security which is reflected in mounting buffer stocks. Yet, there are millions of food insecure and under-nourished people in India. The limitation is not food supply, but food distribution. Careful consideration of food security requires moving beyond food availability and recognizing the low incomes of the poor. It is also important to recognize the choices that households and regions face, including exploitation of natural resources when incomes fall short. Substantial human resources are wasted due to malnutrition related diseases.

Trends in Food Production

India achieved near self-sufficiency in the availability of food grains by the mid-seventies. The annual growth rate of food production including non-cereal food increased from 2.1 per cent during the 1960s to 3.0 per cent in the subsequent decade and further to 3.8 per cent during the 1980s. Between 1960 and 1980, food production barely kept pace with the population but in the 1980s per capita food production increased at a satisfactory rate of 1.6 per cent per annum.

Trends in production of selected food grains and their average annual growth rates are presented in Table 4.1. During the period of triennium ending (TE) 1980-81, rice production was 49.9 million metric tones (mmt) which increased to 89.2 mmt by TE 2006-07. Production of rice increased at a rate of 2.4 per cent per annum during this period. Similarly, the production of wheat nearly doubled from 34.6 mmt in TE 1980-81 to 71.0 mmt in TE 2006-07, at the annual rate of 2.9 per cent over these years. Total production of cereals has also grown at the rate of 2.2 per cent per annum during the 26 year period. However, this growth has been decelerating very fast over the decades. (*Table 6.1*)

Growth in rice production slowed down to 1.8 per cent per annum during the 1990s and has only been growing at the annual rate of 0.1 per cent in the last six years, while the annual growth rate was 3.7 per cent in the 1980s. Overall total growth of cereals declined from 3.1 per cent per annum in the 1980s to 2.0 per cent per annum in the 1990s, and further to 0.2 per cent in the early period of the current decade, because the yield gains for cereals in the post-green revolution era have been low. For pulses and sugarcane also low yield have resulted in low production levels. However, oilseeds exhibited a high annual growth rate of 3.6 per cent in the overall period. But the oilseed sector suffers from the poor performance of the oil processing units.

The relative cereal price which showed a decline in the seventies and eighties, registered a rise in the nineties and also in the early period of the current decade. An increase in cereal price significantly reduces the calorie intake of the poor as their price elasticity of food/calorie estimates of price elasticity is numerically large. The upward trend in the real price of cereals in the nineties and also in the early period of the current decade had coincided with a slowdown in the decline of poverty.

Table 4.1: Trends of Total Domestic Production of Food in India

Food Items	Production (million metric tones)				Annual Rate of Growth (%)			
	TE 1980-81	TE 1990-91	TE 2000-01	TE 2006-07	1980/81-2006-07	1980/81-1990-91	1990/91-2000-01	2000/01-2006-07
Rice	49.9	72.8	86.9	89.2	2.4	3.7	1.8	0.1
Wheat	34.6	53.0	72.4	71.0	2.9	4.1	3.4	-0.5
Total Cereals	113.3	158.8	190.3	194.1	2.2	3.1	2.0	0.2
Pulses	10.5	13.7	13.1	13.1	0.7	2.2	0.3	1.4
Oilseeds	9.4	17.9	21.3	3.6	5.5	2.4	4.5	
Sugarcane	144.9	223.2	294.7	2.6	3.3	2.8	-2.0	

Source: Agricultural Statistics at a Glance, 2007, Directorate of Economics and Statistics, GoI.

Trends in Food Consumption

Cereal Consumption

The NSS data on consumer expenditure for various rounds indicates that per capita consumer expenditure at constant (1990-91) prices steadily increased since 1970 both in rural and urban areas. It increased around 1.5 per cent per annum in both the areas during '70s and '80s; and around 1.2 per cent per annum in rural areas and 2.8 per cent per annum in urban areas during the '90s. It appears that economic reforms benefited the urban households more than the rural ones. But the increase in consumption expenditure did not reflect in food expenditure. Per capita food expenditure at constant prices increased around 0.9 per cent per annum during '70s and '80s while it declined at 0.9 per cent per annum in rural areas and stagnant in urban areas during the last decade.

The consumption of per capita cereal has been declining since the early seventies despite a significant increase in per capita cereal production (Radhakrishna and Ravi, 1992; Rao, 2000). The consumption of per capita cereals declined in rural areas from 15.35 kg per annum in 1970-71 to 11.9 kg per annum in 2005-06 and from 11.4 to 9.8 kg in urban areas. The sharp fall in cereal consumption has been attributed to diversification in food consumption in favour of non-cereal foods, particularly milk and milk products, sugar and gur and other food items, changed tastes and preferences, as well as change in relative prices of food items (Mittal, 2006). Higher economic growth and per capita incomes have contributed to reduction in per capita demand for cereals.

Projections of Food Demand

Demand projections in general are estimated on the basis of assumptions about the base year demand, population, expenditure elasticity and economic growth. The domestic demand projections for rice, wheat and total cereals are arrived at by adding up the Direct Demand (human demand) and Indirect Demand (seed, feed, industrial use and wastage). It is observed that household food demand has been primarily driven by growth in population and income.

The demand and supply projection given below was developed at Indian Council for Research on International Economic Relations. The domestic demand projected under two scenarios of per capita income growth. The two scenarios assume that the gross domestic product (GDP) growth rates to be 8 per cent and 9 per cent. The results of food demand predictions corresponding to scenario of 9 per cent GDP is thought to be most likely in future. As per the projection, the total cereal demand for 2011 is 187.8 mmt if the economy grows at the rate of 8 per cent per annum and 188.5 mmt if the GDP is 9 per cent (Table 4.2). The cereal demand in 2026 will be 273.5 mmt and 277.2 mmt in the alternative scenarios, respectively. During the same period, demand for rice, wheat and pulses is expected to be 102.1 mmt, 65.9 mmt and 57.7 mmt, respectively, under scenario 2. Increase in demand for pulses is quite evident as this is the major source of protein for the vegetarian population. Demand for edible oil is projected to be 40.9 mmt by 2026 and sugar demand is expected to increase almost nine-fold in 2026 from base year demand of 11.9 mmt.

Table 4.2: Projected Domestic Demand for Food Items in India

(million metrisc tones)

Food Items	Base Year	Scenario 1			Scenario 2		
	1999-00	2011	2021	2026	2011	2021	2026
Rice	66.0	94.5	96.9	102.2	94.4	96.8	102.1
Wheat	44.9	60.1	66.8	69.1	59.0	64.3	65.9
Total Cereals	119.0	187.8	242.8	273.5	188.5	245.1	277.2
Pulses	10.4	23.0	38.7	51.0	24.1	42.5	57.7
Edible Oil	8.6	15.7	26.7	35.3	16.8	30.2	40.9
Sugar	11.9	26.7	55.0	81.1	29.3	65.7	100.7

Note: Scenario 1: GDP is 8 per cent per annum; Scenario 2: GDP is 9 per cent per annum.

Source: Surabhi Mittal (2008).

Annual per capita domestic demand presented in Table 4.3 also projects an increase in demand for all the food items. The projected demand in 2026 highlights highest demand rise for oilseeds and sugar *vis-à-vis* total cereals in next two decades.

Table 4.3: Projected Annual Per Capita Domestic Demand for Food Items in India

(Kg/annum)

Food Items	Scenario 1			Scenario 2		
	2011	2021	2026	2011	2021	2026
Rice	80.2	72.0	72.3	80.1	71.9	72.2
Wheat	51.0	49.6	48.9	50.0	47.8	46.6
Total Cereals	159.3	180.4	193.4	159.9	182.2	196.0
Pulses	19.5	28.8	36.1	20.4	31.6	40.8
Edible oil	13.3	19.8	25.0	14.2	22.4	28.9
Sugar	22.6	40.9	57.4	24.9	48.8	71.2

Note: Scenario 1: GDP is 8 per cent per annum; Scenario 2: GDP is 9 per cent per annum.

Source: Surabhi Mittal (2008).

Projections of Food Supply

Medium and long-term supply projections of food have been made using a straightforward approach. Supply projections have been computed using the yield growth for the most recent period of 1993-2003 and taking 2003-04 as the base year for area and production and also assumed that further area expansion will take place. Supply prospects have accordingly been presented in Table 4.4 for selected food items.

If there is no area expansion and future supply is only dependent on yield growth, then total supply of cereals will be 209.7 mmt in 2011, 242.2 mmt in 2021 and 260.2 mmt in 2026. The yield growth of total cereals has been 1.5 per cent in the past decade, according to government estimates.

Table 4.4: Projected Domestic Supply of Food Items in India

(million metric tones)

Food Items	Base Year 2003-04	Supply Projection		
		2011	2021	2026
Rice	88.3	95.7	105.8	111.2
Wheat	72.1	80.2	91.6	97.9
Total Cereals	186.9	209.1	242.2	260.2
Pulses	14.9	16.1	17.6	18.4
Edible oil	8.6 (25.3)	10.1 (29.9)	12.5 (36.9)	13.9 (41.1)
Sugar	24.2 (237.1)	25.0 (245.0)	26.0 (255.2)	26.6 (260.5)

Note: Figures in the parenthes is are the supply projections for oilseeds and sugarcane in respective columns.

Source: Surabhi Mittal (2008).

Rice and wheat production is also estimated to increase to 111.2 mmt and 97.9 mmt, respectively, by 2026. There has been a diversification in the cropping pattern towards high-value commodities in major rice producing regions.

Supplies of pulses are estimated to be of the tune of 16.1 mmt in 2011, 17.6 mmt in 2021 and 18.4 mmt in 2026 under the given assumptions. Oilseed production is projected to go up to 36.9 mmt in 2021 and 41.1 mmt in 2026 over the base year production of 25.3 mmt in 2003-04. Sugarcane has very low yield growth, thus the sugarcane production is estimated to be around 245.0 mmt in 2011, 255.2 mmt in 2021 and 260.5 mmt in 2026. The edible oil production is estimated to be 10.1 mmt in 2011 and 13.19 mmt in 2026. The sugar production is likely to be 25.0 mmt in 2011, 26.0 mmt in 2021 and 26.6 mmt in 2026.

Food Gap

Increase in total demand is mainly due to growth in population and per capita income and as far as supply in concerned, production is constrained by low yield growth. A negative gap indicates that the demand of the commodity is more than its supply and this implies a deficit of the commodity in future (Table 4.5). The gap between supply and demand is narrowing down over the years for all the food items. The supply-demand gap for total cereals is expected to be 21.19 mmt in 2011 whereas it is projected at -16.96 mmt in 2026.

Table 4.5: Supply-Demand Gap for Selected Food Items

(million metric tones)

Food Items	Gap (Supply-Demand)		
	2011	2021	2026
Rice	1.26	8.98	9.13
Wheat	21.21	27.33	32.04
Total Cereals	21.19	-2.94	-16.97
Pulses	-8.05	-24.92	-39.31
Edible oil	-6.66	-17.68	-26.99
Sugar	-4.31	-39.67	-74.13

Note: Demand scenario of GDP growth at 9 per cent is considered here.

Source: Surabhi Mittal (2008).

If we look at the medium-term prospect then in 2011 by the end of the Eleventh Plan, the situation for pulses, edible oil and sugar is alarming. This implies that in the years to come, the country will have to rely on imports of these food items to meet the domestic requirement. Thus, we need to have necessary policy initiatives to increase the supply in future.

Rate of the growth of projected demand for the selected food items is much more than projected supply growths for these. Table 6 shows that in future, for cereals the demand grows at a much higher rate than the domestic supply. This difference in growth rates is much higher for pulses, edible oil and sugar.

Table 4.6: Per cent Annual Growth Rate of Projected Supply and Demand

Food Items	Demand	Supply
Rice	1.55	1.01
Wheat	1.42	1.34
Total Cereals	3.17	1.45
Pulses	6.51	0.91
Edible oil	5.95	2.13
Sugar	8.22	0.41

Note: Growth rate are between base year and 2026. Demand scenario of GDP growth at 9 per cent is considered here.

Source: Surabhi Mittal (2008).

Conclusion

To meet the domestic food requirements, the country either needs to increase agricultural production or depend on imports. Since agricultural growth is limited, imports can help improve the country's supply situation for a short-term. But for the long-term, the country will need to focus on productivity enhancement, through public investment in irrigation, research and efficient use of water, plant nutrition and other inputs. These policies will induce efficiency and can help in maintaining balance between domestic production and demand.

REFERENCES

Bhalla, G.S. (2001) "Demand and Supply of Food and Feed Grains by 2020", *Towards Hunger Free India*, M.D. Asthana and Pedro Medrano, (eds.) New Delhi, Manohar.

Chand, Ramesh Dayanatha Jha and Surabhi Mittal (2004) WTO and Oilseeds Sector: Challenges of Trade Liberalisation India's Oilseed Sector and WTO, *Economic and Political Weekly*, Vol. XXXIX No. 6 February 7, pp. 533-537.

Evenson, R. E., Pray C, and Rosegrant M.W, (1999) "Agricultural Research and Productivity Growth in India". *IFPRI Research Report No. 109*, International Food Policy Research Institute, Washington, D.C.

Fan, Shenggen, Hazell, Peter and Thorat, S. (1999)" Linkages between Government Spending, Agricultural Growth and Poverty in Rural India", IFPRI Research Report 110, International Food Policy Research Institute, Washington, D.C.

FAOSTAT data (2006): http://faostat.fao.org/

GoI (2005 and 2007) *Agricultural Statistics at a Glance*, Directorate of Economics and Statistics, Government of India, New India.

Hanchante, Amresh and Tim Dyson (2004) *Prospects for Food Demand and Supply*, Twenty First Century India, Edited by Tim Dyson, Robert Cassen and L.Visaria, Oxford University Press.

Kumar, Praduman (1998) "Food Demand and Supply Projections for India", *Agricultural Economics Policy Series 98-01*, Indian Agricultural Research Institute, New Delhi.

Kumar, Praduman and Surabhi Mittal (2003) "Productivity and Supply of Food Grains in India", In Towards a Food Secure India: Issues and Policies, S. Mahendra Dev, K.P. Kannan and Nira Ramachandran (eds.), Institute for Human Development and Centre for Economic and Social Studies, Manohar Publishers and Distributors, pp. 33-58.

Mittal, Surabhi (Kuchhal) (2000) "Productivity and Sources of Growth for Major Cereal and Non-Cereal Crops in India: Implications for Food Security and Self-Reliance", Ph.D Dissertation, Dr. Bhimrao Ambedkar University, Agra.

Rosegrant, M.W. and *et. al.*, (1995) "Global Food Projections to 2020: Implications for Investment", *IFPRI Discussion Paper No. 5*, International Food Policy Research Institute Washington, D.C.

Singh, Punjab (2001) *Agricultural Policy Vision: 2020*, Background Paper for Planning Commission Vision 2020.

Thamarajakshi, R. (2001) "Demand and Supply of Food Grains in 2020", *In Towards Hunger Free India*, M.D. Asthana and Pedro Medrano (eds.), New Delhi, Manohar Publishers and Distributors.

http://planningcommission.nic.in/reports/genrep/bkpap2020/24_bg2020.pdf)

5

A Study on Critical Issues and Perspectives of Food Security

V.J.R. Emerlson Moses
D. Ramachandran

INTRODUCTION

When the food prices are spiraling in India and the world, the issue of food security has become more topical. Food security is not merely a physical survival but a complete well-being of all human beings. Second, while massive food production at the national/State level or full buffer stock in godowns even at district level may be necessary, but it is not a sufficient condition for food security that requires purchasing power of a household on the one hand and just distribution within the household on the other. This Chapter discuss the global and national scenario, causes and consequences of food crisis, and policy implications. The national commission on Framers, in its first report (2004) points out five basic factors for agrarian crisis: unfinished agenda in land reform, quantity and quality of water, technology fatigue, access adequacy and timeliness of institutional credit, and opportunities for assured and remunerative marketing. The worst affected in agrarian crisis are small and marginal farmers, landless labourers and women. That is why, long back in 1946 at Noakhali, Mahatma Gandhi had perceptively remarked: "To the hungry, God is bread." After the second World War, US President, Roosevelt, talked of four types of freedom: freedom of expression, freedom of worship, freedom from fear and freedom from hunger. Even Jawaharlal Nehru had announced in 1974: "Everything else can wait, but not agriculture." However, India did not accord the priority to agriculture (in terms of investment) which it deserved. Needless to say that hunger and starvation are violation Declaration of Human Rights. Right to food is a basic birth right of every individual, group, family or community. Supreme Court of India has deliberated in several judicial decisions that right to food is an integral part of right to life enshrined in Article 21 of Indian Constitution. Wheat, rice and maize are three major cereals in the world. Rice is preferred in Asia, maize in America and Africa, and wheat in Europe and Australia. In India, at present maize, rice and wheat are eaten with difference in regional/cultural preference – rice in South and East, wheat and maize in North and West. Robert Zeigler (D.G., International Rice Research Institute, Manila) has said: "In Asia, rice cultural, social and, in many places, even a religious role so it carries much more psychological weight." In 2008, 423 million tonnes of world rice production was estimated. Asia produced 91 per cent of world's rice in 2007 but 4 per cent decrease in global rice trade was projected in 2008. Unfortunately, prices of both rice and wheat spiraled in 2006-07 and 2007-08. India people, like most of Asians, spend almost half of their weekly budget on food-double that in the west.

Causes and Consequences of Food Crisis

Though food production has been increasing, yet its price are spiraling for following reasons:

- Rising long-term demand in developing countries like China and India where rising prosperity has led to eating more. US Department of Agriculture estimates that world-wide rice consumption increased 0.9 per cent in 2007 (about 424 million tones) but production increased less than 0.7 per cent.
- Short-term supply shocks due to unusually cold weather (due to climate change?) and pest infestation in Vietnam,

second largest rice supplier in the world. Aggregate production of maize, rice and soya bean stagnated in 2006 and 2007 due to drought, while drought in Australia led to decrease in wheat production.

- Diversion of a huge chunk of America's corn crop to ethanol production-boosting demand for other staples like rice.

However, Peter Ritter also points out that though trade of food grains was liberalized since 1990's at global level, in recent years there is ban on export of wheat/rice by many developing countries. This was worsened the global food crisis/the Philippines imports only 15 per cent of its rice requirement but it is facing most acute rice shortage in Asia. Consequently, Vietnamese rice is going to the Philippines, thus depriving Africa. We can imagine what is happening in many Sub-Saharan African countries that import up to 40 per cent.

The Global Food Crisis

About 73 million people will be added to the world's population every year between 1995 and 2020, increasing it by 32 per cent to reach 7.5 billion. Much of this population growth will occur in the cities of the developing world. While its rural population is expected to increase by less than 300 million during this period, the developing world's urban population could double to 3.4 billion in 2020. Per capita incomes are expected to increase in all major developing regions over this period. Meeting the food needs of a growing and urbanizing population with rising incomes will have profound implications for the world's agricultural production and trading systems in coming decades. IFPRI research suggests some of the major developments that will characterize the world food situation during the next two decades to 2020. The global financial crisis drew international attention away from the food crisis, but this continues to fester and even grow. When the global food crisis first hit international headlines in 2008, international bureaucrats referred to the current problems in the world food situation as "a silent tsunami", but the truth is that it was not a sudden and unexpected crisis: the signs have been around for some time now and it could easily have been seen to be coming. Even so, its impact has been powerful and already quite devastating, as food shortages and high prices of food have adversely affected billions of people, especially the poor in the developing world.

It is also very much a man-made crisis, resulting not so much from ineluctable forces of global supply and demand as from the market-oriented and liberalising policies adopted by choice or compulsion in almost all countries. These policies have either neglected agriculture or allowed shifts in global prices to determine both cropping patterns and the viability of farming, and also generated greater possibilities of speculative activity in food items. Cultivators in developing countries have been ravaged by the fearsome combination of exposure to import competition from highly subsidised agriculture in developed countries, removal of domestic protection of inputs and reduced access to institutional credit-to the point that even the global increase in agricultural prices after 2002 did not compensate sufficiently to alleviate the pervasive agrarian crisis in much of the developing world.

It is also clear that the global food crisis is not something that can be treated as discrete and separate from the global financial crisis. On the contrary it has been intimately connected with it, particularly through the impact of financial speculation on world trade prices of food.

This is not to deny the undoubted role of other real economy factors in affecting the global food situation. While demand-supply imbalances have been touted as reasons, this is largely unjustified given that there has been hardly any change in the world demand for food in the past three years. In particular, the claim that food grain prices have soared because of more demand from China and India as their GDP increases, is completely invalid, since both aggregate and per capita consumption of grain have actually fallen in both countries. Supply factors have been – and are likely to continue to be – more significant. These include the short-run effects of diversion of both acreage and food crop output for bio-fuel production, as well as more medium term factors such as rising costs of inputs, falling productivity because of soil depletion, inadequate public investment in agricultural research and extension, and the impact of climate changes that have affected harvests in different ways.

The Food Crisis in India

Various studies have pointed out that in India even if the total food production of a small/marginal farmer is not sufficient for the family consumption for a year, he has to sell a part of it in the market due to monetized economy in order to meet his various needs like purchase of utensils, clothes, social obligations, health, education, etc., that is, there exists a compulsive involvement', to use Krishna Bhardwaj's terms (1947), with the market. Thus, almost all the land holders while sowing their crops take into account this very factor. Second, they also grow cash-crops like mustard, rapeseed, peas, potato etc. which are more remunerative than the food grains. Third, while sowing crops they also consider that they have to pay wages to the labourers on time. Earlier for purpose of wages payment, coarse grains used to be sown, but nowadays the trend has changed as the labourers are not willing to accept coarse grains, rather cash is paid after selling food grains or cash-crops. Further, food habits of the farmers themselves have also changed substantially and, therefore, they do not like to grow coarse grains like barley, madua, sawan, koda, ragi, etc., (through these are nutritious). Fourth, most of the farmers also take into account expected social obligations like festivals, religious ceremonies, marriage and birth ceremonies and debt repayment schedule while planning their cropping pattern.

The difference in attitude of the net sellers and petty farmers at the time of sale of food grains is that while the formers (net sellers) keep most of their produce in store after the harvest and sell 90 per cent of the marketable surplus later in lean season (Poush-Magh, *i.e.*, December-January) when the prices rise due to more demand and less supply, the latter have to sell most of the surplus or even out of necessary annual stock just after harvest in order to meet their non-food requirements like medicine, education, clothing, house repair, social function at cheaper rates due to more supply of food grains than the demand in Chaitra (April-May). During the lean season, there is no adequate employment opportunity in the agriculture and the petty farmers purchase food grains at higher rate *i.e.*, they become 'net buyers'. Then even the public distribution system shops do not cope up with the demand more because of corruption and malfunctioning rather than non-availability of food grains in the government stock.

Consequently, either the area under food crops ('acreage response') or the yield of food crops per acre ('yield response') is to be increased to cope up with the demand of the high population growth. For ensuring adequate food production the necessary condition of ensuring adequate inputs in time is necessary. It transpires from discussion with many villagers in U.P., and Bihar that subsidy in seeds, fertilizers, pesticides, irrigation and credit contributes to about 60 per cent of the increase in production and, on the other hand, better remunerative prices contribute to 30 per cent of the increase and an increase in wages of the labour will affect the production to about 10 per cent. Most farmers can not afford costly inputs and high wages, hence agriculture has become a loss-making activity of production. Though India has been providing subsidies on seeds, fertilizers, irrigation (electricity charges), crops loans, etc., yet under pressure of World Trade Organization's Agreement on Agriculture, the Government has reduced the.

However, due to subsidized fertilizers, many farmers use more chemical fertilizers and this trend has to be curtailed by awareness-generation among from chemical fertilizers and soil degradation rather organic manures and green bio-fertilizers for ecological sustainability should be popularised.

Ensuring Food Security in India

It is not surprising that questions of food security and the right to food have become such urgent political issues in

India today. Rapid aggregate income growth over the past two decades has not addressed the basic issue of ensuring the food security of the population. Instead, nutrition indicators have stagnated and per capita calorie consumption has actually declined, suggesting that the problem of hunger may have got worse rather than better.

Consider the evidence on nutritional outcomes from the most recent National Family Health Survey (NFHS) conducted in 2005-06. According to this, 46 per cent of children below 3 years are underweight; 33 per cent of women and 28 per cent of men have Body Mass Index (BMI) below normal; 79 per cent of children aged 6-35 months have anemia, as do 56 per cent of ever married women aged 15-49 years and 24 per cent of similar men; 58 per cent of pregnant women have anemia. The national averages mask locational differences: all these indicators are much worse in rural India.

Further, these indicators have scarcely changed, or have changed very little, since the previous NFHS in 1998-99. In terms of calorie consumption the picture is even worse. According to the National Sample Survey Organization (NSSO) large survey of 2004-05, the average daily intake of calories of the rural population has dropped by 106 Kcal (4.9%) from 2153 Kcal to 2047 Kcal from 1993-94 to 2004-05 and by 51 Kcal (2.5%) from 2071 to 2020 Kcal in urban areas. The average daily intake of protein by the Indian population decreased from 60.2 to 57 grams in rural India between 1993-94 and 2004-05 and remained stable at around 57 grams in the urban areas during the same period.

The all India averages do not capture the wide variation across states and even within states. For example the India State Hunger Index 2008 (brought out by the International Food Policy Research Institute) shows very large differences across 17 major states, ranging from 13.6 for Punjab to 30.9 for Madhya Pradesh. If these states could be compared to countries in the Global Hunger Index rankings, some states in India have index scores at the bottom: Bihar and Jharkhand rank lower than Zimbabwe and Haiti, and Madhya Pradesh falls between Ethiopia and Chad.

Conclusion

Food security in India has to be understood as a distress phenomenon, as with marginal increase in their incomes over time they are forced to cut down on their food consumption to meet other pressing demands of health and education that were not considered important in the past. High economic growth rates have failed to improve food security in India leaving the country facing a crisis in its rural economy.

REFERENCES

Brown, Lester R (2008) "Business as Usual is No Longer a Viable Option," *Indian Express*, 13th June, 2008.

Chakrabarti, M and S.K. Datta (2000), "Agriculture", *in Alternative Economic Survey 1998-2000*, Rainbow Publishers Ltd., Delhi.

Firodia, Arun (2008) "Rising Food Prices: The Blame Game", *The Economic Times*, 9th June 2008.

Government of India (2004) *Servinf Farmers and Saving Farming*, National Commission on Farmers, Ministry of Agriculture, New Delhi.

Guha-Khasnobis, and *et al.*, 2008), *Food Security*, B.davis (ed.) Oxford University Press, Oxford.

Kewalramani, S. (2008) "Green Revolution II Needed, and not Export Curbs", *The Hindu, Business Line*, 7th June 2008.

Ritter, Peter (2008) "No Grain, Big Pain", *Time*, 21st April, 2008.

Sachs, J (2008) "Common-wealth", Allen Lane, Penguin, New Delhi.

Swaminathan, M.S. (2008) "Food for Thought", *Yojana*, Vol. 52, No. 5 June, 2008.

6

Food Security through Government and NGOs
A Study

S. Sivasankaran

INTRODUCTION

India, an agricultural country, is only a bygone story. Fixation of agricultural products by the vendors and not by the agriculturist is the cause for the degradation of agriculture. G. Ramakrishnan, the secretary of Tamil Nadu Communist Party rightly says that the number of persons engaged in the agriculture had been augmented from 60 per cent to 15 per cent.[1] The agricultural lands now have been converted into residential plats and commercial purposes. In the days of monarchy, we safely produced enormous food grains and the granaries in the palaces, temples and huge pots in every houses served as storages. During the famine, the temple granaries rendered a great service to the people to encounter food scarcity. Punjab at national level and Tanjore at State level become the granaries. But due to failure of monsoon, and improper planning on the part of government side, food security has been a long-pending demand of the people. Even during the Second World War, the ever-worst food scarcity occurred in our country. But we were able to tackle the problems by importing rice from Burma, Tailand, French, Indo-China.[2]

The present scenario in the food production and saftey is entirely threatening the society. Food adulteration is a common issue for all countries in the world. The issue persists since antiquity. The governments are very cautious in taking action against the food adulteration by passing legislations. The legislations debases the quality of food offered for sale either by the admixture or substitution of inferior substances or by the removal of some valuable ingredient.[3] The Greek and Roman classics contain allusions to wine makers and dealers who coloured and flavoured their wine. In England as early as the 13th century, bakers cheapened their wares or scanted the weight, and lawmakers for the first time made an effort to prevent fraudulent dealings on the part of butchers and brewers. In the 18th and early 19th centuries, coffee, tea, and cocoa were placed under the protection laws. About the middle of the 19th century chemical and microscopal knowledge had reached the stage that food substances could be analyzed, and the subject of food adulteration began to be studied from the standpoint of the rights and welfare of the consumer. In 1860, the first food law in the interest of the purchaser was enacted. The practical difficulties of enforcing the law had been smeared by appointing administrative officials in 1882. In the United States the Federal Food and Drug Act of 1906 was repealed, as it had some drawbacks, by the more rigorous Food, Drug, and Cosmetic Act of 1938. This law was amended in 1958 and 1962 to define and regulate food additives and food colouring. Imported goods that violate the provisions of the act are denied admittance to the United States. But in the case of India, the adulterators have been backed by the politicians. A few years back, outdated milk powder a large quantity has been shipment from Germany by the private milk producer in Karaikal and mixed it with the milk and sold to the public against their conscience.[4]

Article 39 of the Constitution enshrined in the Directive Principles of State Policy aims to promote welfare of every citizen of the country.[5] Some of the consumer laws are also rooted in the fundamental rights which guarantee right to life, equality, etc. The following laws and Rules concern fair distribution of goods or services to the consumer: The Sale of Goods Act of 1930, Prevention of Food Adulteration Act of 1954, Drug and Magic Remedies (Objectionable Advertisement) Act of 1954, Essential Commodities Act of 1955, The Monopolies and Restrictive Trade Practices Act of 1969, The Water (Prevention and Control of) Pollution Act of 1974, The Protection of Civil Right Act of 1955, The Protection of Human Rights Act of 1993, The Packaged Commodities Regulation Order of 1975, Standards of Weights and Measures Act of 1975, Prevention of Black Marketing and Maintenance of Supplies of Essential Commodities Act of 1980, Bureau of Indian Standards Act of 1986, Consumer Protection Rules of 1987, Tamil Nadu Consumer Protection Rules of 1988, Consumer Protection Act of 1986 (amended in 2002), and Infant Milk Substitutes, Feeding bottles and Infant Foods (Regulation of Production, Supply and Distribution) Act of 1992.

The Food Safety and Standard Act, 2006 was enacted which repealed the Prevention of Food Adulteration Act of 1954, Fruit Products Order of 1955, Meat Food Products Order of 1973, Vegetable Oil Products (Control) Order of 1947, edible Oil Packaging (Regulation) Order of 1988, Solvent Extracted Oil, De-Oiled Meal and Edible Flour (Control) Order of 1967 and Milk and Milk Products Order of 1992. The Act also aims to establish a single reference point for all matters relating to food safety and standards, by moving from multi-level, multi-departmental control to a single line of command.

Ministry of Health and Family Welfare, Government of India is the administrative ministry for the implementation of FSSAI.[6] From the head quarter at New Delhi, the independent statutory organization is enforcing the act with great care. Very recently, the Food Safety Standards Authority of India has claimed that 83 per cent of milk produced and consumed in Jammu and Kashmir is contaminated with components like salt, detergents and several other harmful substances being found in it.[7] Of the 71 samples randomly taken from Delhi for testing by the Food Safety Standards Authority of India, 50 were found to be contaminated with glucose and skim milk powder (SMP), which is usually added to milk in the lean season to enhance volumes.[8] Though the ASSAI performs to ensure providing safety foods to the consumers, most of the vendors never concern about the purity of the commodities.

Usage of Chemicals in the Food Industry

Prevention of Food Adulteration Rules of 1955 ensures the maximum residual limits of pesticide and the presence of heavy metal in the food items. But beyond the level, pesticides[9] are used in management of pests and disease in agricultural and horticulture crops. Heavy metals[10] are present in the Irrigation water and other manures. Infected seeds, irrigation water and soil act as the source of the fungi toxins. Rule 44 AA of the PFA Rules, 1955 prohibits the use of carbide gas for ripening of fruits. But the Ministry of Agriculture has clarified that the fruits are exposed to ethylene[11] in low concentration of 10-100 ppm exogenously to trigger their ripening. Bee wax or Carnauba wax or Shellac wax are permitted to be used in accordance with the good manufacturing practice for use of food additives. However, unscrupulous elements, with the intention of more profit are following the practice of dipping green vegetables in artificial colours to give them a fresh attractive and pleasant appearance. The Prevention of Food Adulteration Act and Rules, now incorporated in the Food Safety and Standard Act, 2006 prohibits the use of colour in fruit and vegetables.

Food Security Bill and the Repercussion of Tamil Nadu

While launching *Food Con 2010* conference in Chennai, K.V. Thomas, Minister of State for Agriculture, Consumer Affairs, Food and Public Distribution said, the centre is keen on piloting the Food Security Bill. He further, pointed out that the food subsidy components was estimated at Rs. 17,000 crore annually. The Hon'ble Minister lamented that the experience with the public distribution system was that subsidized food is not reaching the intended people.[12] In his inaugural address at the Food Con, Mr. K.V. Thomas stressed the need for infusing modern technology into farming, storage and value-addition in the food industry. There are some reasons which spoil the food industry. Though there is a good monsoon, the lack of adequate storage space to stock food grain is the prime most problem encountered by the government. Hence he urged the CII to play a lead role in encouraging private entrepreneurship in food procucts, storage, value-addition and packaging.[13]

Tamil Nadu Chief Minister J. Jayalalitha reacted to the Food Security Bill by writing a letter to the Prime Minster Manmohan Singh. She said: "the centre should not attempt or be seen to attempt encroaching into the domains of the state," and sought exemption of Tamil Nadu from the purview of the proposed measure. She further said: "in a federal structure like ours where the states are in close and direct contact with the people, the choice of designing and implementing popular welfare schemes is at best left to the state." She has opposed the distribution of food items through Targeted Public Distribution System (TPDS), as it is to be mentioned in the National Food Security Bill, and mentioned that under Universal Public Distribution System (UPDS), rice wheat, sugar and other commodities like *toor dal, urad dal,* fortified palmolien and atta, were supplied to the public at heavily subsidized prices through 32,977 fair price shops. The Government of Tamil Nadu allots Rs. 5,000 crore as annual food subsidy.[14]

The National Food Security Mission

To increase productivity, the *National Food Security Mission* (NFSM) has been established under the Eleventh Five-year Plan. It was introduced in eighteen states across India. In Tamil Nadu, the NFSM was lauched in thirty districts mostly for cultivation of rice, wheat and pulse. R.S. Malik, National Consultant of the NFSM, visited to look into the working of the scheme in various fields of Malaipatti, Nainarpuram and Ramasamypuram in Ottapidaram block in February 2012.[15]

International Crops Research Institute for the Semi-arid Tropics (ICRISAT) is one of the private organization working to enhance crop productivity through innovative methods and address food availability and reduce poverty. The institution focus on catalyzing strategic partnership, building research and development capabilities in the agriculture sector that would help boost farm productivity.[16]

CREATE[17]

The Centre for Research, Education, Action, Training and Evaluation (CREATE) is a democratic non-profit organization located in Tamil Nadu. CREATE works to promote democracy among India's rural and poor citizen, and is associated with the Tamil Nadu Theological Seminary, a long-time partner of Global Ministries. The project area includes seven villages of Thenkarai Panchayat of Periyakulam. The agrarian poor of this community face the persistent challenge of maintaining food security.

The villagers, their leaders and the CREATE staff designed agricultural development plans that would be enable all villagers to improve their food security. The programme, so far, dug seven wells with the use of diesel pump. Dry crops like millet, and vegetables like brinjals and bindi have been cultivated. CREATE and the village have also created a Revolving Loan Programme to protect the farmers from the exploitation of local loan agents who charge exorbitant rates for short-term loans. The Revolving Loan Fund is operated by the village associations. Loans are given out at the beginning of the season to enable farmers to plant. The loans are repaid with very low interest or no interest at harvest. The Revolving Loan fund is working very well in most locations.

Cows are also being loaned to landless village women whose families were not eligible to participate in the revolving loan programme. The selected women are receiving cows and cooperate through Self-help Groups in the care, milk and management of the dairy operation with the assistance of CREATE's Programme Co-ordinator for Women and Children. In 2007, several cows suffered from hoof and mouth disease. Most cows and calves died. So the 2008 proposal included funds for building of sheds for the cattle to protect them from excessively damp conditions in the rainy season. The cows were partially insured and so part of the lost value had been recouped. The Programme Co-ordinator for Women and Children encouraged the Self-help Groups to set aside a small serving of milk each village child under the age of five. This distribution to young children has been implemented in each village. The rest of the milk is sold and the profits go to repay the loans and to provide income for the cow owners.

In 2007, CREATE planned to begin developing a direct marketing programme for selling organically grown local rice from these villages to urban consumers who would invest intentionally in local agriculture for the reward of quality rice delivered to them at harvest time. This programme has not gathered enough interest to provide significant support to the agricultural programme. Agricultural Technicians are providing training to farmers to help them learn organic farming techniques, farming techniques which reduce the use of chemical inputs, and effective pest control practices. Some women have been properly trained to produce vermicompost.

The beneficiary from Naranapuram said, CREATE has helped to improve the economic standard of the family through its various schemes. The schemes are substitute for the seasonal employment in agriculture especially transplantation of seeding and weeding operation which would last for four month crop season.[18]

Krish Vigyan Kendra

The Krish Vigyan Kendra is an institutional project of the India Council of Agricultural Research (ICAR) to demonstrate the application of science and technology, input of agricultural research and education on the farmers field. It is imparting technical know-how to the farmers at their doorsteps through various programmes and packages, especially in the field of agriculture, animal husbandry, horticulture, watershed development and soil conservation. The operational area of it encompasses Amaravati, Morshi, Warud, Bhatkuli, Murtizapur, Nandgaon, Khandeshwar, Barshi Takil, Patur, Akola, Daryapur, Balapur, Telhara, Akot and Anjangaon Suri.[19] The KVK is functioning to ensure food security and right price for agricultural products to the farmers.

Food security is a major issue in Tamil Nadu with prices running at an all time high. Climate change affects the region resulting in drought, poor soils, water depletion, farmers need advice, support and information on the latest technological advances to help them cultivate the best crops from the land and to raise health animals.[20] Though we obtained required proportion of growth in the first Green Revolution, the people of Punjab even now suffer from the severe cancer because of excessive use of chemicals in the agricultural fields. Even, the agricultural Scientist M.S. Swaminathan has expressed his regretless for the result of the first green revolution. With out considering the effect of the first one, we attempt to implement the Second Green Revolution. For the effective execution of the green revolution, ATMA (Agricultural and Technological Management Agency) scheme was introduced in Uttar Pradesh and Haryana at first instance. It was introduced in September 2006 in 133 unions of 9 districts in Tamil Nadu. Later it was expanded to 381 unions. The private agency is empowered to appoint the field workers. It is obvious that the ruling party has interfered in the appointments and thus the scheme goes to the dustbin without achieving its goals.[21] The natural scientist Nammalwar condemns the application of chemical in the agricultural fields. Gradually the agriculturists transform into chemical fertilizer to composite manure. The day will come, we hope, we ill be given secured food.

NOTES

1. *Dinamalar, Trichy*, Dated 18 February, 2012.
2. S. Imayavaramban, ' Food Position in Madras During Second World War' in *Thirty First Annual Session Proceedings of South Indian History Congress, Cudappa*, 2011, p. 593.
3. *The Columbia Encyclopedia*, Sixth Edition, Vol. I, 2007, p. 73.
4. *Dinamalar, Trichy*, Dated 23 December 2009.

5. Pon. Thangamani, *Constitutional History of India, 1773-1950,* (Tamil) Chennai, Ponnaiah Pathipagam, 2001, p. 240.
6. ASSAI Means The Food Safety and Standard Authority of India.
7. *Times of India,* New Delhi, Dated 11 January, 2012.
8. *Times of India,* New Delhi, Dated 10 January, 2012.
9. Pessticides Affect the Nervous System and Cause Several Hazardous Diseases Like Cancer, Liver Kidney and Lung Damages, Loss of Weight and Appetite, Irritability, Insomnia, Behavioural Disorder and Dermatological Problems.
10. Heavy Metals Cause Adverse Effect in Human Metabolic System, Skin Disease, Heart Problems, etc.
11. *Ethylene Gas is used for Fruit Ripening Plant Hormone.*
12. *The Hindu,* Chennai, Dated 9 July, 2010.
13. *Indian Express,* Chennai, Dated 9 July 2010.
14. *Times of India,* Chennai, Dated 20, December 2011.
15. *The Hindu,* Tuticorin, Dated 2 February, 2012.
16. *The Hindu,* Chennai, Dated 9 July, 2010.
17. gifts@dom.disciple.org.
18. Interview with Pothumai, One of the Beneficiary from Naranapuram.
19. *Catalog of ICHR's Publication, Amaravati,* 2000, p. 1.
20. *Ibid.,*
21. Dinamalar, Trichy, Dated 19, February 2012.

7

Changes in Cropping Pattern and its Impact on Food Security

M. Samithurai

INTRODUCTION

In India, agriculture being the primary sector accounts for 22 per cent of the GDP and provides direct employment to 58 per cent of the country's population. Frequent monsoon failure leaves the farmers high and dry, caught in debt-traps and there are several incidents of suicide in many parts of the country. Agricultural sector in India is reeling under the pressure of natural calamities on the hand and starving for credit and modernisation on the other. Galloping population and mounting unemployment coupled with ever dwindling jobs in the organized sector compel the masses to fall back on agriculture as the only source to sustain their existence. The annual average growth rate of agriculture sector in India during 1990-99 is 3.4 per cent, we have lower rate of growth in agriculture but population is also increasing. However due to increasing in productivity we could achieve food security. We have land use advantage where we are able to grow two to three crops per year and almost all crops in the world unlike other countries.

At macro level, over the past 40 years, there has been remarkable growth in agricultural production with per capita world food production growing by 17 per cent and aggregate world food production growing by 45 per cent. Between the early 1960s and mid-1990s, average cereal yields grew from 1.2 t/ha to 2.52 t/ha in developing countries whilst total cereal production has grown from 420 to 1176 million tonnes per year. Over the same period, world population has grown from three to six billion, but globally per capita agricultural production has overtaken population growth and for each person today, there is an additional 25 per cent more food compared with 1960. However this is not the case for everyone, it varies regionally and in Africa for example food production per person is 10 per cent lower today than in 1960. Modern agricultural methods have brought spectacular increases in productivity-more cereals and animals per hectare, more meat and milk per animal, more food output per person employed. Any farmer or agricultural system with access to sufficient inputs, knowledge and skills, can produce large amounts of food. However the majority of the chronically hungry are small farmers in developing countries who produce much of what they eat and are often poor and marginalized from input and product markets. The recent advances in aggregate productivity have therefore not brought reductions in the incidence of hunger for all. In the early 21st century, there are still more than 800 million people hungry and lacking adequate access to food. A third are in East and South-East Asia, another third in South Asia, a quarter are in Sub-Saharan Africa, and 5 per cent each in Latin America/Caribbean and in North Africa/Near East.

World population is widely expected then to reach 9 billion by the next generation and by this time, 84 per cent of people will be in those countries currently making up the 'developing' world. At the same time, land and water degradation is increasingly posing a threat to food security and the livelihoods of rural people who often live on degradation-prone lands. Although a combination of increased production and more imports will mean per capita consumption will increase to an average of about 3000 kcal per day by 2015, a developing country person will still only consume half of the cereal and a third of the meat compared with a person in an industrialized country, so food insecurity and malnutrition will still persist.

Food security can be defined as a condition where "all people, at all times, have physical and economic access to sufficient, sage and nutritious food to meet their dietary needs and food preferences for and active and healthy life". Indicators of food insecurity in a given region can include numbers of 'hungry' or malnourished people, of underweight children and of people suffering from micronutrient deficiency. Average per caita food consumption in 2003 was 2780 kcal day^{-1}, yet consumption in 33 poor countries is still less than 2200 kcal day^{-1}. In addition to nearly 0.9 billion people suffering form micronutrient deficiency. Almost 50 per cent of pregnant women in Sub-Saharan Africa are affected by iron deficiency anemia. In the last 10 years progress in the drive to reduce hunger has been slow and has varied around the wrold, in Sub-Saharan Africa the number of hungry people has in fact increased by 20 per cent since 1990. In the period 2000-02, the proportion of under-nourished people in the total people of Kenya was 33 per cent, in Uganda 19 per cent and 44 per cent United Republic of Tanzania. The number of underweight children has also increased in Central, Western Eastern Africa compared to an overall decrease in other developing regions such as Asia. South America and North Africa. The world therefore still faces a fundamental food security challenges, despite steadily falling fertility rates and family sizes, world population continues to increase and so in parallel will the absolute demand for food. Food demand will also shift in the coming decades, as:

1. economic growth increases people's purchasing power;
2. growing urbanization encourages people to adopt new diets;
3. climate change threatens both land water resources.

What makes agriculture unique as an economic sector is that it directly affects many of the natural, social and economic resources on which it relies for success. Agricultural systems at all levels rely on the value of services flowing from the total stock of assets that they influence and control – an agricultural system that erodes soil whilst producing food results in costs that others must bear; another system that sequesters carbon in soils through organic matter accumulation helps to mediate climate change; a diverse agricultural system that enhances on-farm wildlife for pest control contributes to wider stocks of bio-diversity, whilst; a simplified modernized system that eliminates wildlife does not contribute to bio-diversity; and finally, agricultural systems that offer labour-absorption opportunities, through resource improvements or value-added activities, can boost local economies and help to reverse rural-to-urban migration patterns. Agriculture is, therefore, fundamentally multifunctional as it produces many unique food and non-food functions that cannot be produced by other economic sectors so efficiently. Increased food supply is a necessary though not sufficient condition for eliminating hunger and poverty. What is important is who produces the food, has access to the technology and knowledge to produce it, and who has the purchasing power to acquire it. Clearly then there are emergent food poverty and food security challenges; How to find ways to maintain and enhance food production whilst seeking both to improve the positive side-effects and to eliminate the negative ones? This will not be easy, as past agricultural development has tended to ignore both the multi functionality of agriculture and the considerable external costs and what is the best way to increase agricultural productivity in developing countries that still, have hundreds of million people short of food?

These questions are controversial, with widely varying positions about strategies which are likely to be effective including; expanding the area of agriculture; increasing per hectare production in agricultural exporting countries or; increasing total farm productivity in developing countries which are most going to need the food. The conventional wisdom is that, in order to double food supply, efforts need to be redoubled to modernize agriculture – as this has been successful in the past. But there are doubts about the capacity of such systems to reduce food poverty. The great technological progress in the past half-century has not been reflected in major reductions in hunger and poverty in developing countries. Arguably then the most sustainable choice for agricultural development and food security is to increase total farm productivity in situ, in the developing countries which are most going to need the food. The central questions, therefore must focus on the extent to which farmers can improve food production and raise income with *low-cost, locally-available* technologies and inputs and whether they can do this without causing further environmental damages.

The cropping pattern can be considered in the wide perspective of a combination of activities leading to diversification or specialisation in agriculure. It is important both from the individual and national point of view. It is in the pattern of deciding the combination of crops to be grown on limited land area with the available quantities of labour, capital and irrigation. In the latter case, it is the question of determining the cropping pattern encouraged for attaining the nation objective of self-sufficiency in the agriculture sector.

Changing in Cropping Pattern

Changing in cropping pattern means the process of shifting of area under cultivation of major crops. Since 1950-51, area under food grain crops has been decaling in India. It means that either the farmer prefer to grow non-food grain crops or they close down the profession of farming and migrates themselves to urban centres in searching of jobs and livelihood. In 1950-51, area under food grains crops was 74 per cent to total cultivation land, which declining to 72 per cent in 2002-03. The shift in cropping pattern was occurred due the remunerative prices to commercial crops and facility of better market access in the case of those crops.

After 1994-95, there was no specific change in the cropping pattern. In the initial years of Five-year Plan, the cropping pattern between food crops and non-food crops were 74:26. By the year 1980-81, the ratio changed to 80:20 and by the year 1994-95, it changed to 77:23. According to the latest statistical figures, by 2002-03, the ratio between food crops and non-food crops recorded a small change, 75.6:24.4. Generally, the acreage figures shift in favour of food crops.

This is because the prices of food grain have been rising quite fast and the farmers have started growing food grain for the market. Cultivation of food grains has become highly remunerative and productive under the impact of new technology. As indicated already, the largest increase has been recorded by wheat with an increase of 150 per cent, whole the increase in the case of rice has been quite modest, *i.e.* 36 per cent. Acreage under potato has increased by more than 300 per cent during 50 years of planning.

Factors influencing Changing Crop Pattern

Cropping pattern are influenced by some important factors which are:

1. *Natural Conditions*: Natural factors Such as the climate of the country, type of the soil, rain fall and temperature determine the type of crops to be grown.
2. *Irrigation Facilities:* Play a dominant role in determining the crop of a region. It can change the pattern of crops. Assured water supply will enable the farmers to have two three crops in a year.
3. *Prices of Crops*: Prices of different agricultural crops influence the cropping pattern. Changes in the market prices of competing crops will influence the farmer to have that crop in which income will be the maximum per acre.
4. *Size of Farmer and Income of the Farmer:* A subsistence farmer with this small patch of land will grow only food crops for his family. The size of the farm thereby determines the type of crops.
5. *Availability of Inputs*: Availability of inputs like seeds, fertilizers, and pesticides in adequate at a reasonable price will influence the type of crop grown by the farmer.
6. *Government Policy:* The policy of the government may change the crop pattern. This cab be done by supplying the seeds and other inputs at a concessional price to the farmers so as to induce them to grow a particular crop.

The government is aiming to achieve cent per cent food security in the state and also to create revenue for export of agricultural produces for economic upliftment of the farming community; it is aiming an annual growth rate of 4 per cent in agriculture and 8 per cent in the horticulture crops for sustenance agricultural development, employment generation and poverty alleviation. The government is focusing on overall development of agriculture sector in terms of increasing the cropping intensity by bridging every piece of land under cultivation, increasing productivity, maximizing natural resource use with parallel effort to conserve them.

The five types of 'capital' asset include the Natural capital produces environmental goods and services, and is the source of food (both farmed and harvested or caught from the wild), wood and fibre; water supply and regulation; treatment, assimilation and decomposition of wastes; nutrient cycling and fixation; soil formation; biological control of pests; climate regulation; wildlife habitats; storm protection and flood control; carbon sequestration; pollination; and landscape. Social capital produces a mutually beneficial collective action, contributing to the cohesiveness of people in their societies. The social assets comprising social capital include norms, values and attitudes that prompt people to cooperate; relations of trust, reciprocity and obligations; and common rules and sanctions mutually-agreed or handed-down. These are connected and structured in networks and groups; Human capital is the total capability residing in individuals, based on their stock of knowledge skills, health and nutrition. It is enhanced by access to services that provide these, such as schools, medical services, and adult training. People's productivity is increased by their capacity to interact with productive technologies and with other people. Leadership and organizational skills are particularly important in making other resources more valuable; Physical capital is the store of human-made material resources, and comprises buildings, such as housing and factories, market infrastructure, irrigation works, roads and bridges, tools and tractors, communications, and energy and transportation systems, that make labour more productive. Financial capital is more of an accounting concept, as it serves as a facilitating role rather than as a source of productivity in and of itself. It represents accumulated claims on goods and services, built up through financial systems that gather savings and issue credit, such as pensions, remittances, welfare payments, grants and subsidies. As agricultural systems shape these very assets on which they rely for inputs, a vital feedback loop occurs from outcomes to inputs. The basic premise is that more sustainable agricultural systems accumulate stocks of these five assets, thereby increasing all the forms of capital over time. Sustainable agricultural systems tend to have a particularly positive effect on natural, social and human capital, whilst unsustainable systems deplete these assets, leaving less for future generations.

The Food Security Challenge

Sustainability in Agriculture: Many different expressions have come to be used to imply greater sustainability in some agricultural systems over prevailing ones (both pre-industrial and industrialized). These include biodynamic, community-based, eco-agriculture, ecological, environmentally sensitive, extensive, farm-fresh, free-range, low-input, organic, sustainable and wise-use. There is a continuing and intense debate about whether agricultural systems using some of these terms can qualify as sustainable. However agricultural systems high in sustainability can be taken as those that aim to make the best use of environmental goods and services whilst not damaging the five assets particularly natural, social and human capitals. The key principles for sustainability are to integrate biological and ecological processes such as nutrient cycling, nitrogen fixation, soil regeneration, allelopathy, competition, predation and parasitism into food production processes; minimize the use of those non-renewable inputs that cause environmental damage or that harm the health of farmers and consumers; make good use of the knowledge and skills of farmers, so improving their self-reliance and substituting human capital for costly external inputs; by converting new lands to agriculture, but with the result that services from forests, grasslands and other areas of important bio-diversity are lost mostly in industrialized countries, so that food can be transferred or sold to those who need it; make productive use of people's collective capacities to work together to solve common agricultural and natural resource problems, such as for pest, watershed, irrigation, forest and credit management. Sustainability in agricultural systems incorporates concepts of both resilience (the capacity of systems to resist shocks and stresses) and persistence (the capacity of systems to continue over long periods), and addresses many wider economic, social and environmental outcomes. Agricultural systems with high levels of social and human assets are more able to adapt to change and innovate in the face of uncertainty. This suggests that there likely to be many pathways towards agricultural sustainability, and so no single system of technologies, inputs or ecological management is more likely to be widely applicable than another. Agricultural sustainability then implies the need to fit these factors to the specific circumstances of different local agricultural systems.

The measures which are suggested for protecting agriculture from climate change to ensure for the food security include Promoting crop diversification; Devising agronomic practices which may moderate the predicted climate change and promotion of conservation agriculture Practices such as zero tillage, bed planting, residue management and crop rotation; Improve management of livestock population especially ruminants and its diet; and. Change land use by increase area under bio-fuels, agro-forestry-but on the cost of food production to mention a few.

Conclusion

In India the poor farmers would be very vulnerable to change brought about by global warming. Global warming not only leads to loss of life and property, but also might cause a major reshuffle in flora, fauna and cropping pattern in India. India depends heavily on agriculture; the effects of global warming and climate change on the agriculture sector are likely to threaten both the welfare of the population and the economic development of the state. For instance, crop yields are directly affected by changes in climate factors such as temperature and precipitation and the frequency and severity of extreme events such as droughts, floods and cyclonic storms. Changing crops, introducing irrigation or modifying Farm management methods are too costly for many farmers to implement. However, it is fond hope that not only the second green revolution measures can solve the problem of food security by changing the cropping pattern through introducing the packages of inputs and other modern methods of cultivation but also addressing the climatic change and other related issues to reach the sustainable development through ensuring food security.

REFERENCES

Awais, Mohammad and Naheen Haider Zaidi, "Climate Change and its Impact on Agriculture" *Agricultural Finance*. Vol. 42, April. 2010. pp. 9-13.

Kumar, Velu Suresh "Climate Change and Its Impact on India", *Southern Economist*, Vol. 49. May, 2010, pp. 5-8.

Nagaraj, H.V. "Second Green Revolution in India". *Southern Economist*, Vol. 49. No. 9, February 1, 2011, pp. 11-14.

Patri, Neelakant "Global Warming Cap, Trade and Sulk", *Southern Economist*, Vol. 48, Dec,. 2009. pp. 3-8.

Singaraj, A. and Kumar, D. "Economic Impact of Climate Change on Agriculture and Water Resources", *Southern Economist*, Vol. 48, Oct., 2009, pp. 5-8.

8

Cropping Pattern towards Horticultural Crops in India
A Trend Analysis

S. Suganthi
K. Manikandan

INTRODUCTION

Green revolution was aimed at food self-sufficiency and food crops were encouraged during green revolution. However, it is the nutritional security which is considered most important for balanced diet. Fruits and vegetables are also rich source of vitamins, minerals, proteins, and carbohydrates etc., which are essential in human nutrition. Hence, these are referred to as protective foods and assume great importance in the context of nutritional security of the people. Cultivation of horticultural crops plays a vital role in the prosperity of a nation and is directly linked with the health and happiness of the people. In this context, diversification of agriculture assumes greater significance. Diversification is an important strategy from the point of view of agriculture growth (Jha, *et al.*, 2000). Diversification largely depends upon the opportunities and responsiveness of farmers to technological breakthrough, consumers demand, government policy, trade arrangements and development of irrigation and roads and other infrastructure. Changes in cropping patterns are responsive to these factors (Kumar and Mittal, 2003). Cultivation of horticulture plays a vital role in the prosperity of a nation and is directly linked with the health and happiness of the people. In 2005-06 horticultural crops contributed around 28.0 per cent in agriculture from a more 13.0 per cent share of national area under horticulture crops (Singh and Mathur 2008). This shift away from cereals to fruits and vegetable shows that it is economically viable and beneficial to farmers. It is widely recommended that horticultural crops can play a vital role in competing problems of malnutrition, bringing nutritional security, generating greater employment potential in rural areas, profitability and sustainable use of natural resources. The crop diversification towards selective high value crops including fruits and vegetables are effective strategy in raising incomes, generating employment opportunities and alleviating poverty among small and marginal households (Vyas, 1996; Joshi, *et al.*, 2007).

Objectives

1. to analyze the trends in area under different crops;
2. to examine the trends in area under production of horticultural crops and food crop under a comparative framework; and
3. to find out whether small farmers diversify towards horticulture in India.

Methodology

The study makes use of secondary data collected from reports of National Horticulture Board, Government of India. The data used in the study pertain to the period from 1991 to 2010. The variables chosen for the study are: area and production of horticulture crops and food crops. The trends in the variables are analyzed based on calculation of Compound Annual Growth Rate. The formula is as follows:

$$CAGR\,(t_o, t_n) = V\,(t_n) / V\,(t_0)\, 1/t_n - t_0.$$

V (t^0): Start Value; V (t^x); Finish Value, t^n - t^o: Number of years.

The growth rates are computed for decennially for the periods 1991-2000 and 2001-10.

Analysis and Discussion

Trends in Area and Producation of Horticultural Crops

In this section the trends in area and production of horticulture are analyzed juxtaposing the relevant details on food crops. Two variables are considered here. They are area under and production in quantity of horticultural and food crops. The growth rates constructed so are shown in Table 8.1.

Table 8.1: Growth Rate of Area and Production of Horticultural and Food Crops in India

Period	Horticultural Crops		Food Crops	
	Area (million ha)	Production (million tonnes)	Area (million ha)	Production (million tonnes)
1991-2000	2.29	5.2	-0.07	1.7
2001-2010	2.59	5.7	-0.15	0.27

Note: Data Compiled from National Horticulture Board, GoI and Reserve Bank of India.

Table 8.1 shows that growth rate of area under cultivation of horticulturalcrop in India was positive (2.29) in the 1991-2000, and it increased further to 2.59 during 2001-10. It may be inferred that the area under horticultural crop has increased and diversification has given impetus to increase in area under horticulture crop in India. It is clear from the table that the growth rate of the production of horticulture has also increased from 5.2 during 1991-2010 to 5.7 during 2001-10, owing to diversification from low value crops to high value horticultural crops of acreage under cultivation. The growth rate seems to have reclaimed between 1991-2000 and 2001-10. Table 8.1 also provides data on growth rate of area and production of food grains in India for the period of 1991-2010. Table 8.1 shows that growth rate of area under cultivation of food grains in India was negative (-0.07) during

1991-2000. It showed a further negative growth rate of -0.15 during 2001-10. It is also clear from Table 8.1 that the growth rate of the production of food grains has decreased from 1.7 during 1991-2000 to 0.27 during 2001-10. These trends could be noticed more easily from the graphs (Fig. 8.1 and Fig. 8.2) as well.

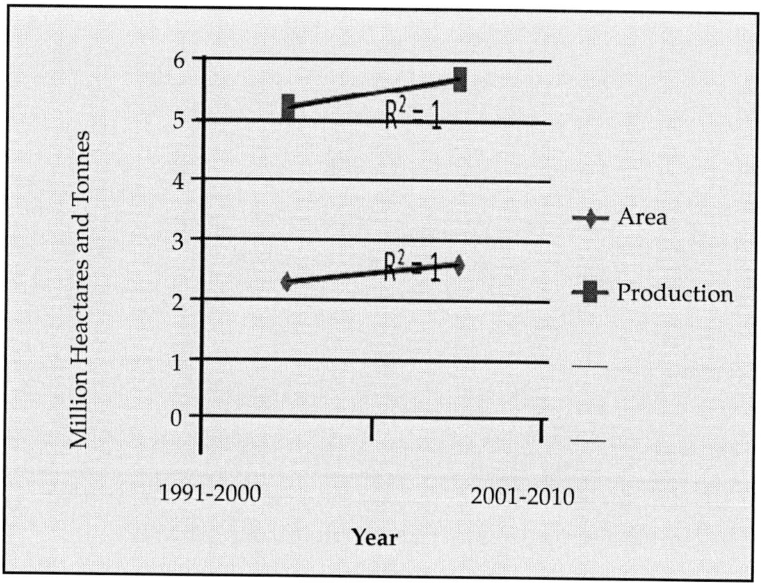

Fig. 8.1: Growth Rate of Area and Production of Horticulture in India from 1991-2010

The decline in the growth rate of area under and production of food grains seem to explain the increase in the growth rate of area under and production of horticultural crops in India. On the whole, it may be stated that the area under and production of horticultural crops have increased over the study period. This is due to diversification of agriculture towards high value horticultural crops. Alongside, it may also be inferred that this trends seem to have been contributing to the nutritional security of the nation.

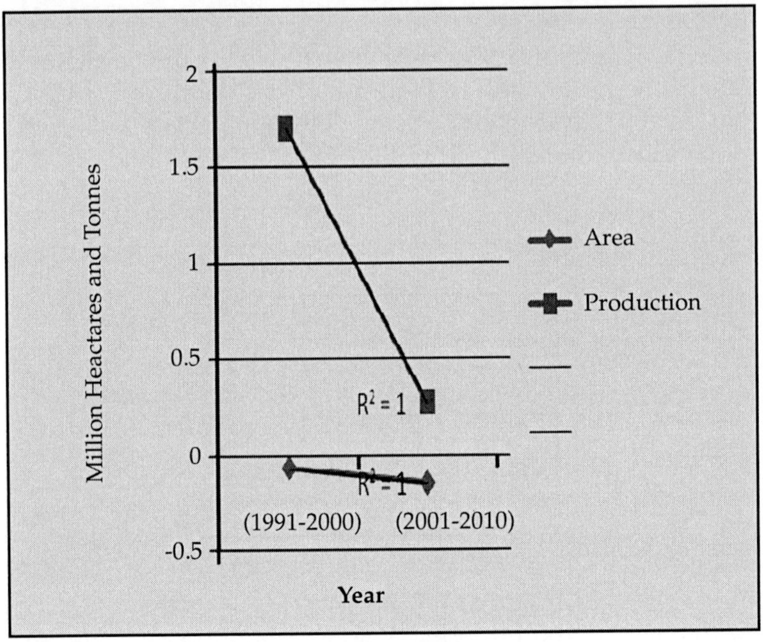

Fig. 8.2: Growth Rate of Area and Production of Food Crops in India from 1991-2010

Do Small Farmers Shift towards Horticulture?

Agricultural Census Data show that there were about 121 million agricultural holdings in India in 2000-01. Around 99 million were small and marginal farmers (Mahendra Dev, 2012). Indian agriculture is predominantly a small peasant based economy with approximately 80. per cent of the operational holdings being below two hectares, and 34. per cent of the agricultural land are cultivated by them (GOI, 1997). As such small and marginal farmers play an important role in sustainable agricultural growth, food security and nutritional security. As discussed earlier diversification towards horticultural crops could improve nutritional security of our nation. In this context, role of small and marginal farmers is crucial. In this section attempt is made so as to find out that small and marginal farmers diversify towards horticultural crops. In terms of production, small and marginal farmers also make larger contribution to the production of high value crops. They contribute around 70. per cent to the total production of vegetables, 55. per cent to fruits against their share of 44. per cent in land area. Thus, small farmers contribute to both diversification and food security. From efficiency point of view, small holdings are equal or better than large holdings. So, horizontal diversification of small and marginal farms towards high value crops is seen to be more than large farms in India. In case of proportion of area devoted to horticulture crops, a positive relationship is observed, but this relationship is not significant because it is also observed that the proportion area devoted to vegetables by large farmers is less compared to marginal, small and medium farming categories. Cultivation of horticulture is labour intensive and small and marginal farmers have family labour at their disposal which large farmers do not, resulting in constraints imposed by availability of family labour in expanding area under horticulture for large farmers (Haque, 2010). (Birthal *et al.*) also show that small-holders tend to have greater labour endowments (*i.e.* larger families), meaning that they may be better suited in cultivating labour intensive high-value crops. (Birthal *et.al.*, 2007). From income point of view it is seen that crop diversification towards high value crops, mainly vegetables and fruits especially by small and marginal holders increases the yield levels of these crops as compared to other crops and it was also reported by farmers that the returns especially from horticulture were more regular as compared to food grains (GOI, 1997). Because of small operational holdings, it is indeed very difficult by the small farmers to improve their earnings only by raising the yields of the existing crops, mainly cereals. However, with the availability of modern farm inputs in the current decades, it was possible for farmers to generate higher levels of income by introducing high value crops commonly known as horticulture crops in their farming units. Thus, the high value crops being more labour intensive may provide stable employment and income to a large section of the rural households who face the severe problem of seasonal unemployment and underemployment under mono-crop economy (Utpal and Chattopadhyay, 2010). Small and marginal farmers really diversify towards horticultural crops. Horticultural crops help to increase employment and income of the farmers on the one hand and on the other helps to achieve nutritional security of the nation.

Conclusion

The study reveals that agricultural diversification has given impetus to area under cultivation and production of horticultural crops in India. Diversification towards horticulture is increasing on the one side and a declining trend is noticed in case of the growth rate of area under cultivation and production of food crops, declining drastically between 1991 and 2010. Thus the study reveals that farmers shift from low value food crops to high value horticulture crops. The paper also shows that small and marginal farmers shift towards horticultural crops. In fact, the horticultural crops help them utilise their family labour optimally and help augment their income. The positive trend in area under and production of horticultural crops as revealed in the study has clear indication of nutritional security, besides employment and income-generation.

REFERENCES

Birthal, P.S., K.P. Joshi and Devesh Roy (2007), "Diversification in Indian Agriculture towards High-Value Crops: The Role of Small Holders," *IFPRI Discussion Paper 00727*, November.

Dev, M (2012), Small Farmers in India: Challenges and Opportunities Indira Gandhi Institute of Development Research, Mumbai, June http://www.igi

Government of India (GOI)(1997), "Operational Land Holdings in India, 1991-92: Salient Features," *NSS 48th Round Report No. 407*, Department of Statistics.

Government of India (2010), *Indian Horticulture Database*, National Horticultural Board. Ministry of Agriculture.

Haque, T. (2010), "Constraints and Potentials of Diversified Agricultural Development in Eastern India," www.ncap.res.in/upload_files/workshop/wsp1.pdf.

Jha, B., N. Kumar, and B. Mohanty (2009), "Pattern of Agricultural Diversification in India," Institute of Economic Growth, *Working Paper* No, E/302/2009.

Kumara, A., Sant Kumara, Dhiraj, Singh, B.K. and Shivjee (2011), "Rural Employment Diversification in India: Trends, Determinants and Implications on Poverty," *Agricultural Economics Research Review,* Vol. 24.

Mittal, Surabhi. (2007), "Can Horticulture be a Success Story for India?, Indian Council for Research on International Economic Relations, " *Working Paper*, August .

Mittal, Surabhi (2009), "Feasibility Check for Diversification Towards Horticultural Production," *Agricultural Economics Research Review,* Vol. 22 January-June.

NAAS (2001), "Diversification of Agriculture for Human Nutrition" Policy Paper-17, National Academy of Agricultural Sciences, India.

Singh, M. and V.C. Mathur (2008), "Structural Changes in Horticultural Sector in India: Retrospect and Prospect for XI Five-year Plan, *Indian Journal of Agricultural Economics*", Vol. 63, No. 3, July-Sep.

Sharma, H.R. (2011), *Crop Diversification in Himachal Pradesh: Patterns, Determinants and Challenges*, India International Centre, New Delhi, November 10-11, naasindia.org

Thaga (2009), "Smallholder Farming in Transforming Economies of Asia and the Pacific: Challenges and Opportunities, Prepared for the Side Event Organized During the Thirty Third Session of IFAD's Governing Council," *Discussion Paper* -18, February.

Utpal, K.D. and Manabendu Chattopadhyay (2010), "Crop Diversification by Poor Peasants and Role of Infrastructure: Evidence from West Bengal," *Journal of Development and Agricultural Economics* , Vol. 2(10), October.

9

Land Utilisation and Cropping Pattern

R. Indumathy

INTRODUCTION

Agricultural crop production is the mainstay of the Indian economy, which supports about 115.5 million farm families. Growth in this sector has a maximum cascading impact on other sectors leading to spread of growth, equality and benefits over the entire economy. Therefore, the need for enhancing agricultural production is very great and very urgent at present. The ability of agriculture to contribute directly to economic growth is, however, dependent on the level of incomes under resultant surpluses in the agricultural sector.

The level of farm incomes, *ceteris paribus*, is the outcome of efficient utilisation of existing resources among alternative production activities. An improper allocation of resources results in output being less than the potential minimum. Quite often farmers are faced with the problem of judicious and efficient use of resources, particularly land, which is in acute short supply. In a State like Tamil Nadu where population pressure is very high and land resources are meager, proper exploitation of land resource is of strategic importance. The wider fluctuations in agricultural output experienced recently are generally attributed to the utilisation of land. Therefore proper land utilisation is very important in planning for higher agricultural production.

Objective

The analysis in this Chapter is intended to focus attention on finding out whether the existing crops involve a misuse of land resource and wastage of productivity resulting in lower yields.

Methodology

The study covers eight major crops: *(i)* Paddy, *(ii)* Cholam, *(iii)* Cumbu, *(iv)* Ragi, *(v)* Sugarcane, *(vi)* Cotton, *(vii)* Groundnut, and *(viii)* Tapioca. All of which constitute 58 per cent of the total cultivated area of 5,82,428 hectares. The data for 32 districts which have been formed from the originally existing thirteen districts are available only for different time periods. Hence to compare the data on an uniform basis, they have been grouped into the original 13 districts. The grouping of these thirteen districts runs as follows:

1. Chengalpattu (Chennai, Kancheepuram, Thiruvallur),
2. South Arcot (Cuddalore, Villupuram),
3. North Arcot (Thiruvannamali, Vellore)
4. Salem (Namakkal),
5. Dharmapuri (Krishnagiri),
6. Coimbatore (Thirupur),
7. Erode,
8. Tiruchirapalli (Karur, Perambalur, Ariyalur),
9. Pudukkottai,
10. Thanjavur (Thiruvarur, Nagapathinam),
11. Madurai (Dindigal, Theni),
12. Ramanathapuram (Kamarajar, Pasumpon Muthuramalingam, Sivagangai),
13. Tirunelveli (Thoothukudi).

In the present study Nilgris and Kanyakumari districts are omitted because the cultivation of selected crops is found to be very meager in these two districts. The basic data for the cropping pattern of each district for each year are taken from Season and Crop Reports of Tamil Nadu. The extent of cultivation of different crops and their average yields have been worked out by averaging the respective data for 28 years from 1981-82 to 2008-09. Since district has been taken as the basic area unit, the data for each crop relate to thirteen districts in the State. The following Tables 8.1 to 9.8 indicate two sets of figures relating to a particular crop namely the extent of cultivation and average yield. The data for the extent of cultivation have been estimated for all the thirteen districts separately and for the state as a whole. They are in terms of percentage of total area under the specific crop to the total cropped area in each district and for the state figure to the total cropped area in Tamil Nadu. Figures 8.1 to 9.8 for the average yield are calculated by taking an average of the actual yields for 28 years for the thirteen districts separately and for the State as a whole and they are in terms of kilograms in tables and maunds (37.324 kg) in graphs. The average yield of sugarcane relates to cane and not to *gur*.

Table 9. 1: District-wise Data for Extent of Cultivation and Yield Paddy

Sl. No.	Districts	Extent of Cultivation %	Average Yield MDS/hec
1.	Chengalpattu	66.01	2984
2.	South Arcot	35.87	3052
3.	North Arcot	27.50	2865
4.	Salem	9.98	2900
5.	Dharmapuri	9.83	2935
6.	Coimbatore	4.99	3382
7.	Erode	16.61	3859
8.	Trichy	22.74	3068
9.	Pudukkottai	52.69	2515
10.	Thanjavur	66.62	2559
11.	Madurai	21.14	3549
12.	Ramanathapuram	51.33	1940
13.	Tirunelveli	27.16	3671
14.	**State**	**31.98**	**2868**

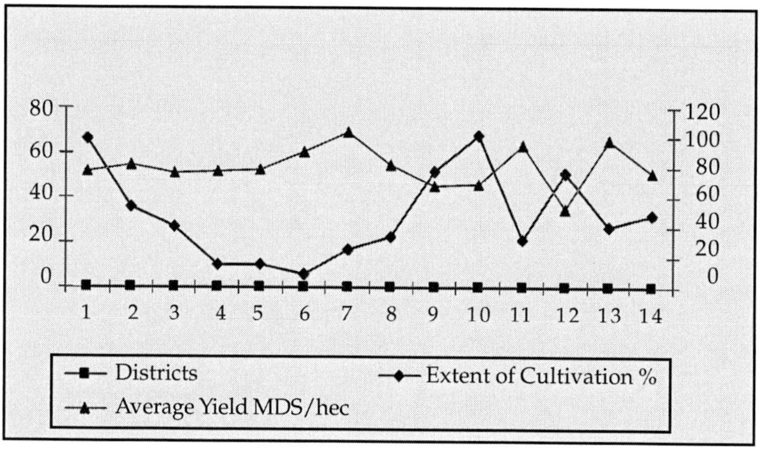

Fig. 9.1: Paddy

Table 9.2: District-wise Data for Extent of Cultivation and Yield Cholam

Sl. No.	Districts	Extent of Cultivation %	Average Yield MDS/hec
1.	Chengalpattu	0.08	1254
2.	South Arcot	1.75	991
3.	North Arcot	0.35	1125
4.	Salem	7.74	509
5.	Dharmapuri	26.65	577
6.	Coimbatore	26.65	577
7.	Erode	9.12	761
8.	Trichy	19.5	1047
9.	Pudukkottai	0.92	—
10.	Thanjavur	—	—
11.	Madurai	15.65	1278
12.	Ramanathapuram	2.45	955
13.	Tirunelveli	3.69	1600
14.	**Tamil Nadu**	**7.44**	**909**

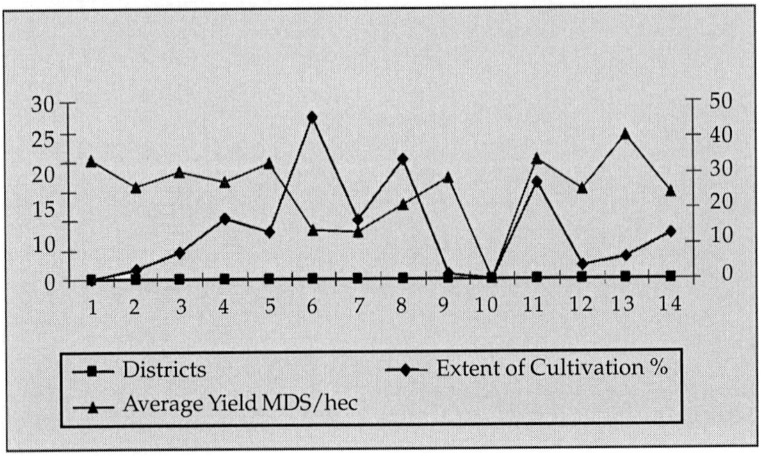

Fig. 9.2: Cholam

Table 9.3: District-wise Data for Extent of Cultivation and Yield Cumbu

Sl. No.	Districts	Extent of Cultivation %	Average Yield MDS/hec
1.	Chengalpattu	0.49	1942
2.	South Arcot	10.06	1316
3.	North Arcot	0.09	1082
4.	Salem	3.17	1421
5.	Dharmapuri	1.11	1559
6.	Coimbatore	0.49	1726
7.	Erode	2.16	1075
8.	Trichy	6.92	650
9.	Pudukkottai	0.35	1415
10.	Thanjavur	0.04	1520
11.	Madurai	2.65	1365
12.	Ramanathapuram	2.56	1209
13.	Tirunelveli	6.88	1411
14.	**State**	**3.09**	**1152**

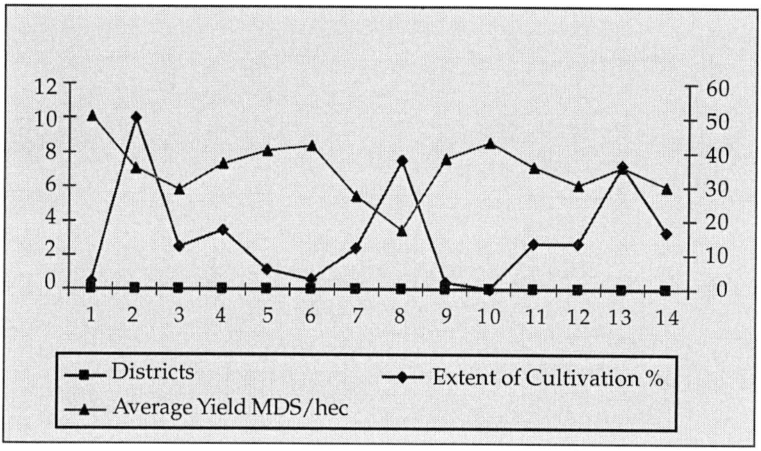

Fig. 9.3: Cumbu

Table 9.4: District-wise Data for Extent of Cultivation and Yield Ragi

Sl. No.	Districts	Extent of Cultivation %	Average Yield MDS/hec
1.	Chengalpattu	1.27	1858
2.	South Arcot	0.87	1986
3.	North Arcot	0.08	1994
4.	Salem	3.39	2119
5.	Dharmapuri	5.71	1638
6.	Coimbatore	0.26	2020
7.	Erode	3.88	1213
8.	Trichy	0.19	1870
9.	Pudukkottai	1.00	1527
10.	Thanjavur	0.03	2292
11.	Madurai	0.32	1963
12.	Ramanathapuram	1.65	1740
13.	Tirunelveli	0.59	2385
14.	**Tamil Nadu**	**2.21**	**1753**

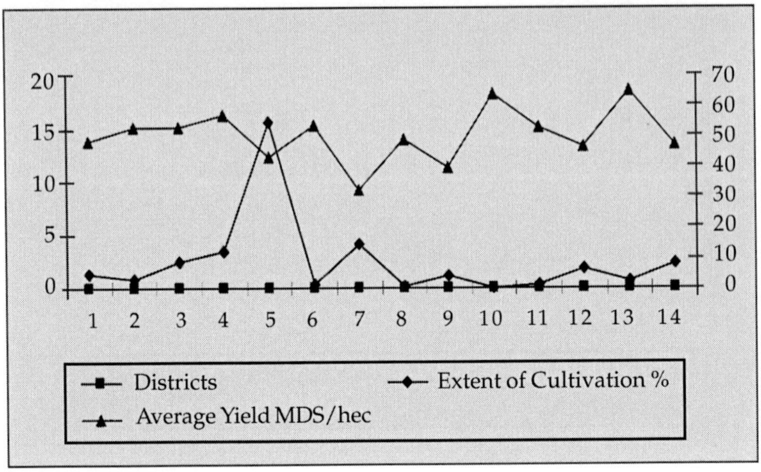

Fig. 9.4: Ragi

Table 9.5: Districts-wise Data for Extent of Cultivation and Yield Sugarcane

Sl. No.	Districts	Extent of Cultivation %	Average Yield MDS/hec
1.	Chengalpattu	3.02	108
2.	South Arcot	7.84	113
3.	North Arcot	0.23	84
4.	Salem	3.77	125
5.	Dharmapuri	3.43	88
6.	Coimbatore	3.54	107
7.	Erode	7.22	120
8.	Trichy	3.89	108
9.	Pudukkottai	1.89	109
10.	Thanjavur	2.36	101
11.	Madurai	3.24	111
12.	Ramanathapuram	1.58	102
13.	Tirunelveli	0.86	105
14.	**State**	**3.99**	**106**

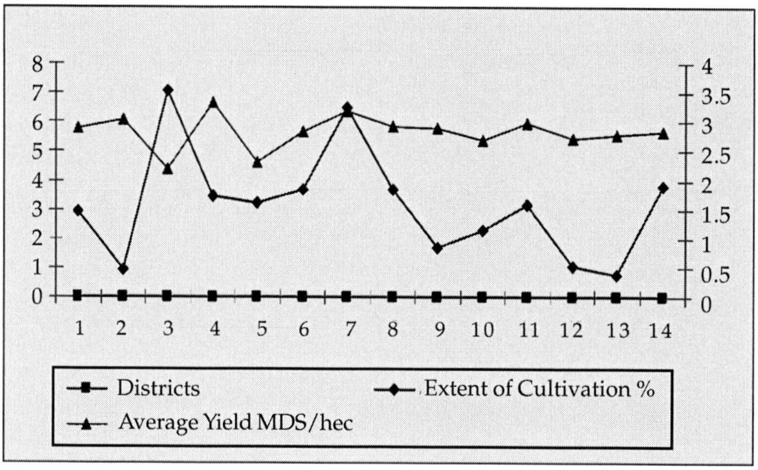

Fig. 9.5: Sugarcane

Table 9.6: District-wise Data for Extent of Cultivation and Yield Cotton

Sl. No.	Districts	Extent of Cultivation %	Average Yield MDS/hec
1.	Chengalpattu	0.04	363
2.	South Arcot	1.38	354
3.	North Arcot	1.06	367
4.	Salem	3.45	337
5.	Dharmapuri	2.52	370
6.	Coimbatore	4.03	370
7.	Erode	2.15	410
8.	Trichy	3.19	265
9.	Pudukkottai	0.29	348
10.	Thanjavur	0.59	393
11.	Madurai	5.35	330
12.	Ramanathapuram	7.24	213
13.	Tirunelveli	9.84	225
14.	**Tamil Nadu**	**3.09**	**276**

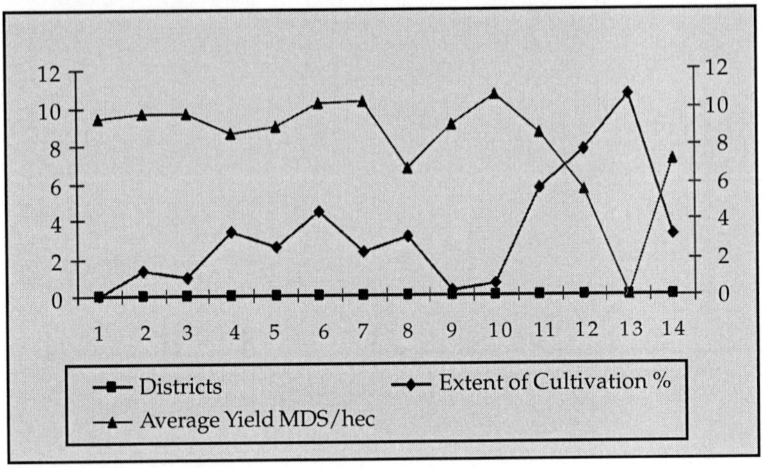

Fig. 9.6: Cotton

Table 9.7: District-wise Data for Extent of Cultivation and Yield Groundnut

Sl. No.	Districts	Extent of Cultivation %	Average Yield MDS/hec
1.	Chengalpattu	16.30	2345
2.	South Arcot	17.77	1689
3.	North Arcot	32.81	1383
4.	Salem	20.72	1440
5.	Dharmapuri	12.22	1491
6.	Coimbatore	10.23	1390
7.	Erode	16.48	1556
8.	Trichy	11.05	1462
9.	Pudukkottai	20.90	1252
10.	Thanjavur	3.11	1714
11.	Madurai	8.73	1596
12.	Ramanathapuram	5.31	1051
13.	Tirunelveli	2.48	1551
14.	**State**	**12.94**	**1511**

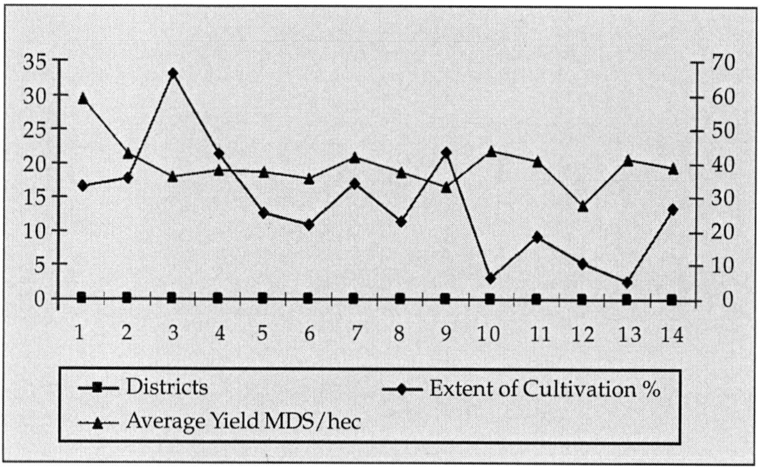

Fig. 9.7: Groundnut

Table 9.8: District-wise Data for Extent of Cultivation and Yield Tapiaco

Sl. No.	Districts	Extent of Cultivation %	Average Yield MDS/hec
1.	Chengalpattu	0.04	32962
2.	South Arcot	2.05	33515
3.	North Arcot	0.15	32957
4.	Salem	6.59	37678
5.	Dharmapuri	2.71	32803
6.	Coimbatore	0.27	40883
7.	Erode	1.14	42546
8.	Trichy	0.02	34398
9.	Pudukkottai	0.02	34398
10.	Thanjavur	0.06	34720
11.	Madurai	0.05	36146
12.	Ramanathapuram	0.01	35149
13.	Tirunelveli	0.05	32185
14.	**Tamil Nadu**	**4.52**	**34275**

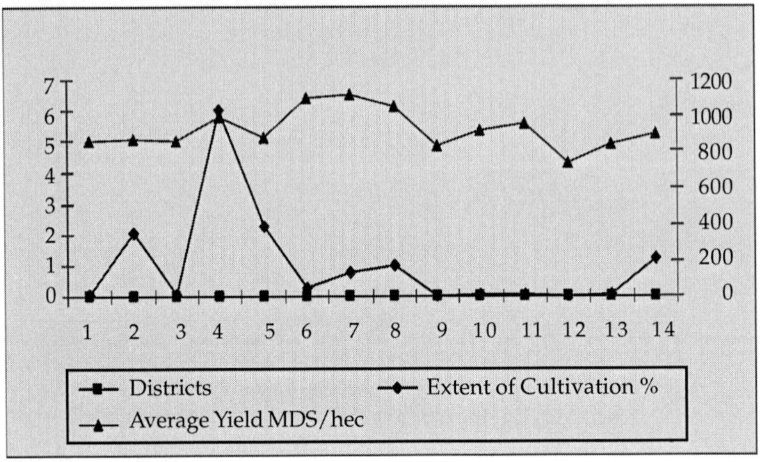

Fig. 9.8: Tapioca

Results and Discussion

A glance at the forgoing graphs present the nature and degree of relationship between area and yield of select crops in Tamil Nadu. To have a more accurate idea about the degree of relationship between area and yields, an alternative detailed approach was further attempted.

As a starting point, for each crop all the thirteen districts were classified in to five groups at suitable class intervals. For the formation of class intervals the average figure for the state as a whole (for each crop) was taken as the base and five groups based on the degree and direction of departure from this base were formed. The following formula was adopted Table 9.9.

Table 9.9: Formation of Groups and Class Intervals

Groups	Extent of Variation (%)
A	More than +15
B	+5 to 15
C	±5
D	-5 to –15
E	Below -15

Source: Compiled by the Researcher.

Table 9.10: Limits Determining the Groups in which Different Districts Fall on the Basis of Degree of Variation in the Extent of Cultivation of Crops and their Yields

Crops	Groups	Limits	
		Extents of Cultivation	Average Yield
1	2	3	4
Paddy	A	More than 35.76%	More than 3298.2
	B	More than 32.57 to 35.76%	More than 3011.4 to 3298.2
	C	From 32.57 to 30.39%	From 3011.4 to 2724.6
	D	Less than 30.39 to 27.20%	Less than 2724.6 to 2437.8
	E	Less than 27.20%	Less than 2437.8
Cholam	A	More than 8.55%	More than 1045.35
	B	More than 7.81 to 8.55%	More than 954.45 to 1045.35
	C	From 7.81 to 7.07%	From 954.45 to 863.5
	D	Less than 7.07 to 6.33%	Less than 863.52 to 772.65
	E	Less than 6.33%	Less than 772.65
Cumbu	A	More than 3.54%	More than 1324.8
	B	More than 3.24 to 3.54%	More than 1209.6 to 1324.8
	C	From 3.24 to 2.94%	From 1209.6 to 1094.4
	D	Less than 2.94 to 2.64%	Less than 1094.4 to 979.2
	E	Less than 2.64%	Less than 979.2
Ragi	A	More than 2.54%	More than 2015.9
	B	More than 2.32 to 3.54%	More than 1840.6 to 2015.9
	C	From 2.32 to 2.10%	From 1840.6 to 1665.4

Contd...

1	2	3	4
	D	Less than 2.10 to 1.88%	Less than 1665.4 to 1490.1
	E	Less than 1.88%	Less than 1490.1
Sugarcane	A	More than 4.57%	More than 121.9
	B	More than 4.18 to 4.57%	More than 113.3 to 121.9
	C	From 4.18 to 3.79%	From 113.3 to 100.7
	D	Less than 3.79 to 3.40%	Less than 100.7 to 90.1
	E	Less than 3.40%	Less than 90.1
Cotton	A	More than 3.54%	More than 317.4
	B	More than 3.24 to 3.54%	More than 289.8 to 317.4
	C	From 3.24 to 2.94%	From 289.8 to 262.2
	D	Less than 2.94 to 2.64%	Less than 262.2 to 234.6
	E	Less than 2.64%	Less than 234.6
Groundnut	A	More than 14.87%	More than 1737.65%
	B	More than 13.58 to 14.87%	More than 1586.55. to 1737.65
	C	From 3.58 to 12.30%	From 1586.55 to 1445.45
	D	Less than 12.30 to 11.01%	Less than 1445.45 to 1294.35
	E	Less than 11.01%	Less than 1294.35
Tapioca	A	More than 5.19%	More than 39416.25
	B	More than 4.74 to 5.19%	More than 35988.75 to 39416.25
	C	From 4.74 to 4.30%	From 35988.75 to 32562.25
	D	Less than 4.30 to 3.85%	Less than 32562.25 to 29134.75
	E	Less than 3.85%	Less than 29134.75

Source: Compiled by the Researcher.

By applying the above formula the exact class limits for five groups were calculated and also for each crop both with reference to the extent of cultivation and the average yield. The results are shown in Table 9.10.

On the basis of the class limits thus fixed, the extent of adjustment and maladjustment of each crop was studied. For determining the degree of adjustment between extent of cultivation and yield perhectare, five adjustment categories were formed and the following procedure was adopted for classifying district into a particular adjustment category.

By applying the above formula the following five 'adjustment categories' were formed:

Table 9.11: Determination of Degree of Adjustment between Extent of Cultivation and Yield Perhectare

AA	BA	CA	DA	EA
AB	BB	CB	DB	EB
AC	BC	CC	DC	EC
AD	BD	CD	DD	ED
AE	BE	CE	DE	EE

Table 9.12: Classification of Paddy Area into Five Classes According to the Degree of Adjustment

Classes	Districts	Area	
		Million Hectares	% to Total
I	South Arcot	0.2485	12.3
II	North Arcot	0.1520	7.6
III	Chengalpattu, Salem. Dharmapuri, Trichy.	0.4401	21.09
IV	Pudukkottai, Thanjavur, Tirunelveli.	0.7001	34.9
V	Coimbatore Erode, Madurai, Ramanathapuram,	0.4701	23.30
	Tamil Nadu	**2.0108**	**100**

Source: Compiled by the Researcher.

Table 9.12 shows that in the case of Paddy, taking the average yield as the basis, it was found that 12.3 per cent was well adjusted, 7.6 per cent sufficiently adjusted, 21.9 per cent tolerably adjusted, 34.9 per cent maladjusted and 23.3 per cent highly maladjusted area.

In the case of Cholam it could be seen that, of the total cultivated area, 19.86 per cent was well adjusted, 12.01 per cent sufficiently adjusted 7.74 per cent tolerably adjusted 5.18 per cent maladjusted, and 55.21 per cent highly maladjusted area (Table 9.13).

Table 9.13 Classification of Cholam into Five Classes According to the Degree of Adjustment

Classes	Districts	Area	
		Million Hectares	% to Total
I	Madurai	0.0907	19.86
II	Salem	0.0549	12.01
III	Dharmapuri	0.0354	7.74
IV	South Arcot, Ramanathapuram	0.0237	5.18
V	Chengalpattu, North Arcot, Coimbatore, Erode, Trichy, Pudukkottai, Tirunelveli.	0.2524	55.21
	Tamil Nadu	**0.4571**	**100**

Source: Compiled by the Researcher.

In the case of Cumbu, 14.1 per cent was well adjusted, 41.7 per cent sufficiently adjusted, 3.9 tolerably adjusted, 7.6 per cent maladjusted and 32.7 per cent highly maladjusted area (Table 9.14).

Ragi shows 27.8 per cent well adjusted area, 2.6 per cent sufficiently adjusted, 12.4 per cent tolerably adjusted, 32.1 per cent maladjusted and 25.1 per cent highly maladjusted area (Table 9.15).

Table 9.14: Classification of Cumbu Area into Five Classes According to the Degree of Adjustment

Classes	Districts	Area	
		Million Hectares	% to Total
I	Tirunelveli	0.0279	14.1
II	South Arcot, Ramanathapuram	0.0825	41.7
III	North Arcot, Erode	0.0078	3.9
IV	Madurai	0.0151	7.6
V	Salem, Chengalpet Dharmapuri Coimbatore Trichy, Pudukkottai Tanjore	0.0647	32.7
	Tamil Nadu	**0.1980**	**100**

Source: Compiled by the Researcher.

Table 9.15: Classification of Ragi Area into Five Classes According to the Degree of Adjustment

Classes	Districts	Area	
		Million Hectares	% to Total
I	Salem	0.0183	27.8
II	Pudukkottai	0.0017	2.6
III	Ramanathapuram	0.0082	12.4
IV	Chengalpet South Arcot, North Arcot, Dharmapuri, Trichy, Madurai,	0.0212	32.1
V	Coimbatore Erode, Thanjavur, Tirunelveli	0.0165	25.1
	Tamil Nadu	**0.0659**	**100**

Source: Compiled by the Researcher.

Sugarcane shows that 16.9 per cent well adjusted area, 11.4 per cent sufficiently adjusted, and 71.7 per cent tolerably adjusted area (Table 9.16).

Table 9.16: Classification of Suracane Area into Five Classes According to the Degree of Adjustment

Classes	Districts	Area	
		Million Hectares	% to Total
I	North Arcot, Coimbatore Trichy,	0.0357	16.9
II	Erode	0.0242	11.4
III	Chengalpattu, South Arcot Salem, Dharmapuri Pudukkottai, Thanjavur Madurai, Ramanathapuram Tirunelveli	0.1520	71.7
VI	—	—	—
V	—	—	—
	Tamil Nadu	**0.2119**	**100**

Source: Compiled by the Researcher.

Table 9.17: Classification of Cotton Area into Five According to the Degree of Adjustment

Classes	Districts	Area	
		Million Hectares	% to Total
I	Coimbatore, Madurai	0.0451	22.9
II	Trichy, Salem	0.0362	18.4
III	—	—	—
IV	Dharmapuri	0.0115	5.9
V	Chengalpattu, South Arcot, North Arcot, Erode, Pudukkottai, Thanjavur, Ramanathapuram Tirunelveli.	0.1037	52.8
	Tamil Nadu	**0.1965**	**100**

Source: Compiled by the Researcher.

In the case of Cotton, it was found that 22.9 per cent was well adjusted, 18.4 per cent sufficiently adjusted, 5.9 per cent mal adjusted and 52.8 per cent highly maladjusted area (Table 9.17).

In groundnut, 10.1 per cent was well adjusted, 33.4 per cent sufficiently adjusted, 7.9 per cent tolerably adjusted 44.3 per cent maladjusted and 4.3 per cent highly maladjusted (Table 9.18)

Table 9.18: Classification of Groundnut Area into Five Classes According to the Degree of Adjustment

Classes	Districts	Area	
		Million Hectares	% to Total
I	Chengalpattu, Ramanathapuram	0.0843	10.1
II	South Arcot, Dharmapuri Coimbatore Trichy. Erode, Tirunelveli	0.2771	33.4
III	North Arcot Salem	0.0653	7.9
IV	Thanjavur, Madurai	0.3671	44.3
V	Pudukkottai	0.0358	4.3
	Tamil Nadu	**0.8296**	**100**

Source: Compiled by the Researcher.

In Tapioca, 47.8 per cent was sufficiently adjusted, 37.2 per cent tolerably adjusted, 0.4 per cent maladjusted and 14.6 per cent highly maladjusted (Table 9.19).

It is possible to draw inferences form these tables that, where localization has been according to the suitability of basic physical factors and where they are being grown because of other considerations, disregarding considerably the suitability of basic physical factors, the land resources are devoted to growing unsuitable crops and hence are misused.

Table 9.19: Classification of Tapioca Area into Five Classes According to the Degree of Adjustment

Classes	Districts	Area	
		Million Hectares	% to Total
I	—	—	—
II	Salem	0.0357	47.8
III	Chengalpattu, South Arcot, North Arcot, Dharmapuri, Ramanathapuram Tirunelveli	0.0278	37.2
IV	Madurai	0.0003	0.40
V	Coimbatore, Erode, Trichy, Pudukkottai, Thanjavur	0.0109	14.6
	Tamil Nadu	**0.0747**	**100**

Source: Compiled by the Researcher.

A consolidated view of the extent of adjustment of all the eight crops however could be studied by grouping all the eight crops as shown in Table 9.20.

Table 9.20: Classification of Area under All Crops into Five Classes According to the Degree of Adjustment

Adjustment Category	Based on Average Yield	
	Area (In Million Hectares)	Percentage (%)
Well Adjusted	0.55	13.6} [30.0]
Sufficiently adjusted	0.66	16.4}
Tolerably adjusted	0.73	18.2
Maladjusted	1.13	28.1} [51.8]
Highly maladjusted	0.95	23.7}

Source: Compiled by the Researcher.

When all the eight crops were taken together it was found that, of the total area based on average yield, 13.6 per cent was well adjusted, 16.4 per cent was well adjusted, 18.2 per cent tolerably adjusted, 28.1 per cent maladjusted and 23.7 per cent highly maladjusted.

In the final analysis, to have a broad outlook of the extent of adjustment and maladjustment of different crops, the five adjustment categories were reduced to only two main classes, by taking the first three in to one representing the extent of adjustment and the last two in to another representing the extent of maladjustment. The result was found to be as follows (Table 9.21).

Table 9.21: Percentage of Total Area under Each Crop (Based on Average Yield)

Crops	Adjusted	Maladjusted
Paddy	41.80	58.20
Cholam	39.50	60.50
Cumbu	62.70	37.30
Ragi	42.80	57.20
Sugarcane	100.00	—
Cotton	41.40	58.60
Groundnut	51.40	48.60
Tapioca	85.00	15.00
All the eight crops	48.25	51.75

Source: Compiled by the Researcher.

Of the total area under specific crops, taking the average yield in to account, 41.80 per cent in the case of Paddy, 39.50 per cent in Cholam, 62.70 per cent in Cumbu, 42.80 per cent in Ragi 100 per cent in Sugarcane, 41.40 per cent in Cotton, 51.40 per cent in Groundnut and 85 per cent in Tapioca was found to be adjusted and to this extent the localization of these crops are according to suitability of basic physical factors.

The remaining area is 58.20 per cent in paddy, 60.50 per cent in cholam, 37.30 per cent in cumbu, 57.20 per cent in

Ragi, 58.60 per cent in cotton, 48.60 per cent in groundnut and 15 per cent in tapioca were found to be maladjusted. The forgoing analysis reveals that the cropping pattern in the state has high degree for maladjustment of crops. Roughly 52 per cent or about half of the cultivated area is being used for growing unsuitable crops. Some broad and specific conclusions derived from the above analysis are:

1. There is considerable misuse of the cultivated area based on crop yields and hence output is affected to a great extent.
2. Roughly 52 per cent or about half of the cultivated area is being used for growing unsuitable crops.
3. There is a possibility of considerable enhancement in agricultural production through the adjustment of various crops in favour of relatively more suitable areas for their growth.
4. The extent of maladjustment was different in different crops in different districts and for the state.

It is but natural that different districts will differ in their response to change in conditions because of uneven distribution of gains of agricultural technology, heterogeneous topography of various geographic regions, climate, varying soil conditions within the regions, irrigation facilities and different levels of economic prosperity among the farm population.

From the above findings from the study, it is clear that farmers generally do not use the available resources efficiently and they would stand to gain through adjustments in respects of crop combination and productive allocation of inputs. What is required for its realization is to strengthen the base for crop production and the real solution lies in efficient allocation of land between various crops and productive adjustment of inputs so as to maximize.

REFERENCES

Books

Aggarwal, A.N.: *Indian Agriculture*, Vikas Publishing House, Delhi, 1980.

Arputharaj, C. : *Indian Agricultural Economy*, Macmillan, Madras, 1982.

Mahajan, Ashwani.: *Agricultural Economics*, Centrum Press, New Delhi. 2010.

Singh, Kavita: *New Dimension in Agriculture for 21st Century*, Mohit Publications, New Delhi, 2010.

Reports

Agriculture Hand Book of Tamil Nadu.

Agro Stat of Tamil Nadu, Directorate of Agriculture, Chennai.

Season and Crop Reports of Tamil Nadu.

10

Precision Farming
A Tool to Achieve Food Security

R. Geetha

INTRODUCTION

Agriculture is the back bone of Indian Economy. Increasing population, changing occupational pattern, shrinkage of arable land and the variations in crop yield has urged the society to lookup for a solution in agricultural sector to achieve high returns with minimal environmental damage As Nehru's opinion 'everything can wait but not the agriculture'. Agricultural sector highly relies on the generation of new technologies and practices to reorient the current and future needs aiming at sustainable development. The concept of precision agriculture first emerged in the United States in the early 1980s. Precision farming is defined as the application of technologies and principles to manage spatial and temporal variability associated with all aspects of agricultural production. Precision farming or precision agriculture is a farming management concept based on observing and responding to intra-field variations. It relies on new technologies like satellite imagery and information technology. It is also aided by farmers' ability to locate their precise position in a field using satellite positioning system like GPS. Precision agriculture aims to optimize field-level management. Precision farming is at infant stage in India.

The present study aims at an enquiry about the status of precision farming in India and in Tamil Nadu in recent past.

Methodology

The information for present study was obtained from the websites.

Objective

The objective of present study is to describe the techniques involved in precision farming along with its merits and demerits.

Precision Farming in Foreign Countries

Remote sensing imagery for Precision Farming can be obtained either through satellite-based sensors or CIR video digital cameras on board small aircraft. The multi-spectral images can be used for anomaly detection. These anomalies can be in the forms of disease/pest, weed growth, water stress, etc. Using the reflectance measurements in the visible part of the spectrum, it has been possible to detect diseases and identify weeds from crops.

Many farm information systems (FIS) are available, which use simple programmes to create a farm level database. One example of such FIS is LORIS for mapping the details from satellite images.

Crop yields for many crops like, rice, wheat etc. have been found to be highly correlated with spectral vegetation index during maximum vegetative cover.

Indian Perspective

The Plasticulture Development Centre (PDC) was established by Indian Government in May 1995 in Dr. Y. S. Parmar University of Horticulture and Forestry, Nauni, Solan Himachal Pradesh under Centrally-sponsored scheme for use of plastics in agriculture under National Committee on Plasticulture Applications (NCPA), and was renamed as Precision Farming Development Centres (PFDC) in 2001-02. The mandate was slightly modified, emphasis was given on the use of right amount of inputs at the right time and right location within a field and management of crops using information technologies Such as GPS, GIS, RS along with appropriate ground level equipments. The existing 17 PFDCs provides necessary technical support and research along with the other operational schemes.

Precision Farming in Tamil Nadu

Tamil Nadu Precision Farming Project is a State sponsored project implemented at Dharmapuri and Krishnagiri districts in 400 hectares with a total budget of 7.20 lakhs for a period of three years. Government of Tamil Nadu had assigned this task to Tamil Nadu Agricultural University. About 23 kinds of crops were selected to grow by precision farming. The State arranged for a mega demo to train the farmers and empower them technically, economically and socially.

Tamil Nadu Precision Farming Project (TNPFP) adopts a location specific, field specific and crop specific approach. The objective is optimisation of inputs use to facilitate optimal output resulting in saving of valuable resources like water and energy. The project had adequately prepared the farmers for market driven production at a time when Multinational Companies set for invasion into retail vegetable market in India.

The first crop has been taken up under the total guidance of Scientists from the University. Subsequent five crops had been taken up by the farmers in 3 years. Demonstration on precision farming in sugarcane (198 hectares), banana (10 hectares), tapioca (100 hectares), coconut (600 hectares), and vegetables (20 hectares), were conducted during first phase of the project. In the second phase, precision farming demonstrations were conducted in sugarcane (237 hectares), banana (65 hectares), tapioca (50 hectares), coconut (1050 hectares), vegetables (200 hectares), flowers (10 hectares) and high value capsicum (5 hectares) was taken up initially. M.S. Swaminathan Research Foundation Chennai, India has joined hands with Israel to initiate PF on an experimental basis in Srirampuram village in Dindigul district of Tamil Nadu, using IRS LISS III (23 m resolution) and Pan (5.8m resolution).

Methodology in Precision Farming in Tamil Nadu

Making use of the GIS, the physiographic map, soil map and land use map for Dharmapuri and Krishnagiri districts were developed. The remote sensing programme enabled the scientists to exactly locate the actual field to scale map its boundary. Two sites were selected for the observation *viz.*, field at Periyammittahalli and a field at Thorapalli. The data on soil nutrient like Nitogen, Phosporous, Potassium, Calcium, Magnesium, Manganese, Iron and Cupper were collected and variability for the field and in the field were assessed. This enabled the scientists to precisely apply the required nutrient in accurate quantities at the root zone during critical phases of crop growth.

The chisel plough technology, raised nursery in portrays, drip irrigation aided with fertigation system, training the farmers to maintain weekly record for future Data Management system are unique features of precision farming in Tamil Nadu. The record also helps to work out the economics of production and arrive at cost benefit ratio and in future will enhance model development for unique situation. The field scientists stayed at villages and extended the technical support to the farmers through out the crop period. The marketing scientists have guided the beneficiary farmers to market them insisting on the importance of minimal grading and sorting and timely delivery at the market. The beneficiary farmers were organized under various commodity forums: The organizations were registered under societies act. They not only imparted skills to develop awareness on latest state of art technologies but also helped them to buy the inputs directly from the manufacturers cutting the cost down to minimum and strengthened their bargaining power while selling their produce.

Table 10.1 to 10.3 give the scenario on precision farming in Tamil Nadu. Department of Horticulture, Agriculture and Tamil Nadu Agricultural University together have brought 27480 hectare of land under Precision farming during the period 2007-10. Invariably all crops have shown increase in yield and income.

Table 10.1: Area covered under Precision Farming in Tamil Nadu 2007-10

Department	2007-08	2008-09	2009-10	Total
	Area in Hectares	Area in Hectares	Area in Hectares	Area in Hectares
Horticulture	6120	4480	2680	13280
Agriculture	6080	4280	2600	12960
TNAU	600	640	—	1240
Total	**12800**	**9400**	**5280**	**27480**

Table 10.2. Yield and Income for Traditional Crops under Precision Farming in 2009

Crop	Normal Yield (ton/ha)	Yield Obtained ton/ha	Yield Increase ton/ha	Increased Income/ha (Rs.)
Tomato	30	53	23	69,000
Chillies	14	20	6	24,000
Brinjal	20	26	6	30,000
Bhendi	12	18	6	24,000
Onion	12	17	5	60,000
Banana	50	80	2	2,40,000

Table 10.3: Yield and Income for Hybrid Crops under Precision Farming, 2009

Crop	Normal Yield ton/ha	Yield Obtained ton/ha	Yield Increase ton/ha
Brinjal	25	78	53
Tomato	80	107	27
Watermelon	30	50	20
Chillies	30	41	11
Sugarcane	110	235	125
Cotton	1.5	2.55	0.05
Groundnut	1.5	3	1.5
Maize	3.5	6	2.5
Sunflower	1.85	2.9	1.05

Among these the Hybrid variety crops have shown higher yield than the normal traditional seeds. Sugarcane has shown 100 per cent increase in yield. Hybrid variety in Brinjal has shown triple fold increase, while traditional variety of tomato has shown 75 per cent increase in yield.

Merits of Precision Farming

1. The Precision Farming project has increased the income levels of the farmers besides empowering them in marketing, forming association.
2. 23 kinds of crops over three years have recorded 60 per cent increase in yield and 90 per cent marketable quality.
3. Farmers were able to save 40 to 60 per cent irrigation water when compared to surface irrigation in vegetables.
4. Tamil Nadu Precision Farming Project areas have become a hot spots for learning to the students of B.Sc (Ag.), B.Sc (Hort.), B.Tech (Hort.) and B.Tech (Agrl.Engg.) of Tamil Nadu Agricultural University. Besides, it has become an activity hub for the rural youth and no doubt, the Precision Farming Project sensitized the young minds about the fruits of modern state of art "micro irrigation techniques".
5. The beneficiary farmers of Dharmapuri and Krishnagiri districts have opted for crop diversification towards vegetable crops owing to high yield and economic returns.
6. Fustigation is an improved method of supplying nutrients through drip system with water soluble fertilizers. The nutrients were supplied in required quantities at critical phases of crop growth to maintain the vigour of the plants throughout the crop period. This method saves 25 per cent of fertilizers and complete utilisation of applied nutrients by the plants.
7. Provision of insurance cover to crops like tomato helped the farmers to overcome the risk of heavy damage due to hailstorm etc.
8. Unlike the conventional method, concentrated harvests in fertigated crop enables the farmer to complete the crop earlier and raise a second short duration crop.

9. Applying the right amount of inputs in the right place and at the right time benefits crops, soils and ground water, and thus the entire crop cycle.
10. Precision farming is the retention of goodness in traditional method and incorporation of scientific methods to suit the local conditions that retains ecological balance the ultimate goal of sustainable development.

Economic and Environmental Impacts

Farmers get good returns by following precision agriculture. Precision agriculture has become a widely acceptable pathway for sustainable agriculture, since it respects crops, soils and farmers. Sustainable agriculture seeks to assure a continued supply of food within the ecological, economic and social limits required to sustain production in the long term. Until now few backdrops have been observed. Traditional varieties are ignored and quick salt deposition in the drip pipes are noticed in drier areas of Tamil Nadu.

Suggestion to Popularize Precision Farming in Large Scale

1. Creation of multi-disciplinary teams involving agricultural scientists in various fields, engineers, manufacturers and economists to study the overall scope of precision agriculture.
2. Formation of farmer's co-operatives since many of the precision agriculture tools are costly (GIS, GPS, RS, etc.).
3. Government legislation restraining farmers using indiscriminate farm inputs and thereby causing ecological/environmental imbalance would induce the farmer to go for alternative approach.
4. Creating awareness amongst farmers about consequences of applying imbalanced doses of farm inputs like irrigation, fertilizers, insecticides and pesticides.

Conclusion

It is mandatory to adopt necessary techniques in agriculture to suit the requirements for the present and future generations. Precision farming is a milestone in the agricultural practices developed by human beings. The greatest advantage of this method is igniting local capacity to produce and distribute food and control food supplies thereby keeping decision-making power within the community. The social well being of the society begins only on the moment when humanity is filled in everyone's heart.

REFERENCES

Maheswari, R., Ashok, K.R. Prahadeeswaran, M., "Precision Farming Technology, Adoption Decisions and Productivity of Vegetables in Resource-Poor Environments", *Journal of Agricultural Economics Research Review*: 2008, Volume: 21.

Ray, S.S. S. Panigrahy and J. S. Parihar, Space Applications Centre, ISRO, "Precision Farming in Indian Context" *GIS and Development*, Ahmedabad.

Tripathi, Santosh "Precision Farming for Small Farmers in Developing Countries" Remote Sensing and Geographic Information Systems, Paper Presented in the Geometric Conference held in Asian Institute of Technology, Feb., 2005.

11

Under Accelaration of Pulses Production Programme in India

C. Sivakozhundu

INTRODUCTION

Pulses is one of the components of the Centrally-sponsored scheme of National Food Security Mission and is under implementation since Rabi 2007-08. This component has undergone a number of changes since its inception and finally has taken the shape of sole Centrally-sponsored scheme on pulses covering all the districts in 14 States by merging all the pulses components of another Centrally-sponsored scheme namely Integrated Scheme on Oilseeds, Pulses, Oil palm and Maize (ISOPOM). Ten districts of Assam and 15 districts of Jharkhand have also been included under NFSM-Pulses. Accelerated Pulses Production Programme (A3P) is another step forward for vigorous implementation of the pulse development under the NFSM-Pulses. A3P has been conceptualized to take up the active propagation of key technologies such as Integrated Nutrient Management (INM) and Integrated Pest Management (IPM) in a manner that creates catalyzing impact by assuring farmers of the higher returns from the identified pulse crops.

Objectives of A3P

The objective of A3P is to demonstrate plant nutrient and plant protection centric improved technologies and management practices in compact blocks covering large area for five major pulse crops namely gram, *urad* (black gram), *arhar* (red gram/pigeon pea), moong (green gram) and *masoor* (lentils) for increasing production and productivity of these crops. Apart from increasing the production and productivity of pulse crops by the participating farmers another objective of A3P is to stimulate other farmers in the adjoining areas to adopt these technologies.

Number of A3P Units

It is proposed to take up 1000 A3P units in the next two years *i.e.* 2010-11 and 2011-12 for active promotion of improved production technologies. Each A3P unit would be in the form of a village level block demonstration covering an area 1 of 1000 hectares. It is proposed to initiate 600 units in the 1st year and 400 units in the 2nd year. Panchayati Raj institutions would be involved in the selection of village level A3P units including the participating farmers. However, states would be given freedom to select the A3P unit based on availability of contiguous area in various villages of different blocks of the selected districts. This should be done well before the start of each season based on the information. States would furnish a final list of districts as well as blocks in each district where A3P will be implemented.

Provision of Inputs to Farmers

Kit containing critical inputs including gypsum, micronutrients, rhizobium culture, phosphate solubilising bacteria (PSB), plant protection chemicals, urea for foliar spray and weedicides are proposed to be given to all the farmers in each A3P unit, free of cost for a maximum area of 2 hectares. The contents of the kit have been kept very broad to accommodate all the pulse crops under A3P. Since all the components of the kit may not be required for all the crops, therefore, states in consultation with SAU/ICAR institutes should modify the contents of the kit as per the recommendations for that area. State Department of Agriculture will finalise the contents for each pulse crop and get the same approved from the National Mission Director. The overall cost of kits should not exceed the specified limit in any case.

Savings on account of reduced cost of kits, if any, can be used for additional area under A3P, providing support for innovative interventions such as crop insurance or any other component state feels fit and adjusts within the savings. However, this utilisation of the savings needs to be approved by the National Mission.

To ensure the timely supply of kits, it is strongly recommended that procurement of inputs may be delegated to district level offices of the Department of Agriculture who in turn would follow the set procurement procedure for the timely supply of inputs. Some of the inputs like gypsum, micronutrients, rhizobium culture and PSB, trichoderma and fungicides for seed treatment, weedicides, Pheromone traps and lure etc., are to be supplied to all the farmers well in advance. However in case of nuclear polyhedrosis virus (NPV)/bio-pesticides and plant protection chemicals, procurement arrangements must be finalised well in advance. About 25 per cent of the required quantity of pesticides should be stored so that in any eventuality of pest outbreak these bio-pesticides/chemicals can be made available to the farmers immediately.

To popularise the improved varieties of various pulse crops in the A3P area, the farmer would also be given seed minikit of improved crop variety for 0.2 ha area for every 1.0 ha of pulse area. The seed minikit together with the extension and institutional support will enable the farmer to apply all the critical inputs and conduct field operations at the right time as per the recommended package of practices. The distribution of seed minikits has dual objective of covering the entire area of the participating farmers under these varieties in the next year and also share/distribute the excess seed with other farmers in the area.

Eligibility for Assistance under NFSM

Whereas the critical inputs are being ensured in the form of free kits to all the A3P farmers, financial assistance for other inputs like additional seed, farm machines and implements, pumps, etc., would be available to the A3P unit farmers under NFSM-Pulses as per their needs.

Hand Holding Approach of NFSM

One of the key constraints contributing to low productivity of pulse crops is inadequate extension services at the farm level. In order to address this issue, existing Project Management Teams (PMT) of NFSM would be further strengthened through provision of need based additional technical manpower at sub district level (one technical assistant for each unit) purely on contractual basis to provide on the spot technical backstopping to the farmers in a hand holding approach. Additional technical manpower proposed to be engaged at unit level will extend technical services to farmers in each unit in close coordination with the input supply agencies. Educational qualification of these Technical Assistants (TA) would be the same as prescribed for TA under NFSM at district level. Special provision for their mobility will also be made under A3P.

Constitution of Farmers, Groups

In order to empower the farmers to help themselves, the farmers of a particular A3P unit should be organized to form small groups/commodity interest groups/joint liability groups so that they may organize various activities of common interest in a systematic manner. These activities are:

- Procurement of various inputs like fertilizers and pesticides.
- Undertaking mass campaigns like Integrated Pest Management (IPM).
- Arranging individual and collective loans including insurance of their crops.
- Establishment of a farm agro centre from where various machines implementscan be taken on custom hire basis, availing of subsidy on various implements which otherwise are out of the reach of individual farmers or his/her requirements like laser land leveller and ridge furrow planter as well as arranging institutional credit etc. State department of agriculture should extend required help in this endeavour.

Capacity Building

All technical assistants appointed under the A3P project will be imparted induction training to carry out various activities proposed under the A3P including distribution of input kits, technical support to farmers and constitution of farmer groups and provide further support to these groups in implementing different activities. All farmers of pigeon pea and chick pea units will be imparted special training on IPM by the National Centre for Integrated Pest Management (NCIPM) and its partner institutes while arrangements need to be made for providing technical training to farmers of A3P units for other three crops *viz., moong, urd* and lentil through trained technical assistants by the States. These trainings will be provided to farmers in groups as well as to individual farmers on one to one basis. Implementation of Farmers Field School will be modified accordingly where instead of 30 farmers a larger group will be taken up with less number of sessions with focussed attention on a few topics. Similarly, strategy to implement A3P should form an integral part of training programme in the state level training for extension workers provided under NFSM-Pulses for which a sum of Rs. One lakh per training is provided.

Convergence of Schemes

There are number of Centrally-sponsored schemes Such as Rashtriya Krishi Vikas Yojana (RKVY), Mahatma Gandhi Rural Employment Guarantee Scheme (MGREGA) National Watershed Development Project for Rainfed Areas (NWDPRA) and other watershed development schemes etc., which can be dovetailed with A3P. State governments through State departments of agriculture/Panchyati Raj institutions may coordinate this dovetailing so that maximum benefits can be provided to these farmers. Most important component which can be dovetailed for promoting the production and productivity of pulses is the rainwater harvesting through the construction of farm ponds for providing life saving irrigation to pulse crops. The new initiative announced in the Union Budget 2010-11 to organize 60,000 'Pulses and Oilseed villages' is another step in promoting pulses production. This initiative should also be dovetailed with the A3P. Details of the 'Pulses and Oilseed villages' are given below:

Beneficiaries of the Programme

Recently an approach to implement the new initiatives announced in the Union Budget 2010-11 to organize 60,000 'Pulses and oilseeds villages' has been finalised. Under this approach a set of implements such as tractor, rotavator and ridge furrow planter along with some working capital at 6,000 designated watershed centric locations will be provided to a nominated agency who would provide the custom hiring services for pulses and oilseed growers. An amount of Rs. 5.00 lakh per agency is proposed for the aforesaid assets with a total amount of Rs. 300 crores under RKVY. The identified agency would provide services to adjoining 10 villages in a hub and spoke model which would serve 60,000 villages. Farmers would be charged an amount of Rs. 500 per hectare for land preparation and sowing which is about 50 of prevailing rate. This amount will be sufficient to meet the operational cost of the service centres such as salary to the driver, cost of POL and other repair and maintenance of the implements. However, states will be free to choose a different set of implements. States should facilitate the convergence of this initiative with the implementation of A3P so that farmers may make use of these machineries in the best possible way for increasing the production and productivity of pulses.

Institutional Support

National Centre for Integrated Pest Management (NCIPM) of Indian Council of Agricultural Research (ICAR) would be associated with the implementation of A3P programme in pigeon pea and chick pea areas. NCIPM will have following four sub-components:

- NCIPM in collaboration with various working partners of various SAUs/ICAR Institutes/Krishi Vigyan Kendras (KVKs) would establish 36 'Nuclear Model units' in selected A3P units for pigeon pea and chick pea. Twenty units of pigeon pea in 10 districts of five States and seventeen units of chick pea in eight districts of five States have been identified to be implemented by NCIPM. Funds for the provision of kits and hiring of Technical Assistants provided under A3P shall be diverted to NCIPM from respective State allocations.

- NCIPM in collaboration with its partner institutes will impart training to all the Technical Assistants recruited under pigeon pea and chick pea blocks in all the districts/ states. In addition, training will also be imparted to different blocks/district/state level officers and farmers to enhance their capabilities towards healthy crop production through IPM strategies. NCIPM will be required to develop a training calendar in this regard.
- NCIPM would also develop and carryout awareness campaigns through conventional (print) and electronic media, to reach the entire areas covered under A3P for pigeon pea and chick pea.
- To establish centralized 'National Pest Reporting and Alert System' through networking of pulse growers, in addition to strengthening of pest diagnostic laboratory.

Action Plans

Tentative annual allocation will be intimated to the states in advance, based on the districts/blocks selected. Each District Agriculture Officer will prepare the action plan of the accelerated pulses projects for the concerned district and forward it to State Mission Director who would compile and prepare the state action plan and send the same to centre for approval and release of funds.

Release of Funds: Fund release mechanism would be on the same lines as being followed under regular NFSM. 814.

Record Maintenance: In each A3p unit, a register will be maintained on the lines of formats developed by the National Productivity Council (NPC) for demonstrations. Documents on soil test reports, dates of supply of seed, INM/IPM kits, date of sowing should be made part of the documents. A board depicting the A3P unit details needs to be displayed at each patch of the unit. Photographs of each stage of crop development should be maintained in the block demonstration register. Production and yield data should also be made part of the register.

Conclusion

A3P will have a strong mechanism of monitoring of the programme. Closing monitoring of the physical achievements in terms of provision of input minikits, seed minikits and overseeing the activities of the technical assistants will be done by the District Food Security Mission Executive Committee (DFSMEC). District level PMT will monitor the programme implementation on regular intervals. State level and National level PMTs would also be involved in monitoring of the programmes. Respective Commodity Development Directorates (CDD) of Government of India would monitor the programme implementation in the states assigned to them. Head of the agriculture department at the district level should ensure the regular monitoring of the programme on daily basis so that tangible results/suggestions for further improvement in the programme can be made. Directorate of Pulses Development (DPD) will be the nodal agency for allocation and monitoring of supply of pulses minikits to states. However, Commodity Development Directorate in-charge of concerned pulses states will provide the information on seed supply position to DPD. State department of agriculture should ensure submission of monthly progress report of A3P along with regular reporting of NFSM-Pulses. Special reporting in terms of crop condition at regular interval as affected by environment will also be ensured. As a part of the regular online reporting of NFSM, efforts shall be made to develop a dedicated web page and data sets with forms to get the information for online reporting the progress of A3P. Required forms and formats for this purpose would be developed. The Project Management Team at the district level will be responsible for online entry of data.

REFERENCES

Aldershot, Surjit, V. (2008) *Farm Business Incomes in India: A Study of Two Rice Growing Villages of Thanjavur Region, Tamil Nadu*, Ph.D. Thesis Submitted to the University of Calcutta, Indian Statistical Institute, Kolkata.

Barddhaman, Sen, Abhijit and Bhatia, M. L. (2004), *Cost of Cultivation and Farm Incomes*, Volume 14, *State of Indian Farmers: A Millennium Study*, Academic Foundation, New Delhi.

Sen, Abhijit (2004) "Changes in Cost Structure and Farm Business Incomes, 1981-82 to 1999-00", Paper Presented in the All-India Conference on *Agriculture and Rural Society in Contemporary India*.

Shetty, S. L (1997), "Financial Sector Reforms in India: An Evaluation", *Prajnan*, 25, pp. 253-287.

Singh, Sukhpal (2002) "Contracting out Solutions: Political Economy of Contract Farming in the Indian Punjab", *World Development*, 30 (9), pp. 1621-1638.

Storm, Servaas (1993) *Macro-economic Considerations in the Choice of an Agricultural Policy: A Study into Sectoral Inter-dependence with Reference to India*, Avebury Press.

Swaminathan, Madhura (2006) "Eleventh Plan Ignores Food and Nutrition Insecurity", *The Hindu*, Sept.

Thulasamma, L. (2003) "Investment in Agriculture: Trends and Issues", Paper Presented in the All-India Conference on *Agriculture and Rural Society in Contemporary India*, Barddhaman, Dec. 17-20.

Vaidyanathan, A. (1986) *India's Agricultural Development in a Regional Perspective*, R.C. Dutt Lectures on Political Economy, Centre for Studies in Social Sciences, Calcutta.

Vaidyanathan, A. (2000) "India's Agricultural Development Policy", *Economic and Political Weekly*, 13 May, pp. 1735-1741.

12

A Study on Irrigational Facilities

S. Muthunagai

INTRODUCTION

Water is an important input for successful agriculture. Water may be available to crops in the nature course by rainfall (or) it may be supplied to the agricultural fields artificially by human efforts man-made arrangements. For supplying water to the fields artificially are known as irrigation. Supplying water to when a region does not have sufficient natural precipitation to meet the plant's moisture requirement artificial supplying water to crops by means of canals, well, and tube-well etc., from the sources of water such as river, tanks, ponds, and underground water.

In geographical conditions, especially the nature of monsoon rainfall, make irrigation indispensable for sustainable agricultural development. Unfortunately, rainfall in India is uncertain, unreliable, irregular, seasonal and unevenly distributed. The main rain bringing northeast monsoon often fails to keep its date of arrival. The amount of rainfall may also vary. Excess rainfall may cause floods. But the less rainfall forces the formers to resort to irrigation. Irrigation has close connection with hydrological circle in which is received in the form of rain. Irrigation is a real consumptive use because of the evapotranspiration losses 90 per cent of water use in India for irrigation in general, the supply of water to the fields in terms of irrigation in scheduled to be 7×5 cm depth of water if nothing percolates or evaporates though this mush application at the time of irrigation in excessive than the actual requirement.

Methodology

The study was supported by the secondary data collected from the census office and from the internet sources to get the updated source for the analytical purposes and for statistical interpretation. Library research is used for the relevant study from different sources for literature purpose and to get the assembly of ideas to visualize the deep study of the area. The secondary data includes the collection of maps from the census and the internet sources for irrigational and agricultural data.

Study Area

The area selected for the study is Thanjavur district of Tamil Nadu. The latitudinal extension of the area, from 9′50 to 11.25 and longitudinal extension from 78.45′ to 79.25′. It has been bounded in the east by Nagapattinam and Thiruvarur districts, in west Pudukottai and Thiruchirapallli districts, in the north by Ariyallur district and the south by half of Pudukottai and half would be covered by east coast of bay of Bengal. The total geographical area is 3396.57 sq. km, with the population of 22,16,138, in the year of (2001 Census). Thanjavur region has extremely rich fertile soils deposited by the mighty rivers. Different sources of irrigation are used depending upon the topography, soils, rainfall, and availability of groundwater requirement of crops. The main sources of irrigation used in different parts of the country are:

1. Canals,
2. Wells, and
3. Tube wells and Tanks.

During the period from 1999-2009 area irrigated from by canals and wells including tubewells increased but the irrigated by tanks are decreased. Percentage of area irrigated by different sources was very high during the year of 2007,

2008 and 2009. Taluks endowed with adequate rainfall and irrigation and productive soils sow more than 50 per cent of their net sown areas more than once.

Table 12.1: Area Irrigated by Source During (2007-09)

Year	Gross Irrigated Area in hec	Gross Sown Area	Percentage
2007-08	207505	252093	82.31%
2008-09	167740	195311	85.88%

Source: Census of Tamil Nadu 2011.

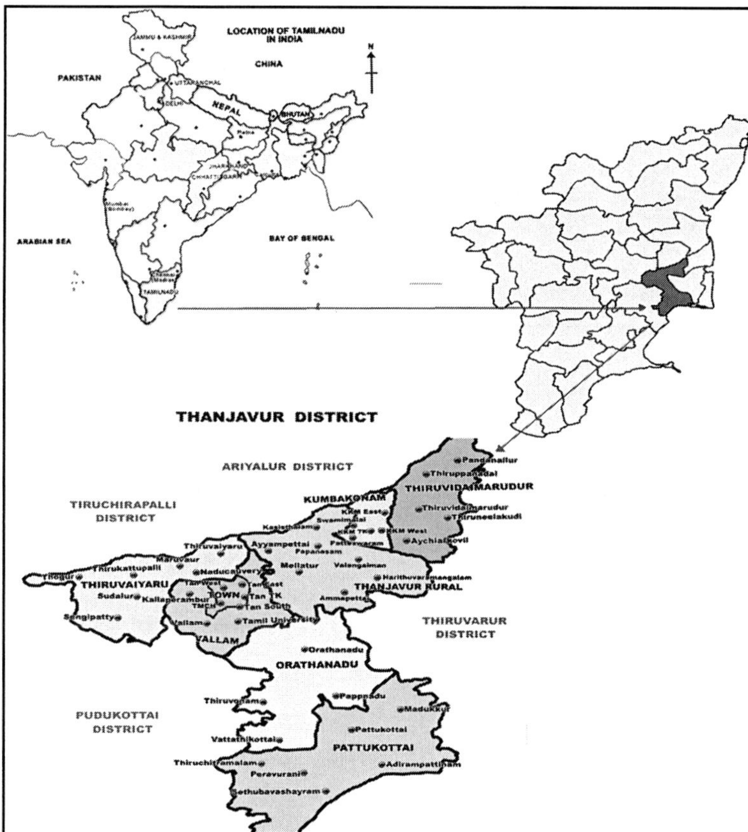

Fig. 12.1: Thanjavore District, India.

Objectives

The main aim of the study is to analyses is the study of irrigation activities in Thanjavur between the year of 1999-2009 and to delineate the details about the irrigation types of canal tanks, well in Thanjavur. The objectives of the study:

1. To describe the details about the types of irrigation in Thanjavur, and
2. To discuss the impact of irrigation on agriculture.

Results and Discussion

Canals

Canal irrigation is a water course which is built to take water from the river to cultivable land irrigation by means of canal is mostly prevalent throughout the year in order to assure supply in dry season the river water is stored in dams and they are brought to the field by canals. Fig. 12.2 shows the net irrigated by canals during the year 1999-2009 it has been observed that the maximum areas under canals have found in Thanjavur. It occupies the moderate area under canal irrigation in the year of 2000, 2006 and 2009. Canal irrigation is highest percentage at Thanjavur in the year of 1999-2009.

Table 12.2: Net Area Irrigated by Canals During the Year from 1999-00 to 2008-09

1999-00	2000-01	2001-02	2002-03	2003-04	2004-05	2005-06	2006-07	2007-08	2008-09
158353	156410	152746	124278	76761	131037	134634	131964	129791	133168

Source: Census of Tamil Nadu 2011.

Monsoon rain deserves the almost importance of irrigation north east monsoon has assured much to the 45 inches of rainfall per annum. The river Cauvery rises in Coorg at on 4.40 feet about the sea level. It is a perennial river to a largest part, it runs through Tamil Nadu. It runs almost all the way of 500 miles through the districts of Tiruchirapalli and Tanjore. Tanjore is gifted with the rice cultivation by the regular flow of Cauvery water in its long course, the Cauvery river irrigation on area 31.00 square miles and confluences with the Bay of Bengal. The reservoir was to have an effective of 80.000 million cubic feet.

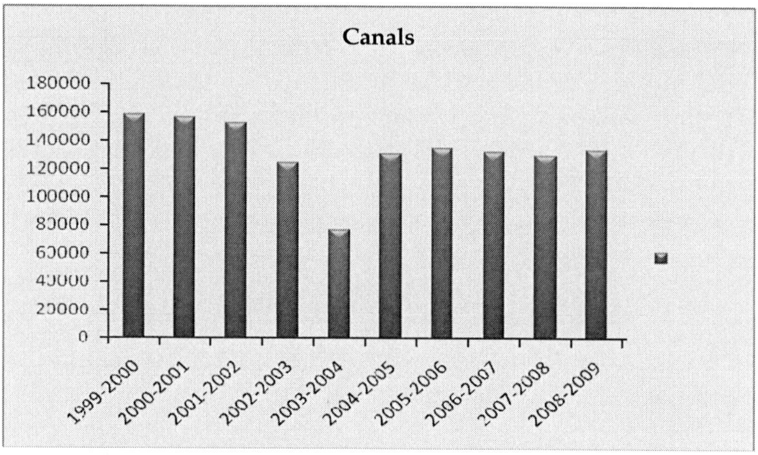

Fig. 12.2: Net Area Irrigated by Canals During the Year from 1999-00 to 2008-09

Tank Irrigation

In the uneven and relatively rocky place, where rainfall is also highly seasonal, people have resorted to tank Irrigation. A small bund of earth, or stones built across a stream impounds water which is go through the narrow channels to the cultivated lands.

Chief Draw Backs of Tank Irrigation Area

- Tanks cover large area of cultivable, and
- Evaporation of water is relatively rapid due to large expanse of shallow water of the tanks.

They do not ensure perennial supply of water sometimes it so happens that .the tanks go dry during the hot period when water is urgently required considering all these tank irrigation is costlier than the tube well irrigation in our study area during the year of 2000-03 the tank irrigation was at maximum level. From, 2004 onwards slowly it has been decreased. During the year of 2001 and 2002 the tank irrigation was little bit moderate in the study area. Considering the larger area which is rendered useless by tanks and a great loss of water evaporation, tank irrigation is costlier than well or tube well irrigation. During the year 2004 onwards only 498 hectares were under the tank irrigation as accounting for very low per cent of net area irrigated by tank. Owing to a pressing demand for irrigation tanks fallen into disuse. Throughout the study the occurrence of the tank irrigation is very low per cent.

Table 12.3: Tank Irrigation 1999-00 to 2008-09

1999 -00	2000 -01	2001 -02	2002 -03	2003 -04	2004 -05	2005 -06	2006 -07	2007 -08	2008 -09
7913	79133	8003	4163	168	358	498	258	306	313

Source: Census of Tamil Nadu 2011.

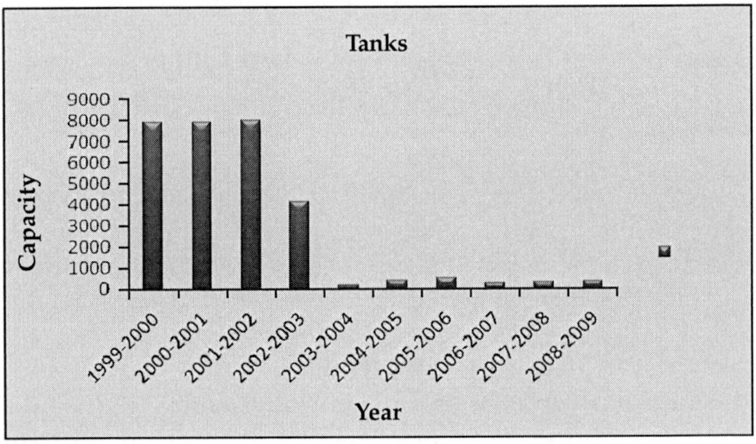

Fig. 12.3: Tank Irrigation 1999-00 to 2008-09

Wells and Tube wells

This source of irrigation is used mainly in the alluvial plains where the soft nature of the soil; wells are easy to dig and the yield of crops from the land after irrigation is rewarding. Wells are dug in the middle of the area to be irrigated and at a place which is relatively at a high level. Well irrigation is quite common in Thanjavur. The underground water has been tapped for drinking and irrigation purposes. A hole is dug in the ground till that sandy acquifer layer is cut which can give a perennial supply of soft water is as tube well. The well wells are dug near ponds, or depressions which collects water for irrigation.

Table 12.4: Area Irrigation by Wells and Tubewells

1999 -00	2000 -01	2001 -02	2002 -03	2003 -04	2004 -05	2005 -06	2006 -07	2007 -08	2008 -09
7116	7864	9221	12531	48011	28389	30034	34357	36602	37077

Source: Census of Tamil Nadu 2011.

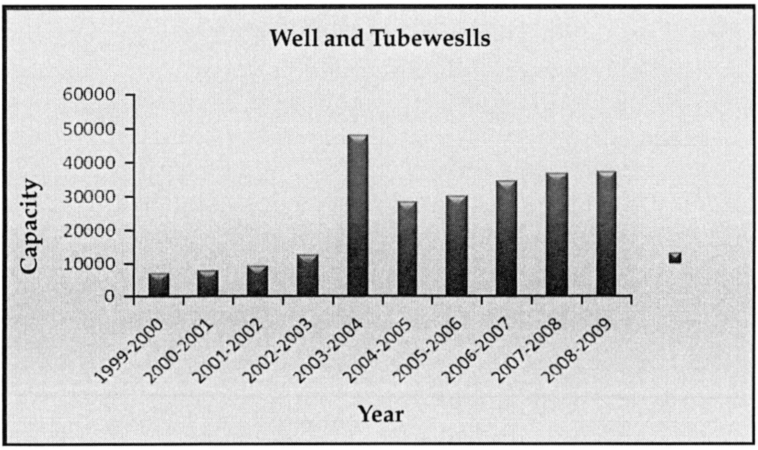

Fig.12.4: Area Irrigation by Wells and Tubewells

This source of irrigation is really rewarding to the study area. Naturally, Thanjavur is getting very good rainfall as well as the alluvial plains. In the year of 2004 the percentage was very high. And slowly became moderate.

Production of food and non-food crops can be stepped by the application of timely irrigation. Irrigation is the most effective and way of increasing agricultural production. Besides, more varieties of crop can be raised in the irrigated areas than in dry places. Use of improved seeds and manures cannot increase the yield to an appreciable extent without requisite supply of water. Another benefit of irrigation is that a crop can be raised during the long dry season.

Production of food and non-food crops can be stepped by the application of timely irrigation. Irrigation is the most effective and way of increasing agricultural production. Besides, more varieties of crop can be raised in the irrigated areas than in dry places. Use of improved seeds and manures cannot increase the yield to an appreciable extent without requisite supply of water. Another benefit of irrigation is that a crop can be raised during the long dry season.

It is seen that from the Table 12.5 there was small increase in the net irrigated area in terms of percentage of net sown area, when compared to 2007 with 2009. During the year of 2000 and 2001 though increase in the irrigated area net sown was also quite significant. The higher area of canal and well irrigation has been occupied by Thanjavur. It is observed that percentage of gross irrigated area on hectare's 82.315 in the year of 2006-07. In 2007-08 it was 85.88 per cent. The range of rainfall during the year 2007-08 was 1001 mm to 1200 mm in Thanjavur.

Table 12.5: Total Sown Area

Year	Net Area	Gross Area	More Than Once
1999-00	5464376	6519109	1054733
2000-01	5303294	6338109	1034815
2001-02	5172492	6226457	1053965
2002-03	4590331	5191108	600777
2003-04	4689156	5316027	626871
2004-05	5097011	5889069	792058
2005-06	5243839	6032718	788879
2006-07	5126072	5842790	716718
2007-08	5061919	5815174	753255
2008-09	**5042896**	**5824248**	**781352**

Source: Census of Tamil Nadu 2011.

Dams and canals were constructed not only during the Biritsh period. In our Ancient period Kallani was built by Raja Raja Chloar for the agricultural development during his period in thanjur. He built the dam with his minimum facilities which serves us even better till today. At present, the whole area is getting very good water source not only from the rainfall and also from very frequent sources of irrigation. The study area is known as a rice bowl of our Tamil Nadu. Cauvery river almost runs through all the taluks of the district. The nook and corner of the study area is getting very good irrigation facilities for almost throughout the year. The canal irrigation covers an area about 75 per cent of the total area. The Cauvery river runs exactly through the middle of the districts.

Conclusion

Thanjavur is an area of high intensity of irrigation which has the fertile soils and fairly good supplies of underground water. The Cauvery river almost covers all the taluks of the district. Canals and wells and tube wells are the principal source of irrigation. Intensity of irrigation is high because of relatively in high rainfall. There are abundant natural depression are in the study area which turned into tanks and ponds. Nowadays, tube wells are the very famous irrigational method almost all the area especially in arable land. In our study area tube well comes after the canal irrigation. From the above, table it is visible that almost the land is irrigated more than once.

REFERENCES

Census of Tamil Nadu 2011: Human Development Report, Tamil Nadu Government.

Dreze, J. and Sen, A., (1996) *Indian Development: Selected Regional Perspectives*. Delhi: Oxford University Press. pp. 420.

Engelman and Roy, (1993) *Sustaining Water: Population and the Future of Renewable Water Supplies*, Washington, DC: Population and Environment Programme, Population Action International, pp. 56.

NCERT (1999) *Sixth All India Educational Survey: Main Report*. New Delhi: National Council of Educational Research and Training.

NSSO (1997) Unemployed in India (1993-94): Salient Features, Fifth Quinequennial Survey, NSS 50th Round, July 1993-June 1994, Report No. 418. New Delhi: National Sample Survey Organization: Department of Statistics, Government of India.

UNDP (1999) *Human Development Report* (1999): New Delhi: Oxford University Press, United Nations Development Programmed.

13

National Rural Employment Guarantee Scheme and Food Security

S. Govindan
Dr. C. Dhandapani

INTRODUCTION

After the notification of the National Rural Employment Guarantee Act on 7th September 2005 a new scheme name National Rural Employment Guarantee Scheme (NREGS) has been launched on February 2, 2006. The ongoing programmes of Sampoorna Grameen Rozgar Yojana (SGRY) and National Food for Work programme (NFFWP) were subsumed with in the NREGS in the 200 districts identified in the initial stage. NREGs implemented by the ministry of Rural Development. NREGs is a flagship Programme of the government that directly touches lives of poor and promotes inclusive growth. Improving the purchasing power of the rural people, primarily semi or unskilled work to people living Below poverty line in rural India. NREGS provides a legal guarantee for one hundred days of employment in every financial year to adult members of any rural households willing unskilled manual work at minimum wage of Rs. 100 per day. The central government outlay for NREGs is 40,000 crores in 2010-11 financial year. 2011 to 2012 year Tamil Nadu touches 1926 crores outlay of NREGS.

Food Security

The food security as access by all people at all times to enough food for an active healthy life (World Development Report 1986). Food and Agriculture Organizations (FAO) defined food security as ensuring that all people at all times have both physical and economic access to basic food they need. The NREGs provides basic food security for the rural livelihoods. Since the launch of the NREGs in February 2006 covering all the 614 districts in the country, the programme has benefited over 10 core rural households and the performance has been found very impressive in connection with right to food. The term food security involves every gaining physical economical, social and environmental access to a balanced diet that includes the necessary macro and micronutrients, safe drinking water sanitation, environmental hygiene, primary health care and education So as to lead a healthy and productive life NREGs are probably the world's largest Ecological security Programme There are Four ways of measuring household and individual food security individual intakes household, Caloric acquisition, diet diversity and indices of coping strategies.

Working of NREGs in Tamil Nadu

Tamil Nadu is India's fifth largest State economy with a Gross Domestic Product of about $50 billion. In the year 2006, NREGs initially implemented in six districts *viz.*, Cuddalore, Dindigul, Nagapattinam, Sivangangi, Tiruvannamalai and Villupuram. Later the scheme was extended to remaining districts. Tamil Nadu has among the highest unemployment rates in the country.

In the year 2010-11 the total fund allotted was Rs. 1613.07 crores. It was considerably increase in the year 2011-12 it is a 1926.86 crores. The data shows that the gain for more in women workers. The data was collected from NREGs website for various aspect like, cumulative number of house holds demanded, number of household provided employment, number of house holds completed 100 days of employment and percentage of household completed 100 days.

Table 13.1: Presents Scenario of MGNRES in Tamil Nadu

Sl.No.	Particulars	2010-11	2011-12
1.	Employment Provided to Households Person days (in lakh)	54.69975	53.50857
2.	Total	1990.89	1820.44
3.	SCs	596.83	528.76
4.	STs	23.41	22.77
5.	Women	1527.4	1373.29
6.	Others	1370.65	1268.94
7.	Total Fund in crores	1613.07	1926.86
8.	Expenditure in crores	1637.02	1720.8
9.	Total works taken up	112418	134743
10.	Works completed	77	3923
11.	Works in progress	112341	130820

Source: www.nrega.nic.in

In this study taken three phases include 31 districts of Tamil Nadu. Phase I include Cuddalor, Dindigul, Nagapattinam, Sivangangai, Thiruvannamalai and Villupuram as on 2-2-2006 on wards. Phase II includes Thanjavur, Tiruvarur, Karur and Tirunelveli on 01-04-2007 onwards. Phase III includes Kanchepuram, Thiruvalur, Vellore, Salem, Namakkal, Dharmapuri, Krishnagiri, Erode, Coimbatore, Nilgiris, Trichy, Perambalur, Ariyalur, Pudukkottai, Madurai, Theni, Ramanathapuram, Virudhunagar, Toothukud and Kanyakumari on 1-4-2008 onwards implemented in NREGs Programme (Table 13.1).

In the year 2009-10, 51,99,861 households demanded employment under NREGs and 51,94,265 households were employed (Table 13.2). Only 5596 households were not employed. In the year 2010-11 59,93,776 households demanded employment under NREGs and 59,66,944 households were employed, only 26,832 house holds were not provided the opportunity. In the year 2011-12 41,95,378 house holds were employee, only 43,053 household were not provided employment (Table 13.3).

Table 13.2: Number of Households Demanded and Provided Employment during 2009-10

Phase	Cumulative No. of Households Demanded	Cumulative No. of Households Provided Employment	Percentage of Employment Provide against Demanded	Households Completed 100 Days	Percentage of Households Completed 100 Days
I	18,45,062	18,43,449	99.91	1,48,702	8.07
II	5,57,255	5,56,475	99.86	33,066	5.94
III	27,97,544	27,94,341	99.89	2,19,469	7.85
Total	**51,99,861**	**51,94,265**	**99.89**	**4,01,237**	**7.72**

Source: www.nrega.nic.in

Table 13.3: Number of Households Demanded and Provided Employment during 2010-11

Phase	Cumulative No. of Households Demanded	Cumulative No. of Households Provided Employment	Percentage of Employment Provide against Demanded	Households Completed 100 Days	Percentage of Households Completed 100 Days
I	19,71,549	19,63,388	98.74	1,553	0.15
II	6,40,606	6,37,199	98.35	297	0.06
III	33,81,621	33,66,357	99.15	3,935	0.17
Total	**59,93,776**	**59,66,357**	**98.97**	**5,785**	**0.14**

Source: www.nrega.nic.in

In the year 2009-10 more than 99.85 per cent of demanded of households were employed in the year 2010-11 more than 98.35 per cent of the house hold that demanded employment in the year 2011-12 all the three phase more than 99.47 per cent of demanded of households was employed.

In the year 2009-10 only 4, 01,237 households received employment for the entire 100 days on 7.72 percentages. In the 2010-11 all the three phase only below 1 per cent to the house hold completed 100 days. It includes 5,785 households are completed 100 days. In the year 2011-12, 6.86 per cent 5.53 per cent and 8.08 per cent of the households competed 100 days of employment in all the three phase (Table 13.4).

Table 13.4: Number of Households Demanded and Provided Employment during 2011-12

Phase	Cumulative No. of Households Demanded	Cumulative No. of Households Provided Employment	Percentage of Employment Provide against Demanded	Households Completed 100 Days	Percentage of Households Completed 100 Days
I	13,70,488	13,53,180	99.59	1,34,713	6.86
II	4,82,881	4,77,872	99.47	37,147	5.83
III	23,42,009	23,21,273	99.55	2,72,110	8.08
Total	**41,95,378**	**41,52,325**	**99.55**	**4,43,970**	**7.44**

Source: www.nrega.nic.in

Participation of Women in NREGs in Tamil Nadu

The share of women in the work force was much more it is around 40 per cent in the phase I districts. The States, specific figures and ranking for 2006-07 and 2007-08 and 2008-09 are fairly stable with Tamil Nadu having the highest participation of women in both years by a long margin. Women dominate NREGs worksite all states. The NREGs have the potential of addressing women's practical needs through wage employment and the creation assets that address basic needs of food water fuel and the fodder. Community based women's group such as Self-help Groups (SHGs) play a very important role. This can help in the more confident and effective expression of needs and affect the selection of works.

Table 13.5 shows in 2009-10 the total women work days of Tamil Nadu is around 14.5 per cent of the total women work days of India and the women share of total persons days is 83 per cent in Tamil Nadu while India holds nearly 48.1 per cent of the women share of total person days. NREGs aims to promote women participation in the work force through a quota to ensure that at least one third of all workers who have registered and requested work under the scheme in each state are women.

Table 13.5: Women Participation under NREGs

Sl. No.	Particulars	India	Tamil Nadu
1.	Total Persons Day lakhs (2006-2007)	950.56	182.79
2.	Total Women Workers (lakhs) (2006-2007)	3679	148.27
3.	Women Share of Total Person Days (Percentage) (2006-2007)	41	82
4.	Total Women Work days Lakhs (2009-10)	13640.48	1982.6
5.	Women share of Total Persons Days (Percentage) 2009-10	48.1	83

Source: NREGs.nic.in

NREGs and Food Security

Work force programmes have been important Programme interventions in India like NREGs. These programmes typically provide unskilled workers with short term employment on public works. They provide involve transfers to poor households during periods when they suffer on account of absence of opportunity of employment. The experience with NREGs so far suggests that it is one of the main planks of rapid poverty reduction in the eleventh five year plan. The programmes has high works participation; of marginalized groups like SC/ST 57 per cent women (43%) in 2007-08. In 2008-09 the participation is SC/ST (54%) and women (49%), strengthening Natural Resource Base of Rural India. It was considerable increasing till now. The NREGs provide more employment opportunities is rural areas they have getting Job and income these income generate food security of rural peoples.

Suggestions for to Improving Successful Implementation of NREGs

- The government has to ensure the benefits are justified and reached.

- The Makkal Nala Paniyalarkal (MNP) has also been made responsible for the implementation of the scheme at the field level.
- Local Government should provide improved work places to the beneficiaries.
- Awareness committee can be formed consisting of educated youth who would bring communication effectiveness of village building initiatives at block/ district level.
- Government should increase the working days of employment from one hundred to two hundred days.
- Increasing infrastructure provision like crèche, water, and first aid box.
- NREGs activities should be undertaken during the off season of Agriculture.
- To create the new employment and increase the wage rate.

Conclusion

NREGs addresses itself chiefly to working people and their fundamental right to live with dignity, economic development and social development must go in parallel way and this may be achieved through NREGs. NREGs are one of the largest schemes in the world and it is the last straw to break the rural poverty. The objectives are good enough to improve the social status of the rural India. In Tamil Nadu this scheme benefited many number of people. This scheme engages people in a constructive way. NREGs made a positive contribution in creating social assets. But they have no significant impact, social and economic standards in the life of rural people in generating employment to the rural poor. Women has benefited more as workers than as a community.

All NREGs works of Tamil Nadu focused on building poverty alleviation initiatives like water harvesting/ renovation of water bodies etc. These works are very much gelling with the visions of the Programme. The Programme should also address specific infrastructure initiatives that would deliver multiplying effect to their village. For a developing rural economy, the Programme is definitely a boon but it needs to metamorphose fitting to the locality needs and there by maturing it's activities from being just a means of short term job provider to long term sustainable livelihood enhancement initiatives.

REFERENCES

Agarval, A.N., *Indian Economy Problems of Development and Planning,* Wishwa Prakasham, New Delhi.

Deas, Mahendra (2005) *Communications of NREGA* Economic and Political Weekly, Vol. XL.

Tamil Nadu Economic Appraisal Department of Evolution, Government of Tamil Nadu 2009-10.

www.nrega.nic.in

www.nrega/tn.nic.in

14

Food Security Through Mahatma Gandhi National Rural Employment Guarantee Programme (MGNREGP) *A Study*

R. Poorani

INTRODUCTION

The National Rural Employment Guarantee Act (NREGA) is an Indian job guarantee scheme enacted by legislation on August 25, 2005. The scheme provides legal guarantee for one hundred days of employment in every financial year to adult members of any rural house hold willing to do public work-related unskilled manual work at the statutory minimum wage of rupees sixty per day. This act was introduced with an aim of improving the purchasing power of rural people, primarily semi or unskilled work to people living in rural India, whether or not they are below the poverty line. Around one third of the stipulated work force is women. It was re-named as Mahathma Gandhi National Rural Employment Guarantee Act (MGNREGA) on 2nd October, 2009.

Implications of MGNREGA

MGNREGA has strong social safety net for the vulnerable groups by providing a fall back employment source, when other employment alternatives are scarce or inadequate. Through the process of providing employment on works that address process of chronic poverty such as drought, deforestation and soil erosion, the act seeks to strengthen the natural resource base of rural livelihood and create durable assets in rural areas. It is rapid progress in recent years. During the period 2006 to 2010, 776.8 cr person-days of employment was generated of which women comprised 50 per cent SCs 21 per cent and STs 20 per cent. Over 9.91 accounts (in banks/ post offices) opened to pay wages transparently. Over 46.95 lakhs works taken up in 619 districts and social audits conducted in 76 per cent of Panchayat. Average wage per day has increased from Rs. 65 in 2006-07 to Rs. 91 in 2009-10. The centre had allocated Rs. 40,100 cr for this scheme for the year 2010-11. The actual expenditure in 2009-10 was Rs. 30,100 cre 44,940,870 rural households were provided job under MGNREGA during 2008-09. In 2010, 179,43,189 families in the country have been provided employment under MGNREGA.

Adult members of a rural household willing to do unskilled manual works, may apply for registration in writing or orally to the Local Gram Panchayat. The gram panchayat after due verifications will issue a job card to the applicant. Employment will be given with in 15 days of applications. Work should ordinarily be provided within 5 km radius of the village. In case work is provided beyond 5 km, extra wages of 10 per cent are payable to meet additional transportation and living expenses. Equal wages will be provided to both men and women. Disbursement of wages has to be done on weekly basis. At least one third beneficiaries shall be women who have registered and requested work under the scheme.

Since, MGNREGA was introduced with the aim of improving the purchasing power of rural people, definitely the village people access to quality and quantity food. The problem of food security comes mainly from the slow growth of purchasing power of the people. It leads to hunger or lack of enough, safe nutritious and socially acceptable food for a healthy and productive life. In developing countries, the root causes of food insecurity include poverty, war and civil conflict, corruption, national policies that do not promote equal access to food for all, environmental degradation, barriers to trade, insufficient supply of protein rich food.

The issue of food security is very much linked with increased agriculture productivity, management of natural resources like land, water, weather, etc., and environmental protection. The MGNREGA is hand in-hand with food security by doing development activities such as water conservation and water harvesting, drought prone (afforestation and tree plantation), irrigation canals, renovation of traditional water bodies, land development, flood control and protection works including drainage in water logged areas, rural connectivity to provide all weather access. MGNREGA has listed working on natural resources and its management as a priority. If this is actually to take place it will not take long to transform the situation in the village through the development of natural resources and the livelihood conditions in the village will improve.

Need for the Study

MGNREGA is important to small and marginal farmers as well as the landless who cannot derive sufficient income in the agricultural sector and also find the sector to be an important safety net to rural households in times of agricultural distress. The importance of MGNREGA in rural areas are poverty alleviation and promotion of livelihood. The successful implementation of the MGNREGA and the Right to Information Act indicates that the climate is conductive for a far-reaching, rights based legislation to eliminate hunger and deprivation. Food access is a function of livelihood opportunities and purchasing power. As early as in 1859, a Famine Commission appointed by colonial government said – Indian famine are not famines of food, but of works, where there is work there is money and where is money there is food. The study on 'MGNREGA' is need of the hour. It is very helpful to understand the status of rural deprived sections.

Objectives

1. To study the impact of MGNREGA on the household income and living standards,
2. To examine the works/activities in the study area, and

3. To know whether the MGNREGA is helpful in securing food security to the workers.

Methodology

The data for the present research study were collected from both primary and secondary sources. The primary data included the information collected directly from the sample respondents through a pre-structured questionnaire by personal interview method. The secondary data were gathered from the records and registers maintained by Block development office, Pudukkottai, Tamil Nadu.

Selection of the Study Area

The researcher selected the Karapattu village, Nirpalani Panchayat, Pudukkottai District, Tamil Nadu.

Selection of the Sample

In Nirpalani Panchayat there are three villages. Among the three villages, Karapattu village chosen for the present study. Out of the total population, hundred respondents was selected for the present study. The collected data have been analysed with the help of statistical tool like percentage analysis and same have been explained through descriptive analysis and narrative procedure.

Summary of Findings

1. It is found that the majority of the respondents (68%) come under MGNREGA. They come for economic necessity and wish to make family life more comfortable.
2. Sixty-one per cent of the respondents said that this scheme is very helpful in poverty alleviation and promotion of livelihood.
3. Under this scheme, beneficiaries are guaranteed to get employment for one hundred days in every year. They could not get employment above hundred days. This will make their family life uncomfortable.
4. Seventy-two per cent respondents perceive that MGNREGA to have helped practically in food security

management. 15 per cent of respondents perceive MGNREGA in no way has to helped in food security management while 3 per cent are not sure.

5. Digging of new tanks/ponds, construction and repair of embankments, land leveling are the main activities in the study area.
6. The study reveals that equal wages are provided to both men and women.
7. Most of the MGNREGA workers represent economically and socially under privileged sections. Mostly, these workers are under-nourished with poor opportunities for healthcare.

Policy Suggestions

- Government should increase the working days of employment from one hundred days to two hundred days.
- Local Government should provide improved work places to the beneficiaries.
- Need to bring about a convergence of child care, nutrition, health (Rural Health Mission) and Education programmes at MGNREGA sites.
- Education can be imparted in the evenings, using the joyful learning techniques available in computer aided literacy programmes.
- There is also a need to raise the self-esteem of MGNREGA workers, making them feel proud of the fact that they are engaged in checking economic destruction.

Conclusion

From the present Study, it is concluded that MGNREGA is important to improve both Income and food security in rural areas and also gives hope to the poorest of the poor. There are uncommon opportunities to erase India's image as the land of the poor, hungry and illiterate.

REFERENCES

Ganesh Sharma and Mona Sharma (2008) "Contemporary Issues in Sustainable Food Security Management," *Kurukshetra, Volume* 56, No. 8, pp. 14-16.

Galasso, E., and Ravallion, M., (2005) "Decentralized Targeting of an Antipoverty Programme," *Journal of Public Economics*, Volume 89, No. 4, pp. 705-727.

Kamboj, Prem Chand *et al.*, (2010) "Impact of NREG Scheme on Agriculture Sector," *Southern Economist*, Volume 48, No. 20, pp. 45-48.

Mukundan, N., (2004) "Environment, People's Participation And Sustainable Rural Development," *Kurukshetra*, Volume. 52, No. 8, pp 4-6.

Mahalingam, N., (2010) "Innovative Use of Water Resources For Food Security and Economic Prosperity," *Kisan World*, Volume 37, No. 10, pp. 3-5.

Singh, P.K., (2007) "NREGA: A New Hope for Rural Employment Generation," *Southern Economist*, Volume 46, No. 4, pp. 27-31.

Swaminathan, M.S., (2009) "Synergy Between Food Security Act and NREGA," *Wastelands News*, Volume. XXIV, No. 3, pp. 1-3.

Vekata Rao, P., and Thandava Krishna,C., (2009) "Food Security in India," *Kisan World*, Volume 36, No. 6, pp. 8-10.

15

Mahatma Gandhi National Rural Employment Guarantee Scheme

Dr. A.M. Ayyothi

INTRODUCTION

Employment is a simple word which can be defined as "an occupation by which a person can earn his living, and unemployment is the inability of providing gainful work to people who are willing to work". Every sixth person in the world is an Indian and every third poor person in the world is also an Indian. Unemployment is the most serious problem facing in our country. A large number of educated and uneducated people loiter about in search of some job. They are willing to work but they can not get it. The population of the country is increasing fast but the jobs can not be increased in that proportion. India's labour force is growing at a rate of 2.5 per cent annually, but employment is growing at only 2.3 per cent. Thus, the country is faced with the challenge of not only absorbing new entrants to the Job market, but also clearing the back log.

An empty mind is devil's workshop. An unemployment person is a nuisance to the society. A hungry man can do any wrong. Therefore, it is the duty of the government to solve the problem of unemployment as early as possible. Government should encourage policies of self employment. In this regard government policies should be liberalized. The

Department of Rural Development is implementing a number of programmes in rural areas through the Central and State Governments for employment generation the important programme presently being implemented by the union Government in India is the Mahatma Gandhi National Rural Employment Guarantee Scheme.

Mahatma Gandhi National Rural Employment Guarantee Act

In 2005, India's parliament passed the National Rural Employment Guarantee Act (NREGA), which is the central governments response to the constitutionally manifested right to work and means to promote livelihood security in India's rural areas. This act was introduced with can aim of improving the purchasing power of the rural people, primarily, semi or unskilled work to people living in rural India, whether or not they are below the poverty line. Around one-third of the of the stipulated work force is women. It was initially called National Rural Employment Guarantee Act (NREGA) but it was renamed on 2nd October 2009 namely, Mahatma Gandhi National Rural Employment Guarantee Scheme (MGNREGS).

The Mahatma Gandhi National Rural Employment Guarantee Act aims at enhancing the livelihood security of people in rural areas by guaranteeing minimum 100 days of wage employment in a financial year to a rural household whose adult members volunteer to do unskilled manual work. The act is applicable to areas notified by the Central Government and will cover the whole country within 5 years of its notification. The act was notified in 200 districts in the first phase with effect from February 2nd 2006 then it was extended to additional 130 districts in the financial year 2007-08. The remaining districts have been notified under the NREGA with effect from 1 April 2008. Thus, NREGA covers the entire country with the exception of districts that have a 100 per cent urban population. For making amendment in section 1(2) of the NREG Act with a view to extend the Act to the State of Jammu and Kashmir, a Bill titled NREG (Extension to Jammu and Kashmir) Bill-2007 was introduced in (Lok

Sabha on 07-03-2007. The Bill was passed by Loksabha on 19-03.2007 and was referred to Raya Sabha for consideration. Rajya Sabha passed the Bill on 27-04-2007. The Bill received the assent of the president of India on 11.05.2007 and has been extended to Jammu and Kashmir with effect from 12-05-2007.

Objectives of MGNREGS Act

1. The Mahatma Gandhi National Rural Employment Guarantee Scheme (MGNREGS) aims at enhancing the livelihood security of the people in rural areas by guaranteeing hundred days of wage employment in a financial year, to a rural household whose members volunteer unskilled manual work.
2. To create durable assets and strengthen the livelihood resource base of the rural poor.
3. The choice of works suggested in the Act address the causes of chronic poverty like drought, deforestation, soil erosion, so that the process of employment generation is on a sustainable basis works.

Salient Features of the Act

(i) Adult members of the rural household may apply for employment in which they are willing to do unskilled manual work,

(ii) The job card with photograph is given at free of cost,

(iii) Employment will be given within 15 days of applying for work by an employment seeker,

(iv) if employment is not provided within 15 days, daily unemployment allowance, in cash is to be paid. Liability of payment of unemployment allowance is of the states,

(v) At least one third of persons are women,

(vi) Panchayat raj institutions have a principal role in planning and implementation of the works in the following areas:

  (a) water conservation;

  (b) drought proofing;

  (c) flood protection;

(*d*) land development;

(*e*) minor irrigation; and

(*f*) rural connectivity.

(*vii*) The District Collector or Chief Executive Office is responsible for the programme at the district level,

(*viii*) The Gram sabha will monitor the work of the Gram panchayat by way of social audit.

Table 15.1: Performance of MGNREGS in Tiruvannamalai District

Sl. No.	Particulars	2009-10	2010-11
1.	Employment Provided to households Person days (in lakh)	3.9004 lakh	3,04382 lakh
2.	Total	176.67	201.58
3.	SCs	39.52 (22.37%)	122.96 (61%)
4.	STs	2.9 (1.64%)	16.13 (8%)
5.	Women	130.32 (73.77%)	169.02 (83.85)
6.	Others	134.25 (75.99%)	62.49 (31%)
7.	Total Funds Rs.	133.09 crore	188.03 crore
8.	Expenditure	127.12 crore	148.42 crore
9.	Total works taken up	133.096 crore	—
10.	Expenditure	127.12 crore	—
11.	Total works taken up	8626	4021
12.	Works completed	0	2730
13.	Works in progress	8625	1291

Source: www.nrega.nic.in/emp Status

Results and Discussion

Table 15.2 presents data on employment generation in Tiruvannamalai Block from 2009-10 to 2010-11. The total number of village panchayats in Tiruvannamalai Block is 69. The highest households registered is 1146 in Pavithram village, but the highest persons registered individually is in Isukalikatteri. The highest number of job cards were issued is in Pavithram village. The lowest job cards were issued in Savalpoondi in the financial year of 2009-10. It was the same trend existed in the financial year 2010-11 also.

Table 15.2: Employment Generation in Tiruvannamalai Block

S.No.	Particulars	2009-10	2010-11
1.	*(i)* No. of Resisted Household	37373	37373
2.	Person	64550	64550
3.	*(ii)* Job Card	37373	37373
4.	*(iii)* Employment demanded	27736	27495
5.	Household	41778	46299
6.	*(iv)* Employment offered Household Person	27736 41778	27494 40298
7.	*(v)* Employment provided Household Person Person days	27663 41617 1194442	29802 44237 1238975
8.	*(vi)* No. of filled muster roll	2961	2317
9.	*(vii)* No. of family completed 100 days	1859	1059
10.	*(viii)* On going works	365	562

Source: www.nrega.nic.in/emp status.

In the year 2009-10 total numbers of employments offered by person was 41,778. The highest employment were in the village of Pavithram *i.e.* 1198 persons. The lowest was in Melathikkan 170 in the year 2010-11. Total number of employment offered in the village was Meyyur *i.e.* 1160 by person, the lowest is Athiyandal 248 persons.

The total number of employment provided by a person days is 12,38,975 in the financial year 2010-11. It was low in 11,94,442 in the financial year 2009-10. The 1859 families have completed 100 days in the financial year 2009-10. But it was low for 1059 families in the financial year 2010-11. The total number of ongoing works in 365 in the financial year 2009-10, but it has increased in 562 in the financial year 2010-11. Tiruvannamalai District has been selected for a national award for successful implementation of the Mahatma Gandhi National Rural Employment Guarantee Scheme (MGNREGS). Tiruvannamalai is among the 10 top districts in the country that has successfully implemented the scheme at the district level since 2006.

Table 15.3 exlibits the employment generation during the year 2010-11. The total number of registered household was 11,59,97,568, by person it is 25,34,31,088. The highest number of registered household were is the state of Uttar Pradesh *i.e.* 1,20,93,103. The lowest number Registered was in the Dadra and Nagar Haweli union territory. The job card issued were 11,51,16,091. In uttar Pradesh it attained the maximum of 1,19,76,817. In Goa it was the minimum of 12,832.

Table 15.3: Employment Generation under MGNREGS in India (2010-11)

Sl. No.	Particulars	2010-11
1.	No. of Register Household Person	115997568 253431088
2.	Job card issued	115116091
3.	Employment demanded Household Person	41878533 66813258
4.	Employment offered Household Person	41775264 66592230
5.	Employment provided Household Persons	42019006 67314680
6.	Person days	1486779860
7.	No. of filled muster Roll	15139254
8.	No. of families completed 100 days	1652166
9.	On Going works	4203478

Source: www. nrega.nic.in.

The total number of employment provided in the financial year 2010-11 in person days was 1,48,67,79,860, In Andhra Pradesh it attained the maximum 27,45,76,369. The lowest was in Goa *i.e.* 1,98,174.

The number of families completed in 100 days were 16,52,166. It was maximum in Andhra Pradesh *i.e.* 16,52,166. In Arunachal Pradesh no one has got 100 days employment.

The total number of ongoing works in India was 42,03,478. The maximum was in Uttar Pradesh *i.e.*, total 9,58,764 works are undergoing. The lowest is in Arunachal Pradesh 309 works are undergoing.

A majority of the poor in rural areas in our country are the wage earners. They earn through unskilled, casual, manual labour. They are often on threshold levels of subsistence, and are vulnerable to the possibility of sinking from transient to chronic poverty. Inadequate labour demand or in predictable crises that may be general in nature, like natural disaster or personal like ill health, adversely impact their employment opportunities.

In a context of poverty and unemployment, MGNREGS provides short term employment on public works such as irrigation, infrastructure, reforestation, soil conservation, rural road construction and connection.

Recommendations

The following are the recommendations to improve Mahatma Gandhi National Rural Employment Guarantee Scheme:

- Communication is very important for the participation of the rural people. Communication channels can be made effective to make rural people understand the processes and futures.
- The Government has to ensure the benefits which are justified and reached to poor peoples.
- Creating awareness of the programme through Self Help Groups (SHGs).

- People are unaware about the unemployment allowance. Hence, the Gram Panchayat Programme officers can provide unemployment allowances.
- To provide job on above 100 days of employment to households and ensure gender equality in rural areas.
- Male members in the village take advantage of women in Gram Sabha meetings. The MGNREGS programme officers should explain the women involvement in Gram Sabha meetings.
- Increasing infrastructure provisions like crèche, drinking water, and first aid box etc. In the work field would ensure efficiency of the programme.
- Programme officers to take work estimation with considering soil texture, climate conditions, etc.
- Government has to increase wage rates in par with price rise.
- The government has to consider for increasing the minimum working days of the programme from 100 days to 200 days in a year.

Conclusion

Thiruvannamalai District is purposively selected for the present research work. A majority of the poor in rural areas in Tiruvannamali, wage earners, they earn through unskilled, casual manual labour. The data base for this research study consist of secondary data. The Mahatma Gandhi National Rural Employment Guarantee Scheme works of Thiruvannamalai is focused on building poverty alleviation on initiatives like water harvesting, renovation of water bodies etc. The programme should also address specific infrastructure initiatives that would deliver multiplying effects to their Thiruvannamalai district.

These act stipulates that priority should be given women in the year 2009-10, the total no of employment provided to households person days was 3.90 lakh it was increasing level. Thiuvannamali District beneficiaries are women who have registered and have requested for work. Against this backdrop, 27 States point out that this has been met in 18 states the highest is being reported in Tripura (85%) and Tamil Nadu (82%) respectively. In Thiruvannamalai District the reported were higher the national coverage which stands of.

This scheme is a historic measure to implement its promise of Right to Work and increasing purchasing power of the rural people in Thiruvannamalai district. This work needs to create sustainable assets that promote the economic and infrastructure development of Thiruvannamalai district. MGNREGs success will depends on the quality implementation. It properly implemented this would provide employment in lean periods to the rural people on the one hand and create really productive assets in the form of infrastructure like roads, irrigation, water harvesting works on the other. This scheme is even excellent initiative that energizes the rural people in building a better sustainable eco-system themselves.

REFERENCES

Bhagawathi, Kumud: *Special Employment and Poverty Alleviation Programme in India,* New Century Publications, New Delhi, 2007.

Datt, Ruddar and K.P.M. Sundharam, *Indian Economy,* S. Chand and Company Ltd., 55th Revised Edition.

Deas, Mahendra (2005) "Communications of NREGA", *Economics and Political Weekly,* Vol. XL, No. 14.

Hook, Alfred *Unemployment its Causes and Cure,* The Labour Publishing Company Ltd., London 1924.

Indian Labour (2010) "New in Brief", *Indian Labour Journal,* Vol. 51, No. 4, Government of India, New Delhi.

Sabha, Dilip (2007) "Planning of NREGS", *Kurukshetra,* Vol. 55, No. 6, Ministry of Information and Broadcasting, Government of India, New Delhi.

16

Mahatma Gandhi National Rural Employment Guarantee Programme and Food Security

A Micro Level Study

P. Veerachamy

INTRODUCTION

As in other developing countries, unemployment is a serious problem of the Indian economy. The poverty of the masses in India closely related to the problem of unemployment. Unemployment is a situation when willing workers fail to get jobs at the prevailing wage rates. In other words, unemployment means involuntary idleness, the time for which individuals are available for and willing to, but are not able to find work. From social point of view, unemployment means wastage of the precious labour resources of the country. For an individual unemployment is a painful and democratizing experience. Employment to be gainful and sustainable has to be productive in character unemployment is a multidimensional phenomenon in India. It is not restricted to one sector or group of population. Instead, it is a widespread disease touching almost every segment of the society.

Statement of the Problem

In order to reduce the level of unemployment rate, various policies and programmes have been introduced and implemented by the Government. But there has not been much more significant reduction in unemployment rate among the poor and uneducated rural people. The unemployment problem has been experienced by them is due to the fact that or either agricultural is a seasonal job provider or the availability of less number of man-days to the workers. In other words, the number of working days to the seasonal workers is uncertain throughout the year. Keeping these economic issues, the NREGP has been implemented in India for the poor people, where 100 man days are guaranteed to the village workers. With this basic brief about the problem of unemployment the researcher has identified that the research problem of the impact analysis of NREGP on various dimensions *viz.*, alternative employment opportunity for the remaining days in a year, on women empowerment household food security and the standard of living of them.

With this practical operation of the NREGP, we tried to test the Nurske theory of capital formation during the Seventh Plan (1985-90). According to Nurske, the excess supply of labour can be transferred for the purpose of capital formation in the form of installing new projects, constructing dams, digging canals, constructing roads, schools and hospitals, etc. But as far as NREGP concerned, they have been concentrating on common properties of the society such as digging and deepening wells, canals, etc. But these activities are helpful for only one year not over a time period. Again they have to do the same work in the next year also. Hence, there is no chance for further more capital formation in future like building, schools, hospital etc. It is the question of the impact of NREGP on capital formation.

Objectives

1. To assess the social economic background of the sample household;
2. To examine the factors responsible for participating NREGP; and
3. To explore the alternative employment opportunities in the study area.

Hypotheses

1. Caste influences the choice of participation of NREGP Scheme.
2. There is significant contribution of earnings of NREGP Scheme income to total house holds income.

Methodology

The researcher selected Kattumannarkoil Taluk for study due to fact that of this scheme was introduced in the phase of Tamil Nadu in the year 2005. Kattumannarkoil Taluk consists of two blocks *i.e.,* Kattumannarkoil and Kumaratchi Blocks. Kattumannarkoil block consists of 55 Panchayat villages and two town Panchayats. Kumaratchi block consists of 57 Panchayats and two town Panchayats. In each block two Panchayats were the scheme has been implemented was selected at random sampling method. According to the Kattumannarkoil block *i.e.,* Melpuliyangudi, and Gunamanagalam Panchayats and in Kumaratchi block *i.e.,* Thavarthampattu and Themmur Panchayats were chosen as representative samples of this study.

In the second stage from each Panchayat 25 beneficiaries on the basis of random sampling, by considering their maximum involvement in the scheme. Thus, the sample size for the study consisted of 100 beneficiaries spread over four Village panchayats. The accessibility to them was made possible with the help of panchayats level officers. Blockwise progress of NREGP works both in physical and financial terms were gathered from DRDA Office and Block Office.

Tools for Analysis

To processed this research work, the researcher was used simple statistical (mean and percentage) as well as econometric tools *viz.,* chi-square test and z-test (large sample).

Analysis and Discussion

Testing of Hypotheses

The hypotheses formulated are tested by analyzing the collected data in this section. The tests are used with appropriate level of significance.

Testing of Hypothesis I

Caste influences the choice of participation of NREGP Scheme.

Framework of Analysis

To test whether there is an association between caste and the choice of NREGP employment, χ^2 test is applied.

H_0: There is no association between caste and the choice of NREGP employment.

H_1: There is an association between caste and the choice of NREGP employment.

$$\chi^2 = \sum ij \frac{(Oij - Eij)^2}{Eij}$$

Where,

O^{ij} = Observed frequency in (ij)th Cell

E^{ij} = Expected frequency

$$E^{ij} = \frac{(\text{ith row total}) \times (\text{jth column total})}{\text{Grand total}}$$

Degrees of freedom = (r–1) (c–1)

r = No. of rows

c = No. of columns

Table 16.1: Caste-wise the Choice of Participation of NREGP Scheme

Sl. No.	Categories-wise	Community			Total
		SC/ST	MBC	BC	
I.	**Kattumannarkoil (Block – I)** a. Melpuliyangudi b. Gunamangalam	34	11	5	50
II.	**Kumarachi (Block – II)** a. Thavarthampattu b. Themmur	18	17	15	50
	Total	**52**	**28**	**20**	**100**

Source: Computed

Calculated value of χ^2 is 11.20

Degrees of freedom = 2

Table value of χ^2 is 5% = 5.991 and at 1% = 9.210.

Since the calculated value is greater than the table value at 1 per cent level of significance, the null hypothesis is rejected. Therefore, the researcher has concluded that there is significance association between caste and the choice of the employment; SC Community (52 out of 100) occupies a predominant role in the both blocks (Kattumannarkoil and Kumarachi). On the other hand, MBC community (28 out of 100) and BC community recorded (20 out of 100). So the researcher concluded that there is a caste influence of choice of employment in NREGP Scheme.

Testing of Hypothesis II

There is significant contribution of earnings of NREGP Scheme income to total household income.

Framework of Analysis

To identify the contribution of NREGP income to the total household's income, Z-test is used.

Z - Test for equality of two mean

$$Z = \frac{\overline{X}_1 - \overline{X}_2}{S.E.(\overline{X}_1 - \overline{X}_2)}$$

$$S.E.(\overline{X}_1 - \overline{X}_2) = \sqrt{\frac{\sigma_1^2}{\eta_1} + \frac{\sigma_2^2}{\eta_2}}$$

Where

$\overline{X}_1$ = Total household income with NREGP (Rs. per year)

$\overline{X}_2$ = Total household income without NREGP (Rs. per year)

σ_1 = Standard Deviation with NREGP

σ_2 = Standard Deviation without NREGP

n = Sample size.

Z-Test for significant contribution of earning of NREGP Scheme income to total household's income.

Since the calculated value (17.98) is greater than the table value (2.58) at 1 per cent level of significance, the researcher has concluded that there is significant contribution of earnings of NREGP scheme income to total household income of all the sample villages selected in both Kattumannarkoil and Kumarachi blocks of Cuddalore District.

Table 16.2: Contribution of NREGP Income to Total Household's Income

Sl. No.	Categories	Mean	S.D	Sample size
1.	Total household income with NREGP (Rs. per year)	71,500	85	100
2.	Total household income with out NREGP (Rs. per year)	48,300	98	100

Source: Computed

Calculated value of Z = 17.98

Standard Error = 12.9

Table value of $Z_{0.05} = 1.96$

$Z_{0.01} = 2.58$.

Summary of Findings

- More than (52%) of them belongs to Scheduled Caste and Scheduled Tribe (SC/ST) and another (28%) belong to Most Backward Caste (MBC). Only (20%) are in Backward community (BC).
- From the responses of the respondents more than (54%) are married and only (46%) are unmarried.
- Most of the respondents of the NREGP scheme are studied between Primary and Secondary level only few (4%) was class the Higher secondary level, (35%) of the respondents are not having any educational status.
- It is inferred that the majority of the household (both Kattumannarkoil and Kumarachi block) was thatched (52%). It shows the majority of the NREGP scheme respondents are very poor and there standard of living also poor in a sample villages.
- The majority of the respondents from Nuclear family system (93%) only (7%) come under joint family system.
- Among the respondents the maximum of 43 respondents was in Agricultural labour, followed by 20 respondents was engaged in Agriculture, 15 respondents was working in the field of Construction, 12 respondents was in

livestock and only 10 respondents was engaged in other workers *i.e.* driver, company workers, tailor and cottage industry workers.

- In case of Kattumannarkoil block, the highly income was recorded (Rs. 13.83 lakhs) in Melpuliyangudi and minimum income was recorded (Rs. 6.96 lakhs) in Gunamangalam village of in agricultural occupation. In Kumarachi block, the highly income was recorded (Rs. 6.57 lakhs in Themmur and (Rs. 5.56 lakhs) in Thavarthampattu in agricultural occupation.
- Recording to Kattumannarkoil block the maximum food expenditure was recorded (Rs. 3.64 lakhs) in Gunamangalam village and (Rs. 3.44 lakhs) was recorded in Melpuliyangudi village. In Kumarachi block maximum food expenditure (Rs. 3.74 lakhs) was recorded in Thavarthampattu village and (Rs. 3.43 lakhs) of food expenditure in Themmur village.
- The highest investment shows in post office savings was (Rs. 0.75 lakhs) in Themmur village followed by highest bank deposits was (Rs. 0.89 lakhs) in Melpuliyangudi, cash in hand was (Rs. 0.46 lakhs) in Themmur, and Investment in SHG was recorded in (Rs. 0.40 lakhs) in Thavarthampattu in Kumarachi block.
- The highest amount of borrowing was recorded in money lenders (Rs. 5.12 lakhs) in Melpuliyangudi village, Kattumannarkoil block. In Kumarachi block the highest amount of borrowings shows in Thavarthampattu village (Rs. 4.95 lakhs). The highest amount of borrowing in banks (31%) in Melpuliyangudi followed by (27%) of highest amount borrowed from relatives and friends.
- Recording other scheme income (expected NREGP scheme), the respondents have IAY scheme the maximum income of (Rs. 18.30 lakhs) about (29.3%) was recorded in Gunamangalam village and minimum income (Rs. 13.50 lakhs) about (21.7%) was recorded in Thavarthampattu village.

Policy Suggestions

The rise in an income of rural poor naturally results in the rise in their level of other employment generation programmes. The rise in an income also lead to rise in savings, repayment of debts, purchase of durable assets and expansion on income. Thus scheme-wise variation is noted in regard to the impact of NREGP on consumption levels.

Conclusion

In spite of difficulties and land ships, the rural poor under the NREGP able to creation of employment opportunities in rural areas. On account of this, income is regenerated the household rural poor and their standard of living. Even though, mostly the government has given employment to the household for the rural areas. With the help of such type of NREGP the social capital can also improved and developed specifically for the rural people. Hence, it is concluded that economic development and social development must go hand in hand with the implementation of social security and development policies.

REFERENCES

Adhikani, Anindita and Kartika Bhatia (2010) "NREGA Wage Payments: We Banks on the Banks? *Economic and Political Weekly,* 45 (1): 30-37.

Chakraborty, Pinaki (2007) "Implementation of Employment Guarantee: A Preliminary Appraisal, *Economic and Political Weekly,* 42 (7): 548-551.

Jain, L.C. (2005) "Employment Guarantee: Putting Panchayats in Charge" *Economic and Political Weekly,* 40 (33): 3649-3650.

Jetli, Narindar K.,(2006) *Man Power Employment Policy and Labour Welfare,* New Delhi: New Century Publications.

Krishnamoorthy (2006) "Employment Guarantee and Crisis Response", *Economic and Political Weekly,* 41 (9): 789-790.

Louis, Prakash (2006) "NREGA Implementation – II Birth Pangs in Bihar", *Economic and Political Weekly,* 41 (48): 4946.

Mehrotra, Santosh (2008) "NREGA Two Years on Where Do we go from here?" *Economic and Political Weekly* 43 (31): 27-35.

Rao, Mohan (2008) "Employment Guarantee Scheme is a Life Line for the Vulnerable Sections", *Kurukshetra;* 56 (8): 46-47.

Reddy, Venkata (1989) "Rural Employment Guarantee Scheme: An Observation", *Kurukshetra*, pp. 39-41.

Shah, Mihi R (2007) "Employment Guarantee Civil Society and Indian Democracy", *Economic and Political Weekly*, 42 (4): 43-50.

Wray, Randall (2006) "Lessons from Argentina's Employment Guarantee" *Economic and Political Weekly;* 41 (23): 2293-2296.

Vaidyanathan. A (2005) "Employment Guarantee: Need for Involvement of States, *Economic and Political Weekly*, 40 (33): 3646-3648.

17

National Rural Employment Guarantee Programme and Food Security
A Micro Experiment

G. Kumar
S.Thamilarasan

INTRODUCTION

Economic security is one of the main components of human security. It constitutes the crux of social security, in the conventional sense. Economic security requires employment and an assured source of a basic income adequate for meeting one's basic needs. A primary objective of state policy should generate greater productive work opportunities in the growth process itself, by concentrating on sectors, sub-sector and technologies which are more labour-oriented, in regions characterized by higher rates of unemployment and under-employment. Recognizing the high incidence of under-employment and increasing actualization of labour, there is a need to enhance employment opportunities for the poor, particularly for those who are in seasonal occupation.

Statement of the Problem

Unemployment in the agricultural sector is the most serious aspect in the Indian economy. First of all, there is open unemployment among the landless agricultural works. With the decline of cottage industries and handicrafts, the rural population has no alternative means of livelihood. They have to fall back on the agriculture sector which is clearly over crowded. There is also considerable disguised unemployment in the agricultural sector. It means more people neglected in agricultural operators than required. In technical language the marginal productivity of many hands in agricultural sector is zero. Another dimension of real unemployment is the problem of seasonal unemployment among the Indian farmers. Agriculture by its very nature is a seasonal activity. For a significant of the part of the year, the Indian farmers are out of work. In the absence of supplementary sources of employment, they have to remain unemployed during slack agricultural season.

Objective

1. To study the working of National Rural Employment Guarantee Programme (NREGP) in the study area between 2005 and 2009.

Methodology

Based on the framed objectives of the study, it is necessary to collect both primary and secondary data with respect to the impact of NREGP on various aspects such as alternative employment opportunity, determination of participating in NREGP and the level of food security between the sample respondents.

Analysis and Discussion

NREGP Scheme Expenditure Statements

It is necessary and general to study the socio-economic background of the sample households. The socio-economic background includes religion, social status, community and size of the family. But along with the general factors, it is also important to know the individual characters like, sex, education occupation, income, expenditure, value of property of the respondents. Because individual and household factors plays predominant role while studying employment. Employment generation programmes includes income, expenditure, borrowings and savings pattern and living conditions of the sample respondents. Kattumannarkoil and Kumarachi Blocks NREGP scheme expenditure statements (year-wise and village-wise) are given bellow. This part of analysis is based on secondary data. The data were collected from Block Development Office (BDO) records of the respective sample villages. Kattumannarkoil block NREGP scheme expenditure statement as follows:

Table 17.1 indicates that Kattumannarkoil Block NREGP statement related to estimated and actual expenditure made during 2005-06 to 2009-10. Recording Melpuliyangudi village in Kattumannarkoil Block, the actual expenditure was recorded in the year 2009-10 is Rs. 27.71 lakhs and it was recorded Rs. 4.48 lakhs in the year 2005-06. It shows the NREGP expenditure was increased during the study period. The percentage share of actual expenditure done in the year 2005-06 to 2009-10. All most covered 92.33 per cent to 99.39 per cent. It shows the efficiency of the programmes in terms of their spending estimated value to actual amount spent in this programmes.

Gunamangalam village, which is also one of the sample village in Kattumannarkoil block. In the year 2005-06 the estimated value was recorded Rs. 2.61 lakhs and expenditure was during the period Rs. 5.88 lakhs. But in the year 2009-10 the estimated value was Rs. 10 lakhs and expenditure made during the period was Rs. 8.85 lakhs. Overall both Melpuliyangudi and Gunamangalam the percentage share of actual expenditure to estimated value was declined. This is mainly attributed to:

(i) during raining season the NREGP was not done in the field;

(ii) postponed the NREGP work due to some internal problems arise in the villages;

(iii) unnecessary delay to the programmes due to the local authority not properly paid the full wage to the NREGP respondents.

Some portion of money taking in the name of 'commission'. This leads to the lack of interest to do the NREGP work.

Table 17.2 shows that Kumarachi block NREGP scheme expenditure statements (year-wise and village-wise).

Table 17.1: Kattumannarkoil Block NREGP Expenditure Statements (Year and Village-wise)

(Value in Rs. 000s)

Sl. No.	Year	Melpuliyangudi			Gunamangalam		
		Estimated Expenditure	Actual Expenditure	% Share of Actual Expenditure to Estimated	Estimated Expenditure	Actual Expenditure	% Share of Actual Expenditure to Estimated
1.	2005-06	521	498	95.58	621	588	94.68
2.	2006-07	600	579	96.33	892	797	89.34
3.	2007-08	1488	1479	99.39	2000	1586	79.30
4.	2008-09	3000	2680	89.33	1700	1204	70.82
5.	2009-10	3001	2771	92.33	1000	885	88.50

Source: Block Development Office, Kattumannarkoil.

Table 17.2: Kumarachi Block NREGP Expenditure Statements (Year-wise and Village-wise)

(Value in Rs. 000s)

Sl. No.	Year	Thavarthampattu		% Share of Actual Expenditure to Estimated	Themmur		% Share of Actual Expenditure to Estimated
		Estimated Expenditure	Actual Expenditure		Estimated Expenditure	Actual Expenditure	
1.	2005-06	671	593	88.37	690	681	98.69
2.	2006-07	878	877	99.88	854	844	98.82
3.	2007-08	1480	1462	98.78	700	689	98.42
4.	2008-09	1921	1876	97.65	2057	1890	91.88
5.	2009-10	1400	1024	73.14	1528	1040	68.06

Source: Block Development Office, Kumarachi.

Kumarachi Block sample villages are Thavarthampattu and Themmur. In Thavarthampattu village, the estimated value of the NREGP was recorded Rs. 6.71 lakhs rather than the expenditure value was made during the year 2005-06 Rs. 5.93 lakhs. The percentage share of actual amount spend in the year 88.37 percentage in the year 2009-10 the estimated value was Rs. 14 lakhs and it expenditure was Rs. 10.24 lakhs. The percentage share of actual expenditure was recorded 73.14 percentage.

Estimated value of actual expenditure of Themmur was Rs. 6.90 lakhs and 6.81 lakhs in the year 2005-06. The percentage share of actual expenditure was 98.69 percentage. In the year 2009-10 the estimated value Rs. 15 lakhs and expenditure was 10.40 lakhs. The percentage share of actual expenditure was 68.06, Overall, the percentage share of actual expenditure to estimated was declining trend during the study period (2005-06 to 2009-10). This is mainly due to:

(a) non-co-operation between local authority to NREGP respondents;

(b) community dispute among the peoples;

(c) lack of integration among the NREGP respondents in the sample villages.

Summary of Findings

- The actual expenditure was recorded in the year 2009-10 is Rs. 27.71 lakhs and it was recorded Rs. 4.48 lakhs in the year 2005-06. It shows the NREGP expenditures were increased during the study period.
- Gunamangalam village, which is also one of the sample village in Kattumannarkoil block. In the year 2005-06 the estimated value was recorded Rs. 2.61 lakhs and expenditure was during the period Rs. 5.88 lakhs.
- But in the year 2009-10 the estimated value was Rs. 10 lakhs and expenditure made during the period was Rs. 8.85 lakhs.
- Estimated value of actual expenditure of Themmur was Rs. 6.90 lakhs and 6.81 lakhs in the year 2005-06. The percentage share of actual expenditure was 98.69 percentages.

- More than half of (56%) the respondents are male members and the remaining (44%) are female which shows the head of the households are male was more members than the female headed households.

Conclusions

The suggestions are made for creation of employment scheme with intention of to gear up the factual achievement to the fullest possible extent. The unemployed beneficiaries should be guaranteed maximum wages and the manual work under the NREGP beneficiaries and also the reduction of migration equal wages for male and female. The NREGP scheme helped to the rural families below the poverty line to get an additional income and the extra income earned through the NREGP beneficiaries was spent towards their income from NREGP.

REFERENCES

Bhatia, Bela and Jean Dreze (2006) "Employment Guarantee in Jharkhand", *Economic and Political Weekly,* 41 (29) pp. 3198-3202.

Dubhashi, P.R., (1970) *Rural Development Administration in India,* Popular Prakasham, Bombay.

Datt, Ruddar and Sundaram, K.P.M. (2004) *Indian Economy,* S. Chand and Company Ltd., New Delhi.

Hirway, Indira (2005) "Enhancing Livelihood Security Through The National Employment Guarantee Scheme Towards Effective Operationalisation of The Act", *Indian Journal of Labour Economics,* 48 (4) 70 pp. 1-14.

Jain, Hemchand (1989) "Enlarging Employment in Rural Areas", *Kurukshetra,* 37(7) p.p. 22-26.

Prasad, Navendra (1990) "Construction of Rural Development", Popular Prakasham, Bombay.

Singh, Katar (2002) *Rural Development Principles,* Policies and Management", Sage Publications, New Delhi.

Singh, Puram (2006) "National Rural Employment Guarantee Scheme", *Kurukshetra,* 54(7) pp. 42-47.

Vanaik, Anish (2008) "National Rural Employment Guarantee Act and the Death of Tapas Soren", *Economic and Political Weekly,* 40(30) pp. 8-10.

18

Agricultural Cooperatives in Food Security Management

R. Velu Raj

INTRODUCTION

Cooperatives operate in all sectors of the economy ranging from small-scale to multi-million dollar businesses across the globe, count over 800 million members and provide 100 million jobs world-wide - 20 per cent more than multinational enterprises. In 2008, the largest 300 cooperatives in the world had an aggregate turnover of US$ 1.1 trillion, comparable to the gross domestic product (GDP) of many large countries. In Brazil, cooperatives were responsible for 37.2 per cent of agricultural GDP and 5.4 per cent of overall GDP in 2009, and earned about US$ 3.6 billion from exports. In Mauritius, cooperatives account for more than 60 per cent of national production in the food crop sector and in Kenya the savings and credit cooperatives have assets worth US$ 2.7 billion, which account for 31 per cent of gross national savings.

Cooperatives are always meant for the sustainable development of the people in the world through polices approved by the members. The movement was begun in India in the beginning of the 19th century and has been functioning continuously with the existence of more than hundred years. From its inception, the movement have strongly been protecting the people especially its members by providing socio-economic status through income generation activities for their livelihood.

Intact, the role of cooperatives in food security, poverty alleviation, and employment generation is well established in India especially in the southern and western parts of the country. According to an estimate, there are more than 500,000 cooperative societies working to bring about a change in the country. The cooperative societies set up shops to sell low priced goods to poor people. In Delhi, Mother Dairy is making strides in provision of milk and vegetables to the consumers at controlled rate decided by Government. Amul is another success story of cooperatives in milk and milk products from Gujarat. It has brought about the White Revolution in the country. These are a few examples of many more cooperatives running in different parts of the country ensuring food security of different sections of society.

Eventually, the cooperative movement in India has a strong platform towards Second Green Revolution – Food Self-sufficiency in our country through its strong rural networks. Therefore, it is assumed that cooperatives are, in one and other way, helping to access by all people at all times to enough food for an active and healthy life (definition on Food Security made by World Bank) through either supply of credit and fertilizer to produce agricultural commodities and/or production of fruits and vegetables, milk and milk products, etc.

This chapter is presented in the following aspects. First, it tries to map out the current status of agricultural cooperatives in India, second, it elaborates the role of agricultural cooperatives in food security and management, thirdly, it focuses on priority issues faced by agricultural cooperatives and finally, it looks at some of the challenging experiences of agricultural cooperatives and lessons learned.

Status of Agricultural Cooperatives in India

About 52 per cent of the total workforce is still employed by the farm sector which makes more than half of the Indian population dependent on agriculture for sustenance. Agriculture continues to be an extremely important sector of India's economy and the cooperative movement has a crucial role to play in bringing about its transformation. Agriculture, including farming, forestry, fisheries and livestock, is the main source of employment and income in rural areas, where the majority of the food producers are the resource – poor farmers. Agriculture contributes to poverty alleviation by reducing food prices, creating employment, improving farm income and increasing wages. Agricultural growth has a strong and positive impact on poverty, often significantly greater than that of other economic sectors. Ameliorating with this context, agricultural cooperatives take part an important role in supporting men and women small agricultural producers and marginalized groups by creating sustainable rural employment and provides the best avenue for mobilizing their resources for enhanced agricultural production.

In this context, agricultural cooperatives in India are very actively and intimately involved in several agriculture related activities. The most important activities are the disbursement of production credit and distribution of fertilizers and other inputs namely seeds, pesticides and agricultural implements, etc. Apart, these cooperatives are also involved in procurement of farm produce, processing and marketing of oilseeds, cotton, sugar, milk and milk products, distribution of essential commodities, clothes, kerosene oil and merchandise, etc.

Apart, these agricultural cooperatives can capture the benefits of value added, because of bulking and take advantages of introducing grades and standards allowing agro processing value addition for the members. In addition, agricultural cooperatives are responsible for stimulating poor farmers to make entry into markets, enhancing demand for standards and grades for perishable commodities (Ortman *et al.*, 2006), such as bananas, onions and tomatoes.

Cooperative movement in India started way back in 1904 through enactment of Cooperative Credit Societies Act which gave path to start Primary Agriculture Cooperative Societies (PACS). Till 1939, these cooperatives were distributing only the credit to the farmers. Its activities got diversified to consumer articles and also some agricultural inputs in the rural areas over a period of time. Subsequently, based on the suggestions made by different committees and commissions, the cooperatives were given a significant role in distribution of fertilizers. Toto, these cooperatives are playing a significant role both in providing credit and fertilizers for production purposes. In this paper, the role of agricultural cooperatives in food security and management is here taken care on the lines of consideration of credit disbursement as well as fertilizer distribution to the farmers of rural India.

Agricultural Cooperatives and Credit Disbursement

In terms of a physical network, India has one of the most pervasive financial sectors in the world including 14,000 cooperative bank branches, 93,413 Primary Agricultural Credit Societies (PACS) and over 32,000 rural branches of commercial banks and RRBs, approximately 1,000 microfinance institutions (MFIs), a large post office network with 154,000 only focused on deposit mobilization and 2.9 million Self-help Groups (SHGs).

The PACS, which are about 93,413 in number, are the major players at the grassroots level and their main functions largely remain confined to the distribution of credit, fertilizers and procurement of farm products for national food stocks. It is to mention that credit is a very powerful instrument for the empowerment of the resource-poor people. It can generate 'accelerated economic growth', when loans are easily available, properly utilised and repaid in time. Usually, cooperatives are disbursing agricultural credit to large farmers of rural areas. The credit needed by the farmers for purchase of fertilizers and other inputs is called 'short-term' credit or 'production credit'. Besides, 'medium-term' and 'long-term' credit is also needed by the farmers' for purchasing agricultural equipments namely tractors, installation of tube wells and land development works etc.

In India, 78 per cent of the farmers belong to the category of small and marginal farmers. They depend heavily on credit for their agricultural operations. These farmers will not be able to adopt the modern agricultural practices unless they are supported by a system which ensures adequate and timely availability of credit on reasonable terms and conditions.

Credit in India is made available to the farmers through a multi-agency network consisting of cooperatives, commercial banks and Regional Rural Banks (RRBs). However, cooperatives accounts for a large proportion of the agricultural credit made available to the farmers. (See Table 18.1)

Credit to buy modern inputs for farming operations is a facilitator in this change. While the overall credit to agriculture has been growing phenomenally during the last five years or so, and the interest rates for farmers have also been reduced to 7 per cent (4 per cent after taking into account the 3 per cent subvention in interest for timely repayment of crop loans), yet the biggest challenge remains in terms of increasing access to credit, particularly for the bottom 40 per cent.

Agricultural Cooperatives and Fertilizer Distribution

Fertilizer use was started in the country with the initiation of the planning process in the early fifties. However, only small quantities were consumed during the initial years. This changed during the green revolution era when the high yielding variety of seeds, irrigation, fertilizer and credit brought about increased food production. Consumption of nitrogenous (N), phosphatic (P) and potassic (K) fertilizers has increased from 1.1 million tonnes in 1966-67, the year preceding the green revolution to 28.2 million tonnes in 2010-11, while the food grain production increased from 74 million tonnes in 1966-67 to 241.56 million tonnes in 2010-11.

Self-sufficiency in food grains has been the basic objective of India's policy on agriculture. The present population of the country is about 1125 million. To feed this level of population, India has to produce 260 million tonnes of food grains from the present level of 241.56 million tonnes. The vital role of fertilizers in increasing agricultural production is well recognized. Since, the land man ratio is declining due to increasing population, the additional food grain production has to come by increasing the productivity of land under cultivation. Adoption of modern agricultural practices is the only way for increasing agricultural productivity. This calls for application of inputs like chemical fertilizers, high yielding

Table 18.1: Share of Cooperative Credit to Agriculture

(Rs. crore)

Year	Cooperative Credit to Agriculture	% Share	Total	% Increase
1985-86	3,87	55	7,005	–
1986-87	44,207	52	8,016	14
1987-88	4420	52	8,429	5
1988-89	4851	53	9,084	8
1989-90	5082	52	9,801	8
1990-91	3408	39	8,846	–10
1991-92	5800	52	11,202	27
1992-93	9378	62	15,169	35
1993-94	10117	61	16,494	9
1994-95	9406	50	18,744	14
1995-96	10479	48	22,032	18
1996-97	11944	45	26,411	20
1997-98	14085	44	31,956	21
1998-99	15916	43	36,897	15
1999-00	18363	40	46,268	25
2000-01	20801	39	52,827	14
2001-02	23604	38	62,045	17
2002-03	23716	34	69,560	12
2003-04	26959	31	86,981	25
2004-05	31424	25	1,25,309	44
2005-06	39404	22	1,80,486	44
2006-07	42480	18	2,29,400	27
2007-08	48258	19	2,54,658	11
2008-09	46192	15	3,01,908	19
2009-10	63497	17	3,84,514	27
2010-11	70105	19	4,46,779	16
2011-12*	53187	20	2,62,129	–

* : up to 30th October 2011.

Source: Economic Survey and NABARD various issues.

seeds and pesticides besides use of mechanical equipments like seed-cum-fertilizer drills, sprayers, pump sets etc. Chemical fertilizers are very costly, particularly the phosphatic and potassic ones which have been decontrolled w.e.f. 25th August, 1992. Urea, of course, is relatively low priced due to grant of subsidy by GoI. However, unless balanced nutrients are applied, the productivity cannot be sustained.

Agricultural cooperatives create the ability for the supply of required agricultural inputs so that production of commodities is done timely to enhance productivity. They also provide an assured market for commodities produced by isolated small farmers in the rural areas. The PACS which are involved in disbursement of agro-inputs also extend production credit to the member farmers for purchasing these inputs. Moreover, in many States a part of the credit is disbursed in the kind form; mainly in the form of fertilizers and also other agro-inputs. The greatest advantage of this arrangement is that farmers are saved from the hassles of getting different inputs from different places. Moreover, these cooperatives are the main agency which alone account for nearly 30 per cent of the total fertilizer business. The total number of fertilizer sale-points in the country is 262,000; out of which about 71,000 (27%) are cooperatives sale-points.

Issues faced by the Agricultural Cooperatives

Some of the problems faced by agricultural cooperatives have been, among others, poor management, lack of capital resources, inadequate training, extension and education programmes, lack of communication and participation among members, feudalistic characteristics of society, unclear and inadequate government policies on the development of agricultural cooperatives, high fragmentation of land holdings, and weak linkages among the activities of the cooperatives *e.g.*, production, credit, marketing etc. To overcome such problems, some of the measures taken by the governments and movements have been: re-assessment and improvement of farm policies, human resource development through formal and informal training of members, development of marketing and agro-processing, implementation of self-reliance projects, diversification of agricultural products including the development of export-oriented crops through contract farming, promotion of universal membership, and strengthening of legal framework of cooperatives.

Challenging Experiences of Agricultural Cooperatives

The former President of India, A.P. J. Abdul Kalam is in the midst of the pioneers in the cooperative sector, he shared few thoughts on the topic 'Cooperatives for Inclusive Growth' on the occasion of the Inauguration of the International Year of the Cooperatives 2012 organized by the National Cooperatives Development Corporation in Partnership with Ministry of Agriculture, on May 15, 2012 are as follows. During the worst of times and best of times, our farmers have produced maximum food-grains and agricultural produce to meet the requirements of the nation. The farming community consists of three types of people namely:

1. Large land holders.
2. Medium and small land holders.
3. Land-less farmers.

We have to ask ourselves a question, what we are doing to reinforce their way of life and agricultural practices from soil testing, seed selection, plantation, provision of fertilizers and pesticides, un-interrupted provision of water and electricity, harvesting and preventing damage due to unseasonal rains, value addition, storage, distribution and marketing systems.

Can the Cooperative Farming Provide a Solution?

In India the advent of planned economic development ushered in a new era for the cooperatives commencing from 1947. Today India is the largest incubator of over 6 lakh cooperative societies with 250 million members. It covers over 97 per cent villages and 71 per cent rural household. The agricultural credit advanced through cooperatives is over rupees 70 thousand crores and it is around 19 per cent of the institutional agricultural credit in the country. The share of the cooperatives in fertilizer distribution is 35 per cent and sugar production nearly 46 per cent. Dairy cooperatives through white revolution have enabled the country to achieve self-sufficiency in milk and dairy products. Housing cooperatives are contributing to the construction of housing units for the economically weaker sections of the society. Moreover, more than rupees three thousand five hundred billion deposits are made in cooperative financial institutions. Thus, we can see that cooperatives are playing an important role in national development and empowering the community.

But much needs to be done to enhance the vibrancy of cooperatives in the country. I would like to discuss some of the possible cooperative structures in the rural sector which can enhance the production of food grains, pulses, vegetables, fruits and floriculture products and enable the farmer to enhance his earning capacity.

Cooperative Structure for Agri-Production-Processing-Marketing

Let us first discuss the challenges of the agricultural sector. India's agricultural sector employs about 50 of the workforce, yet accounts for about 17 per cent of total GDP. Last year, the agricultural sector grew at a rate of 2.7, per cent relative to 11 per cent growth in both the service and industry sector. The country has seen certain successes in Agricultural growth and productivity increase in many parts of the nation. Best insurance to the farmers and to increase their earning capacity is possible only by adopting the techniques such as: multi-cropping with regulated drip-irrigation scientific farming, creation of reliable agro and food processing infrastructure, increased availability of ground water and 24×7 power availability. Such a situation is only possible through creation of responsible agricultural cooperatives which provide the collective wisdom as a business house for planning, managing and marketing the agricultural and agro processed produce for higher levels income to the farmer with assured round the year occupation.

The essential features of such a cooperative would be:

- Create a cooperative in major agricultural centres involving Government, NGOs, Consultancy Services, R & D Organizations and people as partners.
- Farmers will be partners in profit by providing farming inputs to cooperative society.
- R & D Organizations and agricultural universities will provide knowledge inputs for quality agricultural products and technology transfer including training.
- The cooperative will provide finance, critical inputs provision in-time (such as quality seeds, quality fertilizer, and quality pesticides), critical infrastructure, crop insurance and technical guidance such as arrival of monsoon, combating drought etc. to the farmers.
- The cooperative will be responsible for preservation, processing, diversification, quality assurance, transportation, marketing and profitable operation of the overall business.
- The Government will provide policy framework for the smooth transparent operation of the cooperative on the lines of the Amul model, Warna model for safeguarding the interest of the farmers and all other stakeholders. Simultaneously, it will be prudent to create a cooperative for promoting micro enterprises in non-farm sector for creating profitable non-agricultural business in the rural sector.

He also suggested facilitating creation of PURA model (Provide Urban Amenities Rural Areas) in the rural areas in their region as a sustainable development system based on Warana cooperative experience to evolve "Cooperative Based PURA".

Warana PURA: Farmer Cooperative in Action

The Warana PURA mission began as a sugar cooperative movement, as a vision of a great social leader called Sahkaar-shri Tatyasaheb Kore in 1950s to transform the Warana region which was a backward area infested with unlawful activities. The Warana PURA has since then evolved on a cooperative framework and implemented sustainable models based on the core competencies of the rural areas covering 69 villages and about 4 lakh people. This PURA model, which has more than 60,000 farmers, women entrepreneurs and villagers as their members, has been giving consistent dividend of over 25 per cent per annum to all the cooperative society members. The Warana PURA programme has succeeded in creating income generation through value addition to sugar and dairy products, innovative agricultural practices and entrepreneurship, striving towards literacy and healthcare for all. The Warana cooperative sugar factory with about 20,000 farmers as its members has also taken area development as one of its missions and has helped construction of schools, medi-care institutions and libraries. There has been significant effort to upgrade technology and practices, which has reflected in the consistently high sugar recovery rate of more than 12 per cent which is almost 20 per cent higher than the national average. As a result of this, the sugarcane farmers in and around 60 villages near the factory are receiving significantly higher revenues.

For the welfare of landless villagers, Tatyasaheb Kore envisioned and pioneered the creation of the Warana Poultry and Warana Dairy. Warana Cooperative Dairy with more than 16000 milk producers spread over 60 villages, collects and processes more than 500,000 liters of milk every day from it 1753 collection centres. With advanced technologies for value addition and maintaining highest quality standards, the Warana Dairy manufactures and exports many value added products of milk to Middle East. Enhanced income led to better living standards to the rural people of the Warana region the Warana PURA complex evolved innovative models in the service and retail sector in the form of Warana Bazar with its 58 stores. Warana cooperative has provided to its youth a wide spectrum of education to empower themselves and take the vision of the Warana development further. Similarly, the health for the citizen's is supported by initiatives such as the Mahatma Gandhi Hospital and the Dental College.

To inculcate a spirit of saving the Warana PURA complex also started the Warana Cooperative Bank in 1966, which has now more than 18,000 cooperative members and has 24 branches across the Warana valley. The Warana Sugar Parliament, which is a mark of the empowerment in a democratic framework which the Warana PURA complex has provided to the farmers which closely resembled the Indian Parliament, echoing the message of Shri Tatyasaheb Kore which reverberates the faith in democratic, economic, social and educational empowerment of the grass-root level rural population.

Today, Warana is remarkable region which, by following a socio-economic objective in mind has transformed into a rural region with almost none living below poverty line. Now Warana area is thinking in terms of becoming a Carbon neutral PURA by the year 2015. The Warana PURA complex has a message that innovative missions, with focus on better technology and sound management, can fulfill the socio-economic objectives of creating a prosperous and happy society emanating from the bottom of the pyramid. The cooperative model, product diversification, process innovation and market understanding have all been the hallmark of creativity of Warana citizens.

He visualizes the country wide spreading of an integrated and cooperative model for the development of rural India. It should aim at creating a society based on economic competence, pride in Indian culture, and modern education in a variety of streams, empowerment of the women folk and health for all. Such a developed India will mean not only economic development but also integrated development in culture, humanism, education and citizen empowerment.

Conclusion

It is often assumed that world food shortage can be eliminated by increasing food and agricultural production through the application of modern technology. It is also argued that supplying modern inputs such as large-scale irrigation, chemical fertilizers, farm machinery and pesticides can improve the productive capacity of the land. New agricultural technology supported by other factors like, finance resources, creditworthiness, government policies, and political influence makes a lot of difference. In this process of change, the role of agricultural cooperatives have facilitated a lot in agriculture and accelerated the pace of distribution of key inputs of farm production like credit, fertilizers, seeds and equipment, thus contributing to the ushering in of the revolution in agricultural production and productivity in India.

REFERENCES

Abdul Kalam, A.P.J, Cooperatives for Inclusive Growth Synergy and Harmony through Cooperative Movement, *National Cooperative Development Corporation Newsletter,* Vol. XLVI (2), May-June. 2012.

Agricultural Cooperatives in the 21st Century, Cooperative Information Report 60, Rural Business-Cooperative Service, November. 2002.

Bhatt, D.K, IFFCO in the Service of Farmers, *Indian Journal of Fertilizers,* Vol. 2 (1), April. 2006, pp. 11-20.

Dubey, A.K., *et.al.*, Cooperative Societies for Sustaining Rural Livelihood :A Case Study, *Indian Research Journal of Extension Education*, Vol. 9 (1), January. 2009.

Financial Intermediation and Markets, http://indiabudget.nic.in

Government of India, *Annual Report 2010-2011,* New Delhi: Department of Agriculture and Cooperation, March. 2011.

Government of India, *Indian Fertilizer Scenario 2010,* New Delhi: Department of Fertilizers, 2010.

Golait, Ramesh Current Issues in Agriculture Credit in India: An Assessment, *Reserve Bank of India Occasional Papers,* Vol. 28 (1), Summer. 2007.

Mohan, Rakesh Agricultural Credit in India: Status, Issues and Future Agenda, *Reserve Bank of India Bulletin,* November. 2004.

NABARD, Annual Report 2001-02, Mumbai: NABARD, 2002.

Performance of Primary Agricultural Credit Societies in India - 2010-11, Mumbai: National Federation of State Cooperative Banks Ltd., June. 2012.

Reserve Bank of India: *Report on Trend and Progress of Banking in India 2010-11,* Mumbai: RBI, 2011.

Sen, Prabal K. Governance of Cooperatives as Micro Finance Institutions: An Overview in the Indian Perspective, Vilakshan, *XIMB Journal of Management,* 2005.

State of Indian Agriculture Report – 2012, http://agricoop.nic.in/

19

Changing Food Habits
A Case Study

S. Mahima
M. Nandhakumar

INTRODUCTION

The word food refers to the chemical substances taken into the body in order to keep the body in a healthy and active condition. The body requires food for the growth, repair and replacement of its worn out tissues. Hence, food has to provide the required raw-material, energy and other regulating substances like vitamins and minerals for the smooth functioning of the body besides meeting the calorific requirements like carbohydrates, proteins, fats etc. It can be derived from plants, animals or other categories such as fungus or fermented products like alcohol. Although many human cultures sought food items through hunting and gathering, today most cultures use farming, ranching, and fishing, with hunting, foraging and other methods of local nature included but playing a minor role.

Studies on cultures reveals the dietary habits with a view to analyze the change in consumption pattern. While humans are omnivores, religion and social constructs such as morality often affects which foods they will consume. Food safety is also a concern with food borne illness claiming many lives each year. Many plants or plant parts are eaten as food. There are around 2,000 plant species which are cultivated for food, and many have several distinct cultivars. Plant-based foods can be classified as with the nutrients necessary for the plant's initial growth. Because of this, seeds are often packed with energy, and are good sources of food for animals, including humans. In fact, the majority of all foods consumed by human beings are seeds. These include cereals (such as maize, wheat, and rice), legumes (such as beans, peas, and lentils), and nuts. Oilseeds are often pressed to produce rich oils, including sunflower, rape, canola oil, and sesame. One of the earliest food recipes made from ground chickpeas is called hummus, which can be traced back to the Ancient Egypt times.

Pattern of Food Consumption in India

In India, majority of food consumption is still at home. Nevertheless, out-of-home food consumption is increasing due to increase in urbanization, breaking up of the traditional joint family system, desire for quality food, lack of time which translates into an increased need for convenience. Increasing number of working women, rise in per capita income, changing lifestyles and increasing level of affluence in the middle income group have also brought about changes in food habits. In the last two decades, the share of urban population has increased from 23.3 per cent in 1981 to 27.8 per cent in 2001. During the same period the female work participation rate has increased from 19.7 per cent to 25.7 per cent. The per capita income has increased from Rs. 7,328 in 1980 to 10,306 in 2000-01. Indian women of present day have started acquiring education and working at par with their counterparts due to the impact of modernization and scientific advancements. Since they get absorbed into dual role, that is, a housewife and a career woman, they need to make use of some strategies particularly at home by which they are able to provide maximum satisfaction to their each and every family members. Rapid urbanization and sociological changes like the desire on the part of the housewives to spend less time in kitchen, the increased value for leisure, weakening of family ties, increased impact of television and its advertisement as well as changing life styles of the families, have brought about the changes in food consumption pattern. In view of this, the present study made an attempt to find out a case study of Palakkad district in Kerala, with a help of primary data.

Objectives of the Study

1. To analyze the changing food habits among males and females.
2. To examine varies reasons for choosing fast food.
3. To study the level of awareness regarding the problems related to the fast foods.

Data Base and Methodology

The Chapter is based on primary survey data of 100 sample respondents in Palakkad district, Kerala. The questionnaire method was used the collection of data. Simple form of table with the percentages calculated and same have been explained through descriptive analysis and narrative procedure.

Results and Discussion

The respondents attitude towards the choose of the food (Table 19.1) reveals that majority of the respondents opted fast food (64% of males and 74% of females) and only 36 per cent of males and 26 per cent of females think that traditional food is best and it will reduce the health problems.

Table 19.1: Choice of Food by the Respondents

Choice	Males	Females
Fast food	32(64)	37(74)
Traditional food	18(36)	13(26)
Total	**50(100)**	**50(100)**

Source: Primary Data Computed
Note: Figures in the parenthes is percentage

The classification of the males and females on the basis of food habits shows (Table 19.2) that 82 per cent of males were non-vegetarians and 18 per cent of them were vegetarians. However, in the case of females 76 per cent of them were non-vegetarians. On an average majority of the respondents were non-vegetarians.

The respondents schedule for eating fast food (Table 19.3) reveals that 48 per cent of respondents were using fast food

Table 19.2: Classification of Respondents by Food Habits

Choice	Males	Females
Vegetarian	9(18)	12(24)
Non-vegetarian	41(82)	38(76)
Total	**50(100)**	**50(100)**

Source: Primary Data Computed
Note: Figures in the parenthes is percentage

once in a week (22% of males and 26% of females) and 38 per cent of respondents using two or three times in a week. 12 per cent of respondents were using some times in a week and only 2 per cent of respondents were using daily.

Table 19.3: Schedule of Eating Fast Food

Schedule	Males	Females
Daily	2(4)	–
Two or three times in a week	20(40)	18(36)
Once in a week	22(44)	26(52)
Sometimes	6(12)	6(12)
Total	**50(100)**	**50(100)**

Source: Primary Data Computed
Note: Figures in the parenthes is percentage

It is observed that lack of time is the major reasons for choosing fast food (50%) and 20 per cent of respondents opted fast food because it is easily available. 17 per cent of respondents revels some other reasons for opting fast food and only 13 per cent says that fast food is more attractive than traditional food. (Table 19.4) (*See table on next page*)

The level of awareness regarding the various health effects due to fast food and modern food items (Table 19.5) reveals that 63 per cent of respondents were aware about that health problems like cancer and others diseases but the 37 per cent of respondents were not aware about the health problems due to changing food habits. (*See table on next page*)

Table 19.4: Reasons for Choosing Fast Food

Reasons	Males	Females
Easily available	12(24)	8(16)
Lack of time	20(40)	30(60)
More attractive	8(16)	5(10)
Other reasons	10(20)	7(14)
Total	**50**(100)	**50**(100)

Source: Primary Data Computed
Note: Figures in the parenthes is percentage

Table 19.5: Level of Awareness of Respondents about Changing Food Habits

Level of Awareness	Males	Females
Aware	37(74)	26(52)
Not aware	13(26)	24(48)
Total	**50**(100)	**50**(100)

Source: Primary Data Computed
Note: Figures in the parenthes is percentage

Conclusion

On the basis of above analysis, the study concluded that the respondents were having both traditional and new food habits. Majority of the respondents are ignoring their own traditional food trends, but some respondents were still respecting their culture and traditional food items. Effects of other cultures and education were the main reasons of changing food habits. Majority respondents were non vegetarians and opted fast-food culture because of changing life style and lack of time.

REFERENCES

Agrahar, M.D. and Pal, P.P., (2005) "Food Consumption Pattern of the Tribals of Meghalaya and Its Relation With Socio-economic Factors", *Indian Journal of Nutrition and Diet*, Vol. 42(2) pp. 71-80.

Bakshhoodeh, M. and Farajzadeh, Z (2004) "A Study of Households Behaviour in Urban Iron: With Emphasis on Consumption Pattern", *Agricultural Science*. Tech. Vol. 18(2): pp. 39-50.

Chandha, G.K., (2007) "Changing Structure of Demand For Agricultural Commodities: Preparing For The Future", *Indian Journal of Agriculture Marketing*, Vol. 21(1): pp. 18-24.

Datta, T.N. and Ganguly, B.K., (2002) "An Analysis of Consumer Expenditure Pattern in Indian States With Special Reference to Milk and Milk Products", *Indian Dairyman*, Vol. 54(9): pp. 47-56.

Dhuna, M., (1984) "An Analysis of Consumer Behaviour", *Indian Journel of Marketing* ,Vol. 14(7): pp. 26-28.

20

Food Management and Food Insecurity in Star Hotels

G. Mallika
Dr. A. Joseph Xavier
P. Srinivasan

INTRODUCTION

Food Security: The World Food Summit of 1996 defined food security as "All people at all times have access to sufficient, safe, nutritious food to maintain a healthy and active life". Commonly, the concept of food security is defined as including both physical and economic access to food that meets people's dietary needs as well as their food preferences. In many countries, health problems related to dietary excess are an ever increasing threat, In fact, malnutrition and food borne diarrhea are becoming double burden.

Food security is built on three pillars:

- *Food Availability:* sufficient quantities of food available on a consistent basis.
- *Food Access:* having sufficient resources to obtain appropriate foods for a nutritious diet.
- *Food Use:* appropriate use based on knowledge of basic nutrition and care, as well as adequate water and sanitation.

Food security is a complex sustainable development issue, linked to health through malnutrition, but also to sustainable economic development, environment, and trade. There is a great deal of debate around food security with some arguing that:

- There is enough food in the world to feed everyone adequately; the problem is distribution.
- Future food needs can - or cannot - be met by current levels of production.
- National food security is paramount - or no longer necessary because of global trade.
- Globalization may - or may not - lead to the persistence of food insecurity and poverty in rural communities.

Five Key Principles

The five key principles of food hygiene, according to WHO, are:

1. Prevent contaminating food with pathogens spreading from people, pets, and pests.
2. Separate raw and cooked foods to prevent contaminating the cooked foods.
3. Cook foods for the appropriate length of time and at the appropriate temperature to kill pathogens.
4. Store food at the proper temperature.
5. Use safe water and raw materials.

Food safety is a scientific discipline describing handling, preparation, and storage of food in ways that prevent food borne illness. This includes a number of routines that should be followed to avoid potentially severe health hazards. Food can transmit disease from person to person as well as serve as a growth medium for bacteria that can cause food poisoning. Debates on genetic food safety include such issues as impact of genetically modified food on health of further generations and genetic pollution of environment, which can destroy natural biological diversity. In developed countries there are intricate standards for food preparation, whereas in lesser developed countries the main issue is simply the availability of adequate safe water, which is usually a critical item. In theory food poisoning is 100 per cent preventable.

Indian regulations lay down the conditions for food hygiene. A number of legislation governed the food sector including cereals, fruits and vegetables, marine, meat and edible oils. They laid down specifications which were mandatory to be followed and non-implementation attracted punishment and penalties. This legislation has now been replaced by Food Safety and Standards Act. Food Safety Authority has been set up. The Bureau of Indian Standards (BIS) has also laid down specifications which are voluntary. The BIS has specified limits for microbiological parameters for processed foods in respective Indian standards, has also formulated standards on test methods for detection and enumeration of pathogenic microorganisms in food. BIS has also developed code of hygienic conditions for various food industries and has adopted CODEX HACCP and Food hygiene Guidelines as Indian standards.

Regarding implementation, the food inspectors check whether industry is complying with mandatory regulations. BIS inspectors carry on checks only if someone has taken BIS certificate.

The UK Food Standards Agency publishes recommendations as part of its Hazard Analysis and Critical Control Points (HACCP) programme. The relevant guidelines state that:

"Cooking food until the CORE TEMPERATURE is 75°C or above will ensure that harmful bacteria are destroyed. However, lower cooking temperatures are acceptable provided that the CORE TEMPERATURE is maintained for a specified period of time as follows:

- 60°C for a minimum of 45 minutes
- 65°C for a minimum of 10 minutes
- 70°C for a minimum of 2 minutes"

Previous guidance from a leaflet produced by the UK Department of Health "Handling Cooked Meats Safely A Ten Point Plan" also allowed for:

- "75°C for a minimum of 30 seconds
- 80°C for a minimum of 6 seconds"

Note that recommended cooking conditions are only appropriate if initial bacterial numbers in the uncooked food are small. Cooking does not overcome poor hygiene.

Objectives

In general, the star hotels are having high class standard and so they charge more than the regular restaurants or any other outlets. But here the main objective is to find out how far the standard of the star hotels are particular in food security particularly the regulations that have to be adapted as mandatory.

Food insecurity exists when all people, at all times, do not have physical and economic access to the sufficient, safe and nutritious food to meet their dietary needs and food preferences for an active and healthy life. It is said that more than 850 million people all over the world live everyday being food insecure.

Methodology

Secondary data are the main sources for the interpretations carried out especially in the star hotels.

Major Findings of the Study

Nutritional Security

Food safety is an increasingly important public health issue. Governments all over the world are intensifying their efforts to improve food safety. These efforts are in response to an increasing number of food safety problems and rising consumer concerns.

Food and nutritional security can be improved through developments in domestic policies. Although improving and adding domestic policies into the Indian constitution will not directly give the people of India the required food, but it will provide them in the future with means necessary to help themselves and their families become nutritionally stable. The democracy of India is slowly maturing into a prosperous country. The matter of domestic policies is very critical in improving the number of Indians who are food insecure and live in poverty.

Food Insecurity in Star Hotels Problems

The star hotels generally follow the food chain handling in proper way, but still some times, the food handlers may not be aware of the procedures or lack of knowledge on Personal Hygiene or any irresponsible food handlers' mistakes or even sometimes not going for any polices of regulations based on bodies like HACCP (Hazard Analysis and Critical Control Point) will also lead to food insecurity.

Here, there are two comments imprinted in different star hotels. The law says that all food handlers have some food hygiene training relevant to their work activity.

Comment by the Staff

I'm a HR manager at a star hotel (I'd better not say which one) but we get all our staff a food hygiene certificate as part of their induction programme in their first week. They all do it online at www.food-certificate.co.uk and we get the certificates sent to the hotel so that we have got proof that we comply with the law.

Comment by the Guest

We booked and paid for this 4*+ Hotel as part of our Honeymoon package about a year ago and based on the brochure and reviews here we were expecting a 4 star + luxury Hotel where we could relax and enjoy the remaining 13 days of our honeymoon. What we got was an unclean, dangerously unhygienic, and unsafe hotel that after 4 days we said enough was enough, we were so desperate we had to leave, even if that meant returning to the UK early.

Specifically our complaint covers these six main areas:

1. Complete lack of food hygiene standards in the restaurant or any buffet outlet which is making it unsafe to eat.
2. Safety of hotel in general.
3. Lack of cleanliness in the hotel.
4. Lack of cleanliness in the room.
5. Poor standard of the staff.
6. No such good facilities available.

This sample of complaints is not an end, it continues even today in almost all the star hotels. But the real problem is the food Insecurity, with many reasons. The food chain starts from purchase, receiving, storing, during food preparation, Service and even in waste disposal.

The specific ingredients which the purchase department should be careful and that content or goods should be in proper way to receive and identify the right place to store. The storage practice is a difficult task which is in need of knowledge. There should be a more concentration on manipulating the food and the service part is to understand the guest needs and wants on food. It is not fair enough to dispose the waste just like that, since the reaction of bacteria cause the food poison during cleaning and the dish washing. Other food safety problems: some major examples like Naturally occurring toxins, Unconventional agents, Persistent Organic Pollutants (POPs), Metals, etc. Now to some extent, the awareness on organic and non-organic waste is identified and the management is insisting to provide some knowledge on to it.

Implications

Future Directions for Food Safety

In partnership with other stakeholders, WHO (World Health Organization) is developing policies that will further promote the safety of food. These policies cover the entire food chain from production to consumption and will make use of different types of expertise. The Work of the WHO Department of Food Safety and other WHO programmes and departments include strengthening food safety systems, promoting good manufacturing practices and educating retailers and consumers about appropriate food handling. Education of consumers and training of food handlers in safe food handling is one of the most critical interventions in the prevention of diseases like food borne illnesses. Food borne illnesses are defined as diseases, usually either infectious or toxic in nature, caused by agents that enter the body through the ingestion of food. Every person is at risk of food borne illness. WHO is expanding its global network of participating institutions to monitor chemical contamination of the food supply, particularly in developing countries. WHO is promoting the use of all food technologies which may contribute to public health, such as pasteurization, food irradiation and fermentation. WHO has undertaken an important new initiative to strengthen the scientific basis of food safety activities through the establishment of a WHO/ FAO (Food and Agriculture Organization of the United Nations) expert advisory body to assess microbiological risks in food.

Preventive Measures to be taken in Star Hotels

- *Good Hygienic Practices:* All practices regarding the conditions and measures necessary to ensure the safety and suitability of food at all stages of the food chain.
- *Food Safety Management System:* A holistic system of controls that manage food safety in a food business. This includes HACCP system, management policies and trace ability/recall systems.
- *Hygiene and Sanitation in Food Sector:* General principle of food Hygiene, general hygiene practices for commodities, equipment, work area and personnel, cleaning and disinfections (Methods and agents commonly used in the hospitality Industry), safety aspects of processing mater (uses and standards), waste water and water disposal.
- *Food Standards:* The need for food laws, Prevention of food adulteration act standards, fruit product order standards, Agmark standards, Indian standard institution, international – codex, Alimentations, ISO, Regulatory Agencies, WTO, Consumer protection Act.
- *Quality Assurance:* HACCP, Need, Origin, Principles, terminology, steps/stages, benefits. HACCP system which identifies, evaluates and controls hazards which are significant for food safety. A system that is consistent with the seven principles of HACCP to the layout or steps of the Guidelines will be provided. This will be solving the purpose. It should be mandatory for all the star hotels in future.

Conclusion

The food Industry is responsible for controlling the cost and other wastages to bring it out into 32 percentages as food cost, to make their business success. But however everyone should manage, their food right from the purchase to the wastages and also the attention should be taken for the Hygienic part, there starts the security or insecurity of the food which may carry out into nutritive and healthy food because no food is harm. Food is the medicine and the habit of intake stand by the cause.

REFERENCES

Bedi, (Yash Pal) (1974) "*Hand book of Hygiene and Public Health*", Anand Publication Co. Amritsar.

Chakravarty, Sujoy (2006) *Food Insecurity in India: Causes and Dimensions*. Indian Institute of Management Ahmedabad, Research and Publication Department. 22 June.

Gopalan, C. (1995) "Towards Food and Nutritional Security" *Economic and Political Weekly*, Vol. 30, No. 52, December.

Radhakrishna, R. (1991) "Food and Nutrition: Challenges for Policy" *Journal of the Indian Society of Agricultural Statistics*, Vol. 43, No. 3.

Sethi, Mohini Surjeet Malhan, (1993) *Catering Management An Integrated Approach*, New Age International Pvt. Ltd.

Radhakrishna (2001) "Agricultural Growth, Employment and Poverty: A Policy Perspective" Presidential Address, 43rd Annual Conference of Indian Society of Labour Economics, December 18-21.

21

Mushrooming Fast Food Centres
An Emerging Urban Health Problem

S. Vijayalalitha
G. Geetha

INTRODUCTION

A high concentration of people and economic activities have brought considerable changes in day to day life. Recent evidence indicates that the fastest economic growth in urban centres lead to a drastic change in the way of people lives. The emerging trends like IT culture, cultural collaboration and media play a vital role in food habits of people. The mechanized life make people go for fastest way of consumption of food. So they prefer fast food habit to satisfy their hunger. In this paper, we have discussed about the changing food habits among children and its consequences.

Objectives

1. To examine the food habits of the children.
2. To evaluate the BMI index of the children and asses their obesity level.
3. To correlate the relation between the number of fast food centres and incidence of Childhood obesity and
4. To suggest remedial measures to control obesity among children.

Websters Dictionary defines obesity as: "a condition characterized by the excessive accumulation and storage of fat in the body". The increase of childhood obesity is rapidly rising throughout the world. The obesity epidemic is especially evident not only in industrialized nations but also in developing countries where many people live sedentary lives and eat more convenience foods, which are typically high in calories and low in nutritional value. Obese children have higher risks for developing disorders like hypertension, type 2 diabetes, sleep disorders, asthma, orthopedic problems and certain concerns in adulthood or even earlier. A majority of obese children become adults and the complications of adult obesity are worse if the obesity begins in childhood. It is disheartening to note that children, who are obese, are more prone to type 2 diabetes and we come across incidents of the younger generation dying before their parents due to the overwhelming complication of the disorder. The healthcare industry estimates that 20 per cent of Indian's children are overweight or what is defined as 'obese' and many of them are falling prey to the 'Type 2' diabetes.

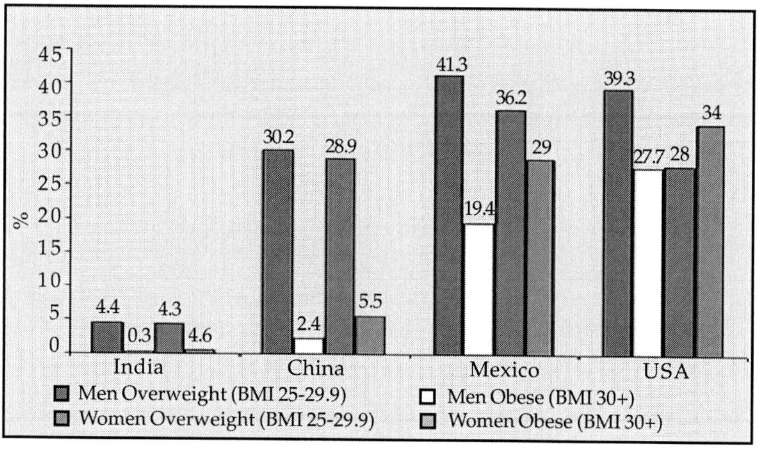

Fig. 21.1: Overweight and Obesity in Adults

Childhood Obesity

Childhood obesity is a medical condition that affects children. It is a characterized by a weight well above the mean for their height and age and a body mass index well above the normal.

Causes for Childhood Obesity

1. Obese parents most often have obese or overweight kids. It is proven that certain genetic factors are also responsible for overweight and obesity.
2. Children who lack in physical activity are prone to become obese. Recent technological advances such as the video games and Internet have an addictive effect of children who tend to spend more time indoor rather than playing outside.
3. Eating fast food, lack of exercise, soft drinks and TV advertisements are the major reasons for increase in childhood obesity. Schools are providing easy access to the high fat, high sugar and salty foods there by encouraging unhealthy diet habits. Television advertisements are playing major role in increasing junk food eating habits.
4. Certain hormonal disorders like hypothyroidism, Cushing syndrome etc., can lead to childhood obesity.

BMI or Body Mass Index is a simple and widely used method for estimating body fat. BMI is calculated by dividing the subject's weight by the square of the height, typically expressed in units.

$$\text{BMI} = \frac{\text{Weight (kg)}}{\text{Height}^2\text{ (m)}}$$

The samples of children ranging with age group of 9-12 were selected the main sample group for the study. The zones of Chennai city were classified and selected as sample areas in such way where the study would give an overview picture of the incidence and distribution of childhood obesity (Table 21.1).

Table 21.1: The Incidence and distribution of Children Obesity

Age Group	No. of Samples
10	25
11	41
12	61
8	11
9	12
Total	**150**

Increase in Fast Food Centres Indirectly Leads to Increase in the Rate of Obesity

The interpretation of these three maps infer that the prevalence of BMI of the three major age group 10 and 12 years are high in Zone V which covers the wards of Anna Nagar (West), Shenoy Nagar, Kilpauk and others. These wards are fast developing with latest fashion and technology. These areas come under the list of posh areas where there are lots of fast food centres mushrooming in a great extent Figure 21.2 indicates the location of fast food centres. The congestion of Fast-food centres is seen high in zone V. The respondents of these zones belong to the commercial and residential areas. Zone X, Zone IX and Zone IV have the second highest prevalence of BMI among the children of the age group of 10 to 12 years. These zones are seemed developing urban centres of Chennai city. The emergence of the IT corridor in the south of Chennai *i.e.* Zone X has brought a drastic development in fashion, technology and their Life style, fast food centres and restaurants. Parents who belong to the IT industry would prefer to have their food and their children's food in these fast food centres. These are the main reasons for the high prevalence of BMI among these zones. Most of the mothers of the respondents belong to the working class.

Therefore, the assumed hypothesis has proven to be true. Higher the fast food centre, higher the prevalence of obesity.

From the analysis, it has been revealed that the fast food centres in zone V, VII, VIII, and X are more in numbers and congested in industrial, educational as well as IT fields. Hence, children in these areas intake junk food from fast food centres like briyani centre, fast food centre, Tiffin centre, restaurant, hot chips, bakeries, chicken centre, café shop, pizza corner, Tiffin stalls etc. According to the BMI index the children fall under the zones V, VII, VIII and X are rich in obesity and also with its related issues. From the findings children coming under the age group 10, 11 and 12 are affected more due to the change in food habits. Also from the average BMI index 20 no. of Children out of 150 come under more affected category and 10 no. of Children come under most affected category.

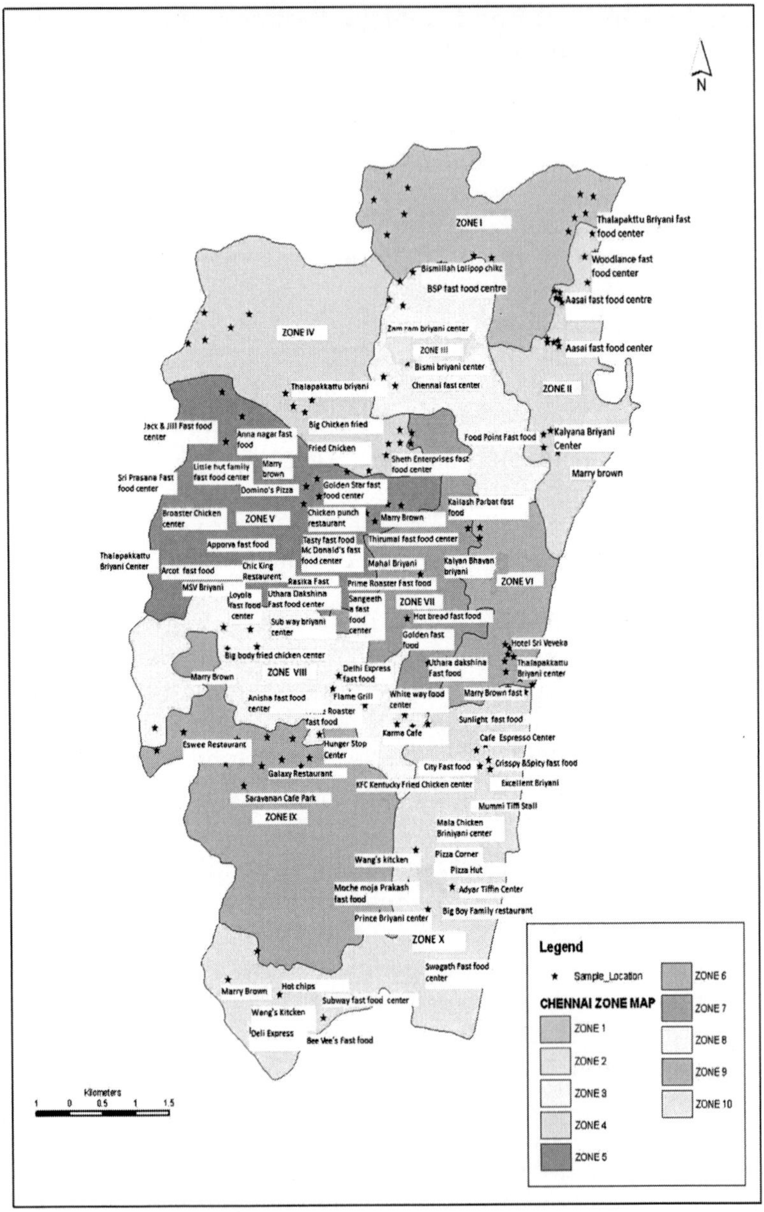

Fig. 21.2: Location of Fast Food Centres in Channai City

Causes of Obestiy

Awareness about the causes of obesity was tested with the respondents and the mothers of respondents. Table 21.2 below explains about the myths and misconception of a person becoming obese or overweight. Though there were options indicating the actual reasons for the causes for obesity, maximum number of respondents had agreed that due to that a person who eats more and constantly would become obese. Overweight in children and adolescents are generally caused by lack of physical activity and unhealthy eating patterns.

Table 21.2: Causes for the Increase in Obesity

Sl. No.	Causes for Obesity	No. of Samples
1.	By eating fast food	1
2.	By eating oily food	1
3.	Fast food	2
4.	After food-sleeping	1
5.	Over happiness	24
6.	By eating heavy food	77
7.	Too much of intake of food	16
8.	No exercise	2
9.	Over sleeping	2
10.	Unknown	22
11.	Due to water content	1
12.	Weakness	1
13.	**Total**	**150**

The respondents are also under the impression that over happiness a person would also be reason to become fat or in other words they would gain weight. Therefore, the awareness level of the respondents seems to be very poor or low. The awareness level, myths and misconceptions, all these would be a reason for the rising trend of childhood obesity. Respondents are not aware that consumptions of fast food items like pizza, burger, chips, chocolates, soft drinks could lead to obesity. Therefore the awareness level is directly related to the increase of childhood obesity.

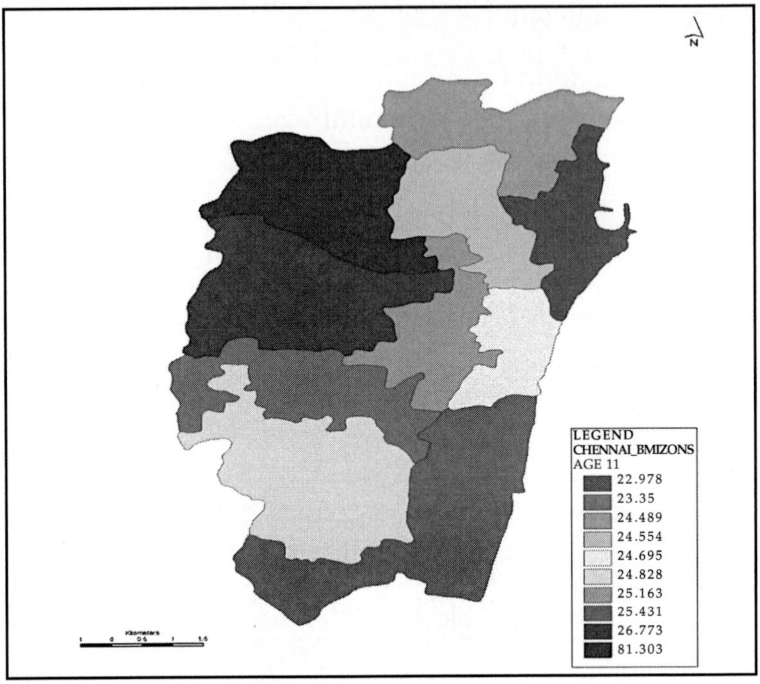

Fig. 21.3: Body Mass Index Age 11

Lower Physical Activity and Higher the Ratio of Obesity

Physical Activity

Physical activity is the best means to overcome obesity especially among the children. In schools Physical Training class are allotted for Children to exercise, but most of these class are utilised by other subject teachers. Thus, exercise for the child comes to an end and increase of weight leading them to edge of obesity. Sports club are must for the children at the age group of 10 to 15 years. Morning exercise can work wonder with children of this age group. The study has inferred that lower the physical activity can increase the rate of obesity. Using Chi-square test the data was used to find the relationship between the physical activity and the rate of increase in obesity. (Table 21.3)

Table 21.3: No. of Hours Spent for the Physical Activity

Physical Activity	No. of Samples
Playing cricket	4
Indoor games	2
Cycling and swimming	2
Cycling and walking	1
Cycling	80
Electric	1
Gymnastics	5
Running	8
Skipping	13
Swimming	23
Tennis	1
Walking and running	1
Walking	10
Total	**151**

Among the 150 samples, the respondents have expressed their different types of physical activities, which they exercise during their spare time. Using Chi-square test the relationship between physical activity and obesity was tested (Table 21.3).

Watching Television

Children spend most of their time watching television; this is the only prime activity which children prefer to do in there spare time. Apart from this, children prefer to spend their time sitting at the computer. Both these sedentary work will lead to increase in childhood obesity as there is lack of exercise. Among the respondents of the study, children belonging to the age group of 12 years spent maximum time watching TV. The second age group, which falls in this category, is 11 years. Table 21.4 represents the hours allotted by the different age for watching TV. This age group is the most delicate group wherein if this age group falls under the category of childhood obesity then they are sure to fall under the category of severe adult-hood obesity. Mothers of these respondents express that they are more comfortable to feed their children while they watch the TV. As a result, the child, from as early as eight months, gets conditioned to this visual stimulus for eating. This again is a bad practice to which the children are addicted, which in due course would lead to childhood obesity.

Table 21.4:

Sl. No.	Observed N	Expected N	(O-E)	(O-E)2	(O-E)2/E
1.	18	14.9	3.1	9.61	0.64
2.	52	14.9	37.1	1.37	0.09
3.	3	14.9	-11.9	141.6	9.5
4.	29	14.9	14.1	198.8	13.34
5.	3	14.9	-11.9	141.6	9.5
6.	12	14.9	-2.9	8.41	0.56
7.	1	14.9	-13.9	193.21	12.96
8.	1	14.9	-13.9	193.21	12.96
Total	**119**	**104.3**			**59.55**

Sl. No.	Observed N	Expected N	(O-E)	(O-E)2	(O-E)2/E
1.	11	36.3	-25.3	640	17.6
2.	72	36.3	35.7	1274.49	36.3
3.	35	36.3	-1.3	1.69	0.04
4.	27	36.3	-9.3	86.49	2.38
Total	**145**				**56.32**

Chi-Square Test

The calculated value of $\chi^2 = 59.55$ which is more than the table value 16.91; H_o per cent is rejected at 5 per cent level. The assumed hypothesis proves that there is relationship of lower between physical activities – higher the obesity level. The calculated value of $\chi^2 = 56.32$ which are more than the table value 16.91, H_o is rejected at 5 per cent level. There is relationship of higher the time spent for watching TV – higher the obesity level.

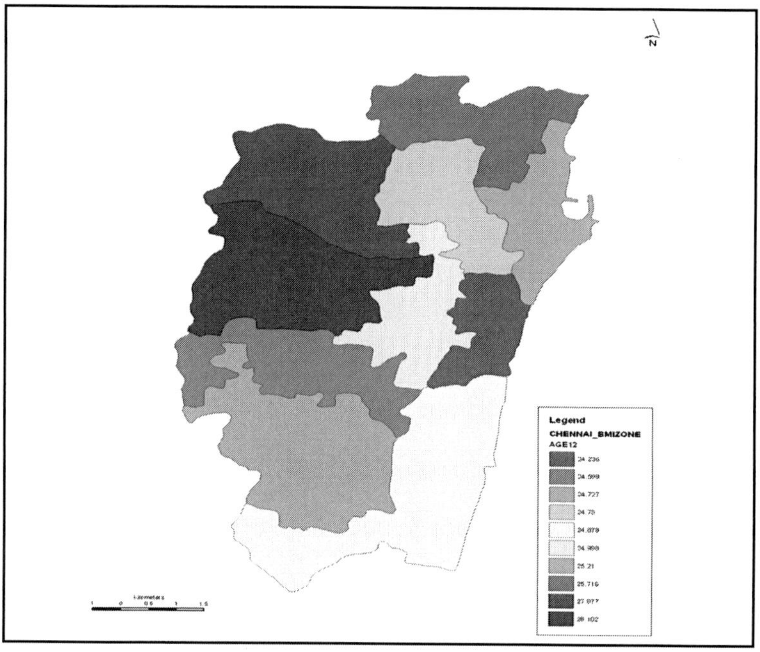

Fig. 21.4: Child's General Health Body Mass Index Map — Age 12

Policy Suggestions

- Governments should ban or limit advertisements on junk food.
- Governments, teachers and voluntary organizations should increase awareness among children on the benefits of eating fruits and vegetables.
- Parents should encourage their children to do more exercise
- Pregnant women must regulate their calorie intake and prevent obesity during pregnancy.
- The infant has to be exclusively breastfed for six months.
- Schools and parents must take initiative in convincing the children that 'junk foods' and too much of carbonated drinks are harmful to their health. Birthday parties and other celebrations in fast food joints should be discouraged or limited.

- Children should also be encouraged to play out door for at least an hour every day. School and civic authorities must take appropriate steps to provide safe playing areas.
- The media should also play a major role in restricting advertisements by the carbonated drinks and the junk food companies that are targeted towards children.
- We can defeat obesity by way of managing our children's diet, motivating them to get off the sofa and get back to riding their bicycle again. We can change our behaviour and our children's too.

Conclusion

The current study is based on relatively a small sample, and as such the results though significant, may have to be looked into with a little bit of caution as the sample study as revealed that Chennai with is its mushrooming of Fast food centres and the copy of western culture is not progressing on a healthy trend, but on a contrary the future adults are all on the verge of the major health problem- Obesity. Among the Chennai city, the income level and the economic power has increased to a great level; this could also be a only reason for the change in life style of the people and children.

REFERENCES

Ammon, Leavy (2002) "Rational Eating, can it Lead to Over Weightness or under Weightness", *Journal of Health Economics,* Vol. 21 No. 5, pp. 887-99.

Anita, F.P, (2002) *Clinical Dietetics and Nutrition*, Oxford University Press, Bombay.

Anderson, P.M, Butcher KF and Levine PB (2003), *Economic Perspective on Childhood Obesity*.

Alanlyles and Zoltan J. Acs (2007), *Obesity Business and Public Policy.*

Brand, Miller Janette C. *et.al.,* (2002) "Glycaemia Index and Obesity" *Am J Clinic Nutrition* Vol. 79.

Baum, Charles L and William F Ford 2004 "The Wage Effects of Obesity A Longitudinal Study", *Health Economics* Vol. 13, No. 9, pp. 885-99.

Cowley, Jehn (2006) "Markets and Childhood Obesity Policy", *The Future of Children,* Vol. 16 No. 1 pp. 69-88.

Ellen, Ben Sefer (2008) *The Childhood Obesity Pandemic: Promoting Knowledge for Undergraduate Nurshing Students*, Sydney, Australia pp. 1-2.

Garrow, J.S. *et al.*, (2000), *Human Nutrition and Dietetics*, Edinburg.

Ghai, D.P, (1993) Essential Pediatrics Institute of Medical Science, New Delhi.

Gopalan, I, Mohan Ram,M. (1981), *Nutritional Disabilities*, National Institute of Nutrition, Hyderabad.

Israel, A.S and Stolmaker L (1980) 'Behavioural Treatment of Obesity in Children and Adolescents, *In Progress in Behaviour Modification*, Vol. 10, pp. 82-106. Academic Press, London.

Kan, Kamhon and Werdertsai (2004) "Obesity and Risk Knowledge" *Journal of Health Economics 23/5)*, pp. 907-34.

Ley, P. (1980), The Psychology of Obesity in Contributions to Medical Psychology. Vol. 2 15. Mitchell E.M. (1980) *Psychological Aspects and Management of Obesity*. pp. 23.

22

Environmental Degradation and Food Security
Issues and Challenges

Dr. K. Joseph Raj

INTRODUCTION

Let us bless the source of life that brings forth bread from the Earth. Let our lives be a blessing to the Earth that sustains us and to all the creatures who like us, call this planet home – John Robbins. Bio-sphere is facilitating for bio-diversity. It covers all organism from microscopic bacteria to more complex plants and animals. The diversity is with in species, between species and among eco-system. The rich bio diversity is damaged by human interference. The human interference focuses on comfort and luxury life. All economics in the world has been exploited more and more resources in the name of development. This development process damages the environment too.

Cases of Environmental Degradation

There are difference sources caused for environmental degradation. All causes are rooter by human activities. The formation of environment took millions of years. But the human inference spoils the environment with in the short spam of time. The modern technologies are invented by human beings which used for exploit the environment and trying to dominate on it. But the environment is to beyond the control of human beings. It has the capacity to tolerate some extent. After a certain level it creates threat against human beings.

Primary Energy Consumption

The primary energy sources are coal, natural gas, oil, hydro, solar, wind geothermal, biomass and waste and nuclear. Of these emission from fossil fuel shares more than other sources. The desirable level of comfort and luxury life, people offer more amount of fossil fuels. It creates more level of air pollution.

Table 22.1 shows that low income countries supply increased to 30.46 per cent in 1990-2006, European Union supply increased to 14.16 per cent in the same period. The world level it increased to 22.19 per cent in 1990-2006.

Table 22.1: Total Primary Energy Supply

Countries	Annual Total Tonnes of Oil Equivalent		
	1990	2006	% Change
Low Income	400.2	575.5	30.46
Middle Income	3797.2	5348.7	29.01
High Income	4479.4	5659.1	20.84
European Union	1324.2	1542.8	14.16
OECD	4521.8	5537.4	18.34
Total	**14522.8**	**18663.5**	**22.19**

Source: Development and Climate Change, World Development Bank, 2010.

Carbon Dioxide Emissions

The main root cause for climate change is too much emission of carbon dioxide. The concentration of CO_2 increased from 280 ppm in 1760 to 379 ppm in 2000. If the trend continues it will increase to 580 ppm at the end of the estuary. The carbon dioxide emission is from the consumption of petroleum, natural gas and coal.

Table 21.2 depicts that, the emissions increased to 14.72 per cent during 1980-90 and declined to 9.19 per cent during 1990-2000, increased to 5.90 per cent in 2004 and it declined to 0.28 per cent in 2009. The declining trend of emissions due to Earth Summit asked the member countries to reduce the emissions. Most of European countries have voluntarily methane and Nitrous Doxide Emissions.

These green house gases are polluting air and impair the environment. Ultimately accelerate the climate change.

Table 22.2: World Carbon Dioxide Emissions (Million Metric Tonnes)

Year	Emissions	% Change
1980	18433.9	—
1990	21616.0	14.72
2000	23803.6	9.19
2001	23949.9	0.61
2002	24681.0	2.96
2003	25891.9	4.67
2004	27518.0	5.90
2005	28366.2	2.99
2006	28939.2	1.98
2007	29724.5	2.64
2008	30399.5	2.20
2009	30313.2	-0.28

Source: US Census Bureau, www.google.com 2011.

Table 22.3 indicates that low income countries emissions increased to 121.99 per cent in 1990-2005. High income and European Union emissions declined to 0.03 per cent and 18.57 per cent respectively. These countries have taken steps to about the both gases CH_4 and N_2O.

Table 22.3: Word Methane and Nitrous Oxide Emissions

Countries	Metric Tonnes of CO_2 Equivalent Million		
	1990	2005	% Change
Low Income	115.5	256.4	121.99
Middle Income	1168.3	1279.4	9.50
High Income	577.2	557.1	-0.03
European Union	142.1	115.7	-18.57
OECD	644.6	651.4	1.05
Total	**2647.7**	**2860.0**	**8.02**

Source: Development and Climate Change, World Development Bank 2010.

Emissions and its Impact on Climate

The emissions of CO_2, CH_4 and N_2O increase the temperature *i.e.* Global Warming. The global warming has been brought changes in biosphere. The biosphere is the dwelling place for all living organism. There is a threat to the universe. The following are the important effects.

Sea Level Rising

Sea level is raising due to global warming. The thermal expansion of oceans is melting the glaciers and ice caps. The average rate of global mean spectral rise is estimated to be 1.8 ± 0.5 mm/year. Each millimetre rise in sea level will retreat on an average of 1.5 metres. The Inter-governmental Panel on Climate Change assisted that the sea level could rise by one meter during 21st century. Thus one metre rise in sea level will retreat 1500 meters or nearly one kilometre.

Global Temperature

The global average surface temperature has increased and the 100 year (1906-2005) indicates an increase of temperature $0.74°C \pm 0.18°C$. If the concentration of CO_2 reaches 560 ppm, the temperature is projected to increase 1.4 to 5.8°C.

Changes in the Hydrologic Cycle

The increase in the global mean temperature result in increase in the evaporation rates resulting in an increase in humidity levels. The upper tropospheric water vapour absorbs radiation and amplifies the warming rates. These changes bring changes in the energy balance.

Heat Waves

Climate change is indicated by the heat waves. As a result of global warming, the number of days per year is increasing continuously. The recent heat waves killed about 70000 people in 2003. IPCC report indicated that Romunia will have 28.9 days in 2050. Majority of the countries will have more than 10 days of heat waves in near future. It affects human and eco-system of the world.

Environmental Degradation and Bio-diversity

Bio-sphere is the place where living organism are interacting with them. The earth supports a web of a 5 million to 10 million species of plants and animals. A few dozen species provide basic nutrition, 20 per cent of human caloric intake from rice, 20 per cent comes from wheat, a few species of cattle, poultry and pig supply 70 per cent of animal protein. Only among the 20 per cent of animal protein from fish and shell fish is a diversity of dietary species found.

Global warming has significant impact on the timing of species life cycle. In many plant species, the timing of spring growth such as budding, flowering and fruiting is a response to temperature. In animals, the timing of migration, breeding, and metapmorphasis has changed. These phonological events have been happened earlier periods. Most of the insects grow faster and have shorter generation time at higher temperature. Under warmer conditions the plants have flowed earlier, insects have emerged earlier and non migrant birds have nested earlier. There can be longer breeding periods far both plants and animals.

Environmental Degradation and Marine Eco-system

Climate change is already changing the distribution of eco-system. The increase in green house gases with in the earth's atmosphere is set to change fundamental variables associated with oceanic environments. The increase in calcium carbonate saturation state, sea level and temperature of the earth oceans bring negative impact on marine bio-diversity.

The marine eco-system provides a very huge amount of food to all sections of the people especially protein nutrient provider to the entire mass of the world. Fish and shell fish currently supply about 8 per cent to the world population. A rise in temperature 1°C could have rapid effect on the mortality of fish and geographical distribution. If the trend continues, the stock of fish will fall. There is treat to food security especially less developed countries and poor people of the countries of the world.

Environmental Degradation and Agriculture

Ever since human beings first began domesticating plants and animals some 12000 years ago, agricultural bio-diversity has played a vital role in sustaining and strengthening food, nutrition, health and livelihood security all over the world. There is a direct and indirect relationship between agriculture sector and environmental degradation. One tonne of grain production requires 1000 tonnes water. The temperature, monsoon and availability of irrigation facilities are very close to agriculture production. The global warming speed up the hydrologic cycle and increase evaporation will make draught conditions.

The changes in hydrologic cycle create stress on water. It will lead to shortage of water for all purposes. Agriculture sector consumes 70 per cent of water throughout the world. Some of the world's major rivers are being drained dry, failing to reach the sea. The Colorado (USA) Yellow river (China), Amu Darya (Central Asia) are failed to reach the sea. Climate change reduces the water availability in some rivers on the other hand there are rivers facing problem of flood. The both extreme situations affect agriculture production. The increasing trend of global temperature is resulted in dry rivers, lakes, ponds in the local areas. As a result, the expansion of arable land and desert in the world will be increased.

The modern technology is used in agriculture production throughout the world. As a result, the food production is shown increasing trend. But the availability food is not fed to all section of people in the world.

Table 22.4 indicates the all the food production is increasing trend all over the world and besides population is increasing. The growth rate of food production is not sufficient to meet the demand for all section people in the world. Food is not secured to all section of people in the world.

Table 22.4: World Food Production

Crops	1970	1980	1990	2000	2009-10
Wheat	310.7	440.2	592.3	586.5	648.2
Coarse grain	565.5	713.1	841.1	875.5	1084.6
Rice	316.4	396.9	518.2	599.0	—
Meat	100.7	136.8	180.1	235.0	573.2
Fish	65.2	71.9	97.9	131.0	142.2*
Oil crops	34.9	49.3	75.4	110.0	157.3**
Cereals	1192.5	1569.9	1951.7	2060.5	2489.3**
Vegetables	—	—	—	—	941.1**
Milk – Eggs	—	—	—	—	67.4**

Source: 1. FAO Report 2011., 2. U.S. Census Survey, *- 2008 Figure, ** - 2009 Figure

Food Production in India

Indian agriculture sector is struggling with many problems. Investment on agriculture has been declined. Many farmers were committed suicide due to financial crises. The main causes of problem in agricultural sector are: monsoon failures, unseasonal rainfall, flood, land acquisitation for special economic zones, urbanization poor pricing and soon. These problems bring negative impact on agricultural sector. As a result, people are forced in the line of lack food security.

Table 22.5 indicates that, wheat, rice, cereals and pulses are increasing trend over the period of time. The rice production increased from 22.90 million tonnes in 1952-53 to 9.32 million tonnes in 2011-11, wheat production increased from 7.50 million tonnes to 85.93 million tonnes in the same period and total production increased from 59.20 million tonnes in 1952-53 to 241.56 million tonnes in 2010-11. The per capita availability is not increased due increase population. Therefore, a section people in the country are keeping away from food security.

Table 22.5: Food Production in India

Year	Rice	Wheat	Cereals	Pulses	Total
1952-53	22.90	7.50	19.61	9.19	59.20
1970-71	42.22	23.83	30.55	11.09	105.17
1980-81	53.63	36.31	29.02	10.63	129.59
1990-91	74.29	55.14	32.70	14.26	176.39
2000-01	84.98	69.68	31.08	11.07	196.81
2010-11	95.32	85.93	42.22	18.9	241.56

Source: Ministry of Agriculture Government of India, 2011.

Environmental Degradation and Agriculture Production in 2050

In the world all nations are not getting adequate water to grow all their food crops. With 40 per cent of the world food supply is coming from irrigated land. If water is scarce it will affects food production and it creates food shortage throughout the world. Environmental degradation directly as well as indirectly affect the food production in near future.

Table 22.6 depicts that change in temperature will be realised in all countries. The heat waves will be increased all the countries if the trend continuous. The output of all countries shows negative impact due high temperature. Therefore, both developed and developing countries will face food crisis. Thus food security is the world wide problem in near future.

Table 22.6: Climate Change and Agriculture Production

Countries	Agriculture Output 2000-50	Agriculture Yield 2000-50
India	-38.1	-12.2
Bangladesh	-21.7	8.9
China	-7.2	8.4
Russian Federation	-7.7	10.0
Pakistan	-30.4	-32.9
United States	-5.9	-1.7
Australia	-26.6	-16.4

Source: Development and Climate Change World Development Bank, 2010.

World Undernourished

Food and Agriculture Organization estimated that 850 million people were undernourished in 2007. Climate change is expected in increase the number of undernourished people between 35 and 170 million people in 2080. The food security pushes additional 600 million people worldwide at risk of hunger by 2080.

Table 22.7 indicates that land locked developing countries and small island developing countries number of people undernourished are higher than developed regions. The developing regions it declined from 20 per cent in 1990-92 to 15 per cent in 2006-08. The developed regions a negative changes *i.e.* 30.8 per cent. The world it declined from 16 per cent in 1990-92 to 13 per cent in 2006-08. If environmental degradation continues, there will be a drastic change in climate and as a result shortage of water for irrigation and shrink the cropped area. It will increase the food shortage and food crisis.

Table 22.7: Number of People Undernourished (Million)

Region	Total Population	Number of People Undernourished			
		1990-92	1995-97	2000-02	2006-08
Developed Regions	1231.3	15.3	17.5	15.4	10.6
Developing Regions	542.0	833.2	774.0	820.8	839.4
Least Developed Countries	796.7	211.2	249.4	844.7	263.8
Land locked developing countries	382.8	90.2	101.6	102.5	98.3
Small Islands developing countries	52.2	9.6	10.9	9.7	10.7
World	6652.5	848.4 (16)	791.5 (14)	836.2 (14)	850.0 (13)

Source: FAO Report 2011.

The global agriculture sector faces significant challenges in the coming decades. Continued population growth will drive up food demand, while climate change and natural resource of degradation will create challenges on the supply of food articles in term of average production and in terms of production volatility. FAO estimates that global agriculture. Production will need to increase by 70 per cent between 2005-07 and 2050. Almost 100 per cent in developing countries will to feed a population of more than 9 billion people in 2050. Insufficient growth in production will lead to higher prices. It will create adverse effect on food security. FAO estimates that 1.3 billion tonnes of food are lost and wasted globally every year. The losses are carried out both developed and developing countries.

Conclusion

Food security is not less than the national security. It needs to be given top priority in the national planning all over the world. The countries should not depend on imports for maintaining food security and mitigate food inflation. The maintain the food security, all the nations should come forward to protect the environment and safeguard the agro bio-diversity. The policy decisions will induce the investment in agriculture sector. Investment is to create a more productive and efficient agriculture sector and will make food more affordable for the poor and reduce the price as well. On the whole food security could be maintained by protection of environment, mitigate green house gases and increase the investment in agriculture sector. All section of people in universe come under the term of good security and serve the planet without hunger.

REFERENCES

Climate Change, Water and Food Security, FAO, Rome, 2008.

Development and Climate Change, World Development Bank Report, 2010.

Go Lay Pamuk Mengo *et al.*, *Effects of Global Climate Changes on Agriculture and Water Resources*, Ohrid, Republic of Macedonia, May 2008.

Hugh Turral *et al.*, Climate Change Water and Food Security, FAO, Rome 2011.

Kumar, Ravi K.S. Climate Changes Studies in Indian Agriculture, *Economic and Political Weekly*, Nov. 17, 2007.

Parry, M.L, *et al.*, *Effects of Climate Change on Global Food Production Under SRES Emission and Socio-economic Scenarios*, Elsevier 14, 2004.

Rashmi R R and Satapathy, Facing the Challenge, *Yojana*, April, 2010.

Simplifying Climate Change Based on the Findings of IPCC Fourth Assessment Report, Tata Energy and Research Institute, TERI Press, New Delhi, 2009.

The State of Food Insecurity in the World. FAO, Rome 2011.

23

Environmental Degradation and its Impact on Food Security

S. Lourdu Initha

INTRODUCTION

Environmental degradation is caused by human activities in the name of development. The development process accelerated the in climate change. The main evil of development is emitting green house gases. Among the gases CO_2 plays a vital role to change the climate. The concentration of CO_2 in the atmosphere increased from 280 ppm in 1760 to 379 ppm in 2000. If the trend continues, the end of the century it will increase to 560ppm. The CH_4 and N_2O increased from 770 ppb to 1774 ppb and 270 ppb to 319 ppb respectively during the same period. The other green house gases namely methane, black carbon and nitrous oxide which currently contribute about 25 per cent of the total warming. The higher level of concentration of carbon dioxide makes the earth hotter and it is termed as global warming.

The nexus between agriculture and food security is one of the quintessential challenges of sustainable development. Rapid growth in many of the world's population and economies are increasing the demand for food, energy, fiber, water and for housing. Environmental Degradation directly affects food production by change in agro ecological condition and indirectly by affecting growth and distribution of income. These changes will bring food insecurity in near future. There are 1.2 billion people do not most basic needs for sufficient food every day. Of these the largest segment are 800 million poor women, men and children who live in rural environment (Eva Ludi 2009). The climate change decreases the availability of food grains and it leads to increase number of people without food. Consequently people face the problem of food insecurity.

Environmental Degradation and Food Grain Production

Environmental degradation induces the temperature and change the climate. There is a direct and indirect relationship between agriculture sector and climate change. The temperature, monsoon and availability of irrigation facilities are very close to agricultural production. The high level concentration of CO_2 reaches 560 ppm; the temperature is projected to increase 1.4 to 5.8 degree Celsius. As a result water cycle will be affected. While the world as a whole will get wetter as warming speeds up the hydrologic cycle, increase evaporation will make drought conditions. The following figure explains the global warming and hydrologic cycle which affect food production.

The changes in hydrologic cycle create stress on water. It will bring shortage of water for all purposes. The agricultural sector is facing threat because 70 per cent of the water consumed worldwide, including that diverted from rivers and pumped from underground is used for irrigation, while 20 per cent is used by industry and 10 per cent for residential purposes. In the increasingly intense competition for water among these sectors, the economics of water do not favour to agriculture (Lester R. Brown 2001).

The climate change reduced the water availability in some rivers on the other hand there are rivers facing problem of flood. The high level of temperature resulted in dry river, lakes and ponds in local areas. As a result, the increasing trend of arable land and expansion of desert in the world.

Table 23.1 indicates that the arable land has been increased both in developing and developed countries. As a whole the total area under arable land is increasing trend in the world. If it continues, the production and the yield will decline in near future.

Table 23.1: Irrigated Land Area and as Percentage of Arable Land

World/Region	Irrigated Land					
	(Area 1000 ha)			As% of Arable Land		
	1980	1990	2002	1980	1990	2002
Developed countries	58926	66286	68060	9.1	10.2	11.1
Developing countries	151296	178702	208659	21.9	24.1	26.3
World	210222	244988	276719	15.7	17.6	19.6

Source: FAO (2008).

Ecological Consequences of Climate Warming

The characteristics of all individual, animals and plants are determined by the interaction between their genes and environment. The physical environment experienced by each individual includes temperature, rain fall, day length and geological subtract, while the biotic environment includes the presence of food, competitors and natural enemies. Phenotype of organism may change indirectly by environmental changes. Under warmer conditions, plants have flowered earlier, insects have emerged earlier in the season, amphibians have returned to earlier, breeding earlier, migrant birds have returned earlier in spring. There can be longer breeding periods for both plants and animals. The largest phonological changes will be more at higher latitudes and altitudes because the warming of the globe is more intense in these areas. The phonological changes are caused by climate change. These changes continue in the world, the food production will be declined. As a result shortage of food grains will lead to emerging crisis for food insecurity.

World Food Production

Stability of food supplies is affected by climate change. Weather conditions are expected to become more variable that at present with increasing frequency of and severity of extreme events. Greater fluctuations in crop yields and local supplies can adversely affect the stability of food supplies and food security. Climate change fluctuations will be most pronounced in semi-arid and sub humid regions are likely to reduce crop yields and live stock numbers and productivity. Many irrigation projects and new technology in crop production have been adopted in the world wide to meet the increasing demand for agriculture products.

Table 23.2 shows that all food production are increasing trend all over the world. Per person food availability increased from 2410kg in 1969-71 to 2790 in 2000-02. The availability of food is not eventually distributed to all countries. There are countries facing shortage of food grains therefore they are forced to import food grains from other countries.

Table 23.2: World Food Production (Million Tons)

Crops	1970	1980	1990	2000	2003
Cereal	1192.5	1549.9	1951.7	2060.5	2080.0
Wheat	310.7	440.2	592.3	586.1	560.0
Paddy	316.4	396.9	518.2	599.0	583.1
Coarse grain	565.5	713.1	841.1	875.5	938.0
Meat	100.7	136.8	180.1	235.0	253.4
Oil crop	34.9	49.3	75.4	110.0	123.2
Coffee	3849.6	4836.9	6072.1	7550.0	7175.2
Fish	65.2	71.9	97.9	131.0	132.5

Source: FAO, Rome, 2005.

World Hunger

FAO estimated that 850 million people were under-nourished in 2007. Climate change is expected to increase the number of undernourished people between 35 and 170 million people in 2080. The food security pushes additional 600 million people worldwide at risk of hunger by 2080 in addition to projected revenue losses of 26 per cent by 2060 for dry land areas in sub-Sharan Africa. These figures are calculated at a threshold of 2°C (UNDP 2007-09).

Table 23.3 shows that the under nourished ranges from 4 per cent to 15 per cent both in Africa and developing world. The developed countries were 16 per cent of the population undernourished and African countries were more than developing countries.

Table 23.3: Hunger in Africa and the Developing World

Region	Total Under-nourished	Total Under-nourished as to Total Population
North Africa	61,000,000	4
West Africa	34,400,000	15
South Africa	35,700,000	39
East Africa	92,400,000	40
Central Africa	45,200,000	55
Developing World	797,900,000	16

Source: UNDP Report – 2007-09.

Climate Change and Agriculture Production in 2050

As a result of global warming the number of days per year is increasing continuously. Majority of the countries in the world will have more than 10 days of heat waves in near future. Some parts of the world will not have enough water to always grow all of their food. With 40 per cent of the world food supply coming from irrigated land, water scarcity directly affects food security.

Table 23.4 indicates that the heat waves will be increased all the countries and reduce the agriculture output and yield. The output of all countries shows negative impact due high temperature. Therefore food insecurity will be faced by both developed and developing economies of the world. (*See table on next page*)

Climate Change and Marine Food Production

At about 70 per cent of the earth's surface is covered by sea water. Climate change is already changing the distribution of eco-system. The Inter-Governmental Panel on climate change

Table 23.4: Climate Change and Agriculture Production

Countries	Change in Temperature °C 2000-50	Change in Heat Waves 2000-50	Agricultural Output 2000-50	Agl yield 2000-50
India	1.6	10.8	-38.1	-12.2
Bangladesh	1.4	8.7	-21.7	8.9
China	1.7	16.1	-7.2	8.4
Russian Federation	2.2	29.1	-7.7	11.0
Pakistan	1.8	19.8	-30.4	-32.9
United States	1.8	24.4	-5.9	-1.7
Indonesia	1.2	0.4	-17.9	-17.7
Zimbabwe	1.5	12.3	-37.9	-10.6
Morocco	2.1	21.1	-39.0	-25.2
Australia	1.5	10.9	-26.6	-16.4

Source: World Development Report, world Bank 2010.

2001 assessed that the sea level could rise by as much as one meter during 21st century when the present global warming continues. Thus one meter rise in sea level will retreat 1500 meters or nearly one mile.

The bio-diversity of coral reef is extra ordinary with an estimated million species of plants, animals. This was estimated to spread at about 400000 km. The loss of bio diversity in marine certainly will reduce the breeding fish. In the course of time the fish population will decline and it leads increase the problem of food insecurity throughout the world.

Conclusion

There is a close nexus between water and crop production and there is a relationships between climate change and food production. There are countries took steps to increase production. But at the same time, there are countries faced food crisis. These countries are forced to import grains from other countries to meet the requirement. Even though the world food production has been increased, millions of people live with hunger. If the climate change reduces the food production again, more number will fall in hunger. There is threat to the food security. The world has experienced the food insecurity. This will increase in near future. This problem could be minimized with the help of mitigation of green house gases and cope up with the existing environment.

REFERENCES

Christoph Bals *et al.*, "Climate Change and the Right to Adequate Food", W.W.W Google, 2008.

Climate Change, Water and Food Security, FAO, Rome, 2008.

Daniel Pauly, *et al.*, "Global Warming Effects on Sea and Food Security" W.W.W .Google, 2009.

Eva Ludi, Climate Change, Water and Food Security, Overseas Development Institute, 2009.

Hugh Turral *et al.*, *Climate Change, Water and Food Security*, FAO, Rome, 2011.

Mall, R.K., "Water Resources and Climate Change: An Indian Perspective", *Current Science,* 2006.

Ravi Kumar, K.S "Climate Change studies in Indian Agriculture", *Economic and Political Weekly,* November 17, 2007.

Thomas, E. Lovejoy and Lee Hannah (Edi.) *Climate Change and Bio-diversity*, TERI, 2005.

World Development Report, World Bank 2010 Food and Agriculture Organization, Rome, 2005.

24

One Rupee Rice Scheme under Public Distribution System

M. Soundarapandian
A. Saltheen

INTRODUCTION

Poverty is measured as either absolute or relative poverty. Absolute poverty refers to a set standard which is consistent over time and between countries. The World Bank defines extreme poverty as living on less than US $1.25 (PPP) per day, and moderate poverty as less than $2 a day (but note that a person or family with access to subsistence resources, *e.g.*, subsistence farmers, may have a low cash income without a correspondingly low standard of living – they are not living 'on' their cash income but using it as a top up). It estimates that "in 2001, 1.1 billion people had consumption levels below $1 a day and 2.7 billion lived on less than $2 a day."

PDS with a network of about 4.51 lakhs fair price shops (FPS) has distributed commodities to about 18 cr households. The Indian public distribution system (PDS) is designed to help both the producers and consumers of food grains by linking procurement to support price and insuring their distribution along with other essential commodities at affordable price throughout the country. PDS, therefore, continues to be a major instrument of Government's economic policy for enhancing food security for the poor. Government of Tamil Nadu has been implementing universal public distribution system in the state instead of the targeted public distribution system advocated by the Government of India. Tamil Nadu is a State where failure of monsoon and frequent droughts and cyclone affect large number of potentially vulnerable families. The universal distribution system in Tamil Nadu envisages that every family living and cooking separately is entitled to a family card and thus assures universal food security. It is left to the choice of the families themselves to by rice or other commodities according to their need.

The Government of Tamil Nadu State has implemented many measures for the eradication of rural poverty in India. Supply of essential commodities through ration shop is one of the measures for the poverty eradication. The Government of Tamil Nadu has supplied the rice at the rate of Re. 1 per kg to the poor family since 2007. The present study attempt to analyse the impact of Rs. 1.00 rice distribution in ration shop on poverty eradication in Tamil Nadu state.

On September 15, the then Tamil Nadu Chief Minister launched 'One Rupee a Kg Rice Scheme', a 'revolutionary scheme' in memory of his Mentor and Former Chief Minister C N Annadurai even as the Government of Tamil Nadu kick-started the centenary celebrations of the Dravidian Stalwart who helped party storm to power in 1967.

The Government of Tamil Nadu was already providing rice at Rs. 2 a kg at fair price shops. The further subsidized rice would benefit 1.86 cr cardholders in the State. The government was already incurring a food subsidy of more than Rs. 1,950 cr on food items supplied in fair price shops and the new scheme would entail the government an additional burden of Rs. 400 cr.

Objectives of the Study

1. To study the performance of one rupee rice scheme under PDS in Tamil Nadu.
2. To analyse the supply of essential commodities in Tamil Nadu.

Methodology

The secondary data were used for the present study. In order to analyse the functionary and impact of one rupee rice scheme under PDS in Tamil Nadu, date for 6 years from 2005-06 to 2010-11 were collected from the department of civil supplies corporation ltd. (TNCSC Ltd.) and Department of statistics in Tamil Nadu.

Results and Discussion

Table 24.1 shows the procurement of paddy in Tamil Nadu as the period of study from 2005-06 to 2010-11. The procurement of paddy had increased from 13,81,570 million tones to 18,37,540 million tonnes in the same period. The growth performance of procurement of paddy by Government of Tamil Nadu shows the positive trend during the study period.

Table 24.1: Procurement of Paddy in Tamil Nadu

(in million ones)

Year	Procurement of Paddy	Trend Value
2005-06	13,81,570	2381570
2006-07	16,07,803	2387157.53
2007-08	14,49,464	2387161.631
2008-09	16,46,819	2387165.67
2009-10	17,54,321	2387169.74
2010-11	18,37, 540	2387173.82

Source: Tamil Nadu Civil Supplies Corporation, Government of India, 2011.

Table 24.2 gives the details about the food subsidy under PDS in Tamil Nadu state. The food subsidy provided by the Government of Tamil Nadu was increased from Rs. 61559.64 cr in 2005-06 to Rs. 3078.00 crores in 2010-11. During the period of 10 years period, the food subsidy for PDS in Tamil Nadu state was increased in six times. It is inferred that the Tamil Nadu state is interested in the best performance of PDS.

Table 24.2: Food Subsidy in Tamil Nadu under PDS

(Rs. in crores)

Year	Subsidy	Trend Value
2005-06	1559.64	2715.23
2006-07	1833.02	1817.62
2007-08	1961.06	3011.74
2008-09	2988.00	3168.97
2009-10	2997.00	3882.69
2010-11	3078.00	4596.41

Source: Tamil Nadu Civil Supplies Corporation (TNCSC), 2011.

Table 24.3 shows the number of ration cards in Tamil Nadu during the period of 2005-06 to 2010-11. The number of ration cards under circulation was increased from 169.30 lakhs in 2005-06 to 170.23 lakhs in 2010-11. It is clear that there is a steady growth in the family cards under circulation for Public Distribution System in Tamil Nadu.

Table 24.3: Number of Ration Cards in Tamil Nadu

Year	No. of Cards (in lakhs)	Trend Value
2005-06	169.30	276.26
2006-07	169.34	303.04
2007-08	169.42	329.82
2008-09	169.84	356.6
2009-10	170.11	383.38
2010-11	170.23	410.16

Source: Tamil Nadu Civil Supplies Corporation, Government of India, 2011.

In Table 24.4 the number of ration shops in Tamil Nadu was 27,510 in 2005-06 and it was increased to 30019 in the year 2010-11. Of the total ration shops, 27,843 ration shops were run by the cooperative sector. It shows the major role of running the fair price shops in Tamil Nadu. But the ration shop run by the SHGs has been increased from 131 to 324 during the study period 2005-06 to 2010-11.

Table 24.4: Number of Ration Shops in Tamil Nadu

(in number)

Year	Cooperative Shops	TNCSC Shops	Other Shops	Total Shops	Trend Value
2005-06	26341	1022	131	27510	27750.00
2006-07	26556	988	107	27651	30188.97
2007-08	25486	1027	101	26614	32627.94
2008-09	26942	1150	88	28180	35066.91
2009-10	27004	1248	106	28358	37505.88
2010-11	27843	1852	324	30019	39944.85

Source: Tamil Nadu Civil Supplies Corporation, Chennai, 2011. Department of Statistical of Economics, Tamil Nadu, 2011.

Table 24.5 shows the growing trend of the rice off takes under PDS in Tamil Nadu State. The rice off-take was increased from 32,23,508 million tonnes in 2005-06 to 37,44,402 million tonnes in 2010-11. It is inferred that there is a positive growth of PDS rice off take in Tamil Nadu State due to the increase in the number of cards holders.

Table 24.5: Rice off-takes under PDS in Tamil Nadu

(in million tonnes)

Year	Rice	Trend Value
2005-06	32,23,508	3043763.88
2006-07	33,62,789	3053686.5
2007-08	33,84,251	3063609.12
2008-09	36,32,017	3073531.74
2009-10	34,79,304	3084541.36
2010-11	37,44,402	3093376.98

Source: Food, Civil Supplies and Consumer Protection Government of Tamil Nadu, 2011.

Table 24.6 analyses the wheat off-takes level in Tamil Nadu state during the period from 2005-06 to 2010-11. It shows that the wheat off take level was increased from 71,007 million tonnes in 2005-06 to 1,27,474 million tonnes in 2010-11. The two fold increase in the off take of wheat in Tamil Nadu state during the study period. It is clear that due to the awareness among the people of Tamil Nadu regarding the health status of wheat, the off take level has been achieved in a better way in the PDS of Tamil Nadu state.

Table 24.6: Wheat Off-takes under PDS in Tamil Nadu

(in million tonnes)

Year	Wheat	Trend Value
2005-06	71,007	82999.1
2006-07	75,077	95776.55
2007-08	91,167	108554
2008-09	98,874	121331.45
2009-10	1,23,305	134108.9
2010-11	1,27,474	146886.35

Source: Tamil Nadu Civil Supplies Corporation, Government of Tamil Nadu, 2011.

Table 24.7 shows that sugar off-take under PDS in Tamil Nadu state was increased from 3,30,515 million tonnes in 2005-06 to 3,88,271 million tones in 2010-11. Despite, there was gradual rise in the price of sugar in ration shops, the off take level was also increased year by year. It is inferred that the sugar off take increase is inevitable in Tamil Nadu state.

Table 24.7: Sugar Off-take under PDS in Tamil Nadu

(in million tonnes)

Year	Sugar	Trend Value
2005-06	3,30,515	302512.5
2006-07	3,53,000	306485.8
2007-08	2,90,048	310459.1
2008-09	3,48,220	314432.4
2009-10	3,71,945	318405.7
2010-11	3,88,271	322379

Source: Tamil Nadu Civil Supplies Corporation, Government of Tamil Nadu, 2011.

Table 24.8 shows that kerosene off-take under PDS in Tamil Nadu state was increased from 6,86,018 kilolitre in 2005-06 to 6,18,447 kilolitre in 2010-11. Despite, there was gradual rise in the price of kerosene in ration shops, the off take level was also increased year by year. It is inferred that the kerosene off take increase is inevitable in Tamil Nadu State.

Table 24.8: Kerosene Off-takes under PDS in Tamil Nadu

(in kilolitre)

Year	Kerosene	Trend Value
2005-06	6,86,018	670865.3
2006-07	6,58,835	781866.14
2007-08	6,62,987	892866.98
2008-09	7,21,621	1003867.82
2009-10	6,22,225	1114868.66
2010-11	6,18,447	1225869.5

Source: Government of Tamil Nadu, 2011.
Department of Food, Civil Supplies and Consumer Protection Department.

Table 24.9 reveals that the allocation of kerosene under the PDS of Tamil Nadu state has been increasing year by year and it shows the positive trend of growth during the study period. The allocation of kerosene was increased from 5,58,929 million litres in 2005-06 to 5,68,947 million litres in 2010-11. It is inferred that the allocation of kerosene under PDS encourage the sugar option to the card holders and issue of kerosene reduced from 10 litres to 5 litres per card holder.

Table 24.9: Allocation of Kerosene Oil in Tamil Nadu

(in million tonnes)

Year	Allocation	Trend Value
2005-06	5,58,929	1416582.16
2006-07	5,58,929	1628401.37
2007-08	5,58,929	1840220.59
2008-09	5,58,929	2052039.81
2009-10	5,64,841	2263859.02
2010-11	5,68,947	2475678.24

Source: Tamil Nadu Civil Supplies Corporation, Chennai, (TNCSC), 2011.

Table 24.10 reveals that distribution of PDS commodities were *Tur dhall, Urid dhall,* Fortifed *Atta, Rava, Maida.* Distribution of commodities year by year increased in PDS of Tamil Nadu. The supply of dhal has been increased from 19728 tonnes in 2005-06 to 135421 tonnes in 2010-11 tonnes. *Urid dhall* supply was also increased from 10328 tonnes in 2005-06 to 59482 tonnes in 2010-11 tonnes. The distribution of Palmolin oil was increased from 21642 kilo litres in 2005-06 to 1,24,827 kilolitres in 2010-11 tonnes litres. Similarly, the supply of Fortified *Atta* was increased from 2347 from in 2005-06 to 6749 tonnes in 2010-11. At the same period, the supply of *Maida* was increased from 5428 tonnes in 2005-06 to 23,541 tonnes in 2010-11.

Table 24.10: Distribution of PDS Commodities

(quantity tonnes)

Sl. No.	Years	Tur Dhall	Urid Dhall	Palmolin Oil (Kl)	Fortifed Atta	Rava	Maida
1.	2005-06	19728	10328	21642	7521	2347	5428
2.	2006-07	20174	11724	23462	8436	2562	5942
3.	2007-08	21912	12029	24725	534	1889	5864
4.	2008-09	76058	29630	83238	27225	2246	8597
5.	2009-10	114954	55318	118191	34348	5627	19744
6.	2010-11	135421	59482	124827	36485	6749	23541

Source: Tamil Nadu Civil Supplies Corporation (TNCSC), 2011.

Summary of Findings

- The procurement of paddy had increased from 13,81,570 million tones to 18,37,540 million tonnes in the same period in India.
- The food subsidy provided by the Government of Tamil Nadu was increased from Rs. 1559.64 crores in 2005-06 to Rs. 3078.00 crores in 2010-11.
- The number of ration cards under circulation was increased from 169.3 lakhs in 2005-06 to 170.23 lakhs in 2010-11. There is a steady growth in the family cards under circulation for Public Distribution System in Tamil Nadu.

- The number of ration shops in Tamil Nadu was 27,510 in 2005-06 and it was increased to 30019 in the year 2010-11. Of the total ration shops, 27,843 ration shops were run by the cooperative sector.
- The rice off-take was increased from 32,23,508 million tonnes in 2005-06 to 37,44,402 million tonnes in 2010-11.
- Sugar off take-under PDS in Tamil Nadu State was increased from 3,30,515 million tonnes in 2005-06 to 3,88,271 million tonnes in 2010-11.
- The wheat off-take under PDS in Tamil Nadu State was increased from 71,007 million tonnes in 2005-06 to 1,27,474 million tonnes 2010-11.
- The kerosene off-take under PDS in Tamil Nadu State was increased from 6,86,018 kilolitre in 2005-06 to 61,8,447 kilolitre 2010-11.
- The Allocation of kerosene in Tamil Nadu under PDS in Tamil Nadu State was increased from 5,58,929 million tonnes in 2005-06 to 5,68,947 million tonnes in 2010-11.
- The supply of Tur dhal has been increased from 19728 tonnes in 2005-06 to 135421 tonnes in 2010-11. *Urid dhall* supply was also increased from 10328 tonnes in 2005-06 to 59482 tonnes in 2010-11. The distribution of Palmolin oil was increased from 21642 kilolitres in 2005-06 to 124827 kilolitres in 2010-11.

Conclusion

The one rupee rice scheme of Government of Tamil Nadu has the positive impact on the eradication of poverty in the study area. While concluding, it is suggested that the Government has to take necessary step to identify the needy people of one rupee rice and proper distribution at required level of the poor people.

REFERENCES

Department of Statistics in Tamil Nadu.

www.worldbank.com

www.tncsc.com

www.facmin.com

www.tngov.com

25

Food Security
A Study

P. Matheswaran
S. Ponnarasu

INTRODUCTION

Food security refers to the availability of food and one's access to it. A household is considered food-secure when its occupants do not live in hunger or fear of starvation. According to the World Resources Institute, global per capita food production has been increasing substantially for the past several decades. In 2006, MSNBC reported that globally, the number of people who are overweight has surpassed the number who is undernourished - the world had more than one billion people who were overweight, and an estimated 800 million who were undernourished. According to a 2004 article from the BBC, China, the world's most populous country, is suffering from an obesity epidemic. In India, the second-most populous country in the world, 30 million people have been added to the ranks of the hungry since the mid-1990s and 46 per cent of children are underweight. In developing countries, often 70 per cent or more of the population lives in rural areas. In that context, agricultural development among smallholder farmers and landless people provides a livelihood for people allowing them the opportunity to stay in their communities. In many areas of the world, land ownership is not available, thus, people who want or need to farm to make a living have little incentive to improve the land. Two commonly used definitions of food security come from the UN's Food and Agriculture Organization (FAO) and the United States Department of Agriculture (USDA):

- Food security exists when all people, at all times, have physical, social and economic access to sufficient, safe and nutritious food to meet their dietary needs and food preferences for an active and healthy life.
- Food security for a household means access by all members at all times to enough food for an active, healthy life. Food security includes at a minimum:
  1. the ready availability of nutritionally adequate and safe foods; and
  2. an assured ability to acquire acceptable foods in socially acceptable ways (that is, without resorting to emergency food supplies, scavenging, stealing, or other coping strategies). (USDA)

Objectives

1. To analyze the various issues prevalent in India relating to Food Security.
2. To study the various challenges faced by during the implementation of Food Security in India.
3. To analyze the various issues relating to the Global Food Crisis.
4. To study the various Food Schemes in India.

Food Security Issues in India

Food security has been a major developmental objective in India since the beginning of planning. India achieved self-sufficiency in food grains in the 1970's and has sustained it since then. But the achievement of food grain security at the national level did not percolate down to households and the level of chronic food insecurity is still high. Over 225 million Indians remain chronically under nourished. In 2000-01, about half of the rural children below five years of age suffered from per cent malnutrition and 40 of adults suffered from chronic energy deficiency. Such a high level of wasting away of human resources should be a cause for concern.

In recent past, there has been a shift in policy focus towards household level food security and per capita food energy intake is taken as a measure of food security. The government has been implementing a wide range of nutrition intervention programmes for achieving food security at the household and individual levels. The Public Distribution System (PDS) supplies food items, such as food grains and sugar, at administered prices through fair price shops. There have been a range of food-for-work and other wage employment programmes. Another approach adopted by the government is to target women and children directly; this includes mid-day meal programme for school going children and supplementary nutrition programme for children and women.

High economic growth rates have failed to improve food security in India leaving the country facing a crisis in its rural economy, warns the latest report released by the World Food Programme and the M S Swaminathan Research Foundation (MSSRF). According to the GOI Economic Survey, foodgrain production in India has declined from 208 kg per annum per capita in 1996-97 to 186 kg only in 2009-10, a decline of 11 per cent. Despite reduced production, India has been exporting on an average 7 million tonnes of cereals per annum, causing availability to decline further by 15 per cent from 510 g per day per capita in 1991 to 436 g in 2008.

Food Security Challenges In India

The most important challenge is to increase the energy intake of the bottom 30 per cent of the population and at the same time facilitate diet diversification to meet micro-nutrient deficiency. The food gap can be met from the existing foodgrain stocks in the medium term and by increasing their purchasing power in the long run through increasing job opportunities. The micronutrient deficiency can be rectified through supplementary nutrition and supply of fortified food. There is also a need to improve the efficiency of the various food schemes initiated by the government and make it more available and free of corruption and urban bias. However for those who are around the poverty line, this has to be understood as a distress phenomenon, as with marginal increase in their incomes over time they are forced to cut down on their food consumption to meet other pressing demands of health and education that were not considered important in the past. Food is still needed, but not demanded for lack of money. Endemic hunger continues to afflict a large proportion of Indian population. Internationally, India is shown to be suffering from alarming hunger, ranking 66 out of the 88 developing countries studied by IFPRI in 2008. India as part of the world community has pledged to halve hunger by 2015, as stated in the Millennium Development Goal 1, but the present trends show that this target is unlikely to be met.

The Global Food Crisis

The global financial crisis drew international attention away from the food crisis, but this continues to fester and even grow. When the global food crisis first hit international headlines in 2008, international bureaucrats referred to the current problems in the world food situation as-a silent tsunami, but the truth is that it was not a sudden and unexpected crisis: the signs have been around for some time now and it could easily have been seen to be coming. Even so, its impact has been powerful and already quite devastating, as food shortages and high prices of food have adversely affected billions of people, especially the poor in the developing world.

It is also very much a man-made crisis, resulting not so much from ineluctable forces of global supply and demand as from the market-oriented and liberalising policies adopted by choice or compulsion in almost all countries. These policies have either neglected agriculture or allowed shifts in global prices to determine both cropping patterns and the viability of farming, and also generated greater possibilities of speculative activity in food items. Cultivators in developing countries have been ravaged by the fearsome combination of exposure to import competition from highly subsidised agriculture in developed countries, removal of domestic protection of inputs and reduced access to institutional credit - to the point that even the global increase in agricultural prices after 2002 did not compensate sufficiently to alleviate the pervasive agrarian crisis in much of the developing world.

Food Schemes in India

India has the largest food schemes in the world:

- Entitlement Feeding Programmes;
  - ICDS (All Children under six, Pregnant and lactating mother).
  - MDMS (All Primary School children).
- Food Subsidy Programmes;
  - Targeted Public Distribution System (35 kg/month of subsidised food grains.
  - Annapurna (10 kgs of free food grain for destitute poor).
  - Employment Programmes.
  - National Rural Employment Scheme (100 days of employment at minimum wages).
  - Social Safety Net Programmes.
  - National Old Age Pension Scheme (Monthly pension to BPL).
  - National Family Benefit Scheme (Compensation in case of death of bread winner to BPL families).

Policy Suggestions

- *First,* as the net sown area and crop intensity increases more opportunities for wage employment are created, which may also increase the wage rate besides the number of days of employment.
- *Second,* increased water availability and reduced soil erosion increases production on small and marginal farmers' lands. And last, the higher productivity of Common Property Resources improves access of the poor to more fodder, fuel wood, water and NTFPs. NREGA assets should be monitored for at least five years to establish their links with drought proofing and enhanced availability of water.

- *Third,* start a drive to plant fruit trees on degraded forests and homestead lands that belong to or have been allotted to the poor. This will not only make the poor people's diet more nutritious, but will also diversify their livelihoods and reduce seasonal vulnerability.
- *Fourth,* create more job opportunities by undertaking massive public works in districts with low agricultural productivity. The upper limit of work guarantee of 100 days per worker should be enhanced to 150 days through an amendment in the Rules in the poorest 200 districts.
- *Fifth,* improve the skills of the poor for market oriented jobs, so that they are absorbed in the sunrise industries such as hospitality, security, health, and construction.
- *Sixth,* launch a drive in collaboration with civil society to cover the poorest, as a large number of homeless and poor living in un-authorised colonies in urban areas have been denied ration cards, and are thus not able to avail of PDS, on the ground that they do not have an address! In Rangpur Pahadi, a slum area just two km away from Vasant Kunj (Delhi), people living since 1990 have not been given even voter ID or any ration card. Thus their very existence is denied by the Delhi Government.
- *Seventh,* give shops to Panchayats, women's self-help groups, or to those who already have a shop so that it remains open on all days. Making it obligatory for dealers to sell non-cereal items will ensure better communication between the dealer and the card holders.
- *Eighth,* prepare a comprehensive list every two years of all destitute needing free or subsidized cooked food. Open up mid-day meals kitchen to these old, destitute and hungry in the village. This is already being done in Tamil Nadu, and its replication in other states should be funded by the GoI. Establish community kitchens across cities and urban settlements to provide inexpensive, subsidised nutritious cooked meals near urban homeless and migrant labour settlements.

- *Last*, India requires a significant increase of targeted investments in nutrition programmes, clinics, disease control, irrigation, rural electrification, rural roads, and other basic investments, especially in rural India, where the current budgetary allocations are inadequate. Higher public investments in these areas need to be accompanied by systemic reforms that will overhaul the present system of service delivery, including issues of control oversight.

Conclusion

Food insecurity and hunger is caused by a large number of factors and hence solutions too have to be multi-sectoral in nature. Because of stagnating growth in agriculture after the mid-1990s there has been employment decline, income decline and hence a fall in aggregate demand by the rural poor. The most important intervention that is needed is greater investment power, and roads in the poorer regions. It is essential to realize the potential for production surpluses in India.

REFERENCES

Dev, S. Mahendra (2003) *Right to Food in India,* Working Paper No. 50, Centre for Economic and Social Studies, Hyderabad.

Dev, S. Mahendra (2008), *Inclusive Growth in India: Agriculture, Poverty and Human Development*, Oxford University Press, Delhi.

Dev, S. Mahendra, K.P. Kannan and Nira Ramachandran (2003) *Towards a Food Secure India*, Institute for Human Development and Centre for Economic and Social Studies, New Delhi.

Dyson, Tim and A. Hanchate (2000), India's Demographic and Food Prospects: State Level Analysis, *Economic and Political Weekly,* Novmber 11, Vol. 35.

GoI (2007), *Economic Survey 2006-07*, Ministry of Finance, New Delhi.

Menon, Purnima, Anil Deolalikar and Anjor Bhaskar (2008) *The India State Hunger Index: Comparisons of Hunger Across States*, IFPRI, October 14, New Delhi.

Rao, C.H.H. (2005), *Agriculture, Food Security, Poverty and Environment*, Oxford University.

Swaminathan, M.S. (2000) *Weakening Welfare: The Public Distribution of Food in India,* Left Word Books, New Delhi.

26

A Study on Malnutrition in Rural

A. Kalaiselvi
R. Kunjammal

INTRODUCTION

The role of healthcare in economic development has received increasing attention in recent years. There is a general agreement that economic growth is not merely a function of incremental capital-output ratio. Investment on education, imparting skills and health care plays a significant role in fostering economic growth. Over the years there has been an overall improvement in the state of health of the people of India. The substantial improvement is the result of many factors including improvement in public health, coupled with infectious disease prevention and control and also application of modern medical practices in diagnosis and treatment of various ailments. In spite of overall improvement in socio-economic conditions and increasing life expectancy, the prevalence of malnutrition continues to be an area of major concern in health sector. India is home to 57 million of the world's 146 million malnourished children. This menace continues to remain a silent emergency in the country, with 47 per cent of children under five either underweight, stunted, wasted or with micronutrient and malnutrition.

Malnutrition not only enhances their susceptibility to infection, but it also affects their educational achievements, health and overall productivity when they grow up.

Consequently, child malnutrition is not only responsible for 22 per cent of the country's disease burden and half of the 2.3 million child deaths annually, but it also costs India at least 10 billion per year in terms of lost productivity, illness and death. Such a colossal loss is unacceptable for a growing global power like India. The tragedy of persistent child malnutrition in the country, despite steady economic growth, reflects not only the inequitable character of this growth but also the failure of health and nutrition delivery mechanisms, to the poor. It also indicates a lack of political will to deal with the crisis on a priority basis. In fact, child malnutrition in India is among the highest in the world along with Bangladesh, Ethiopia and Nepal.

Statement of the Problem

The recent report of the National Family Health Survey reveals the status of the child malnutrition in the country. About 45.9 per cent children under underweight and, 38.4 per cent are stunted. China, the world's most populous country, has less than 10 per cent of its child population underweight. More humiliating is the discovery that even sub-Saharan Africa has almost half our percentage of underweight children. Skepticism in accepting this disturbing statistics on malnutrition in India is because we have been made complacent by the plentiful food stocks and over-loaded. Food Corporation of India (FCI) god owns, we take pride in our Midday Meal Scheme for school children which is the largest nutritional programme in the World. The 30 year old Integrated Child Development Service (ICDS) is another flagship project. It has now about six lakh centre with some seven lakh Anganwadi workers and an equal number of helpless catering to over four cr pre-school children as well as pregnant and lactating mothers. But despite all these things, malnutrition rates in India over the past 10 years have declined at the very modest pace of a mere two per cent per annum, lower than many countries with a comparable socio-economic profile. Bangladesh has brought down its malnutrition rates by about six per cent a year. The recent report of the World Food Programme (WFP), about 18,000 children die due to hunger and malnutrition everyday, a fact which underscores the urgent need for the government to respond to poverty in all its manifestations.

Severe malnutrition is more frequent among girls (19.1%) than boys (16.9%). While most infants in India are initially breast-fed, only 37 per cent children are exclusively breast-fed for four months. Malnutrition rates among children of 0-3 years vary greatly across States, *i.e.* Madhya Pradesh (55.1%), Bihar (54.4%), Orissa (84.4%), Uttar Pradesh (51.7%) and Rajasthan (50.6%) to Goa (28.6%), Manipur (27.5%) and Kerala (26.9%).

Malnutrition continues to be equated with food shortage and the solution canvassed is to supply increased caloric intake not realising that the *Khichdi-Dalia* staple provided at such meals is inadequate. Children require special food in small quantities which is dense in energy and nutrients and not adult food, since children consume much smaller quantities. This explains why 75 per cent of Indian children under three suffer from iron deficiency (anaemia), fifty per cent from vitamin A deficiency, apart from very high rates of zinc deficiency. In this context, the present study was an attempt to find out the prevalence of malnutrition among rural children in Tamil Nadu.

Area of the Study

The researchers selected Mangudi Panchayat, which is most backward Panchayat among 13 Panchayat unions, Pudukkottai District, Tamil Nadu. The researchers selected purposively Mangudi village because the village is familiar to the researchers and easily access to this area. There is one government school in Mangudi village. Out of 400 students, 256 students are male children and 144 are female children. One hundred children were selected under simple random sampling method.

Methodology

The present study is based on both Primary and Secondary data. Primary data have been collected from 100 children through personal interview method. Secondary data have been collected from Internet service, journals, magazine and also various anthropometric indicators used for classification of malnutrition. The present study is focused on children aged 8-14 years studying in class 1st to 8th standard in government schools, Pudukkottai District, Tamil Nadu.

Objectives

1. The main objective of the present study to identify the prevalence of malnutrition among sample student respondents.

Hypotheses

- There exist a positive relationship between father's occupation and malnutrition.
- There is an insignificant relationship between sex and malnutrition.

Findings

- The study reveals that 35 per cent of children are underweight (low weight for age). Twently per cent of children are stunted (low height for age) 13 per cent of children are wasted (low weight for height). Thirtly-two per cent of children are healthy.
- Poor nutritional status was associated with socio-economic variables such as sex of the child and father's occupation. Female gender and father's occupation were significant factors for malnutrition.
- Lack of toilets, poor toilet facilities, lack of clean water are also responsible for poor nutritional status.
- Malnutrition dulls motivation and curiosity and reduces play and exploratory activities. Poor nutrition of children do not only affect the cognitive development of children but also reduce the work capacity in future.

Conclusions

Eradication of malnutrition also makes sound economic sense. In countries with widespread deficiencies of the three major nutrients, it is estimated that micro nutrient malnutrition results in a loss of about five per cent of the Gross Domestic Product (GDP) whereas solving the problem would cost less than 0.3 per cent of the GDP. The study suggested to a need for intensive nutritional programmes targeted towards poor female children and their mothers which is very important for human resource development. In this backdrop, government as well as the Non-governmental Organizations (NGOs) to put greater effort and resources on malnutrition prevention and take early action rather than coping with malnutrition.

REFERENCES

Hanumantha Rao, C.H, (2005) "*Agriculture, Food Security, Poverty and Environment*", Oxford Publication: New Delhi.

James, Philip, *Ending Malnutrition by 2020: An Agenda for Change in the Millennium*", Final Report to the ACC/SCN by the Commission On The Nutrition Challenges of The 21st Century, 2000.

Tim Dyson and Amresh Hanchante (2000) "India's Demographic and Food Prospects-state-level Analysis", *Economic and Political Weekly,* Nov. 11.

www.akshayapatra.org

en.wikipedia.org/wiki/malnutrition-in-India

web.worldbank.org>countries>southAsia

27

Women, Food Security Issues and Agricultural Sector

A. Sulthan Mohideen

INTRODUCTION

Regardless of the level of development achieved by the respective economies, women play a pivotal role in agriculture and in rural development in most countries of the Asia-Pacific Region. Evidently there are serious constraints which militate against the promotion of an effective role for women in development in those societies which were bound by age-old traditions and beliefs. Patriarchal modes and practices motivated by cultures and/or interpretations of religious sanctions and illiteracy hinder women's freedom to opt for various choices to assert greater mobility in social interactions. Resulting from these situations, women's contribution to agriculture and other sectors in the economy remain concealed and unaccounted for in monitoring economic performance measurement. Consequently, they are generally invisible in plans and programmes. They were, in fact, discriminated against by stereotypes which restrict them to a reproductive role, and denied access to resources which could eventually enhance their social and economic contribution to the society. In developing countries, among the poor, rural women are the poorest and more vulnerable. Empirical evidences suggest that women in rural areas are more adversely affected by poverty than men. The incidence of poverty among rural women is on the rise in most of the developing countries. The issues of gender bias and equity point to the double burden women have to bear – that on being poor and being a woman. Further strategies and programmes for development had largely overlooked the question of gender equity. Projects aiming to reduce poverty view the poor rural women as the recipient of benefits of development, instead of active participant and still poor rural women have the least access to basic needs such as food, health and education.

Hunger and Poverty

Hunger, which usually follows food shortages, is caused by a complex set of events and circumstances (social, economic and political factors) that differ depending on the place and time. Although hunger has been a part of human experience for centuries and a dominant feature of life in many low-income countries, the causes of hunger and starvation are not very well understood. Our understanding of the main causes of hunger and starvation has been hampered by myths and misconceptions about the interplay between hunger and population growth, land use, farm size, technology, trade, environment and other factors. Poverty cannot be defined simply in terms of lacking access to sufficient food. It is also closely associated with a person's lack of access to productive assets, services and markets. Without access to these, it is unlikely that production and income-earning capacities can be improved on a sustainable basis. Rural poverty is related to food insecurity, access to assets, services and markets: income-earning opportunities; and the organizational and institutional means for achieving those ends. Throughout the history and in many societies, inequalities of women and men were part and parcel of an accepted male-dominated culture. It is a complex historical process, which requires detailed study before one can conceive of a viable strategy to improve and sustain the status of women in society. One of the basic factors causing unequal share of women in development relates to the division of labour between the sexes. This division of labour has been justified on the basis of the child-bearing function of women and this is biologically important for survival. Consequently, distribution of tasks and responsibilities between men and women in a given society has mainly restricted women to the domestic sphere. Mass poverty and general backwardness has further aggravated the inequalities. While the women's child-bearing and child-rearing functions are respected in many countries, there has been very little recognition of women's actual or potential contribution to the economic, social and cultural states. The role of women within the family combined with high level of unemployment and underemployment of the population in general, has led to the unequal state of priority to men in matters of employment. It is understandable that women cannot be expected to join the army, for instance, as foot soldiers but Israel's well-known and rightfully feared sabrahs or women commandos have shattered the myth of man's physical superiority and thus priority for most jobs.

Discrimination of Women

It is relevant to consider some aspects of the marginalization of the status of women in the world by having a look at the figures which are based on the documents of the United Nations. Women do almost all the world's domestic work and coupled with their additional work in the productive spheres - this means most women work a double day. Unpaid domestic work is regarded as women's work. Though it is vital work, it is invisible work, unpaid, undervalued and unrecognised. Yet, the women's contribution to society in this regard is enormous:

Agriculture: Women grow about half of the world's food, but own hardly any land, have difficulty in obtaining credit and are overlooked by agricultural advisors and projects. In Africa, three-quarters of the agricultural work is done by women while in Asia, Latin America and the Middle-East, women comprise half of the agricultural labour force;

- *Health*: Women provide more health care than all health services combined and have been major beneficiaries of a new global shift in priorities towards prevention of disease and promotion of good health;
- *Education*: Women continue to out number men among the world's illiterates by about 3:2 ratio, but school enrollment boom is closing the education gap between boys and girls;
- *Political Affairs*: Due to poorer education, lack of confidence and greater workload, women are still under-represented in the decision-making bodies of their countries.

The effects of the long-term cumulative process of discrimination against women have been accentuated by under-development. Graphically, while women represent nearly 50 per cent of the world's adult population and one-third of the total labour force, they labour nearly two-thirds of the total working hours but receive only one-tenth of world income and own less than one per cent of property. The story of overworked women in the rural areas of the developing and underdeveloped countries of the world is too well known. The type of agricultural activities generally expected of women is highly labour-intensive and the rural women generally do not enjoy the benefits of new technologies. Their wages are generally less because it is assumed that the efficiency of women's labour is poor compared to that of men. Regarding ownership of land, women do not enjoy equal rights, particularly in the developing countries where most of the production, processing, storage and preparation of food is carried out by the women. These account for 50 per cent of the total labour required for food production. Many of these tasks are performed by children, especially the girls. Besides helping the menfolk in many farm operations, women have to shoulder the entire responsibilities for household chores. Bringing water from far-off wells and rivers and gathering fuel wood from forests are also part of their daily duties. Such enormous waste of human energy is unnecessary in this technological age.

Women, Food Security Issues and Agricultural Sector

Not only do women produce and process agricultural products but they are also responsible for much of the trade in these and other goods in many parts of the third world. In many parts of the world, women continue to play an important role as rural information sources and providers of food to urban areas. This may involve food from the sea as well as from the land. Although women rarely work as fisher people they are often involved in net-making and the preparation and sale of the catch. Women's roles and status all over the world are generally determined by social institutions and norms, religious ideologies, eco-systems and by class positions. The Indian social systems exhibit such grave disparities. Indian women are not a homogeneous group. Their traditional roles are not identical in all strata of society. Norms and taboos governing their roles and behaviours within and outside the family, the structure of family organizations and social practices and the positions accorded to women in a community differ considerably across regions, cultures and levels of socio-economic development. It is needless to emphasise on the significant contribution of women to agricultural production and household food security. In the process of production, handling and preparation of food, women play a multiple role throughout the sequence. They are said to be 'feeding the world'. Do women really feed the world? Let us consider the evidence. On a global scale, women produce more than half of all the food that is grown. In sub - Sahara Africa and the Caribbean, they produce up to 80 per cent of basic foodstuffs. In Asia, they provide from 50 to 90 per cent of the labour for rice cultivation. And in Southeast Asia and the Pacific as well as Latin America, women's home gardens represent some of the most complex agricultural systems known. In countries in transition, the percentage of rural women working in agriculture ranges from about a third in Bosnia and Herzegovina to more than half in Poland. Across much of the developing world, rural women provide most of the labour for farming, from soil preparation to harvest. After the harvest, they are almost entirely responsible for operations such as storage, handling, stocking, marketing and processing. Women in rural areas generally bear primary responsibility for the nutrition of their children, from gestation through weaning and throughout the critical period of growth. In addition, they are the principal food producers and preparers for the rest of the family. Despite their contributions to food security, women tend to be invisible actors in development. All too often, their work is not recorded in statistics or mentioned in reports. As a result, their contribution is poorly understood and often underestimated. There are many reasons for this. Work in the household is often considered to be part of a woman's duties as wife and mother, rather than an occupation to be accounted for in both the household and the national economy. Outside the household, a great deal of rural women labour – whether regular or seasonal – goes unpaid and is, therefore, rarely taken into account in official statistics.

In most countries, women do not own the land they cultivate. Discriminatory laws and practices for inheritance of and access and ownership to land are still widespread. Land that women do own tends to consist of smaller, less valuable plots that are also frequently overlooked in statistics. Furthermore, women are usually responsible for the food crops destined for immediate consumption by the household, that is, for subsistence crops rather than cash crops. Also, when data is collected for national statistics, gender is often ignored or the data is biased in the sense that it is collected only from males, who are assumed to be the heads of households. These handicaps have contributed to an increasing 'faminisation' of poverty. Since the 1970s, the number of women living below the poverty line has increased by 50 per cent , in comparison with 30 per cent for their male counterparts. Women may feed the world today, but, given this formidable lists of obstacles placed in their path, will they be able to produce the additional food needed for a world population expected to grow by three billion in 2030? During the FAO-sponsored World Food summit of 1996, world leaders from 186 countries adopted the Rome

Declaration on World Food Security and a Plan of Action. These international agreements specified that the role of women in agriculture and food security must be emphasised, in order to create the enabling political, social and economic environment required for the eradication of hunger ad poverty. Under Commitment-I of the World Food Summit Plan of Action agenda, governments committed themselves to:

Women play an indispensable role in farming and in improving the quality of life in rural areas. However, their contributions often remain concealed due to some social barriers and gender bias. Even government programmes often fail to focus on women in agriculture. This undermines the potential benefits from programmes, especially those related to food production, household income improvements, nutrition, literacy, poverty alleviation and population control. Equitable access for rural women to educational facilities would certainly improve their performance and liberate them from their marginalised status in the society. Other areas where women's potential could be effectively harnessed are agricultural extension, farming systems development, land reform and rural welfare. Landmark improvements have been recorded in such cases as the extension of institutional credit and domestic water supplies where women's potential have been consciously tapped. Socio-economic goals of productivity, equity and environment stability are closely woven around the agriculture sector policies and new dimensions in programmes implemented are already emerging as new values. Regardless of the level of development achieved by the respective economies, women play a pivotal role in agriculture and in rural development in most countries of the Asia-Pacific Region. Asia-Pacific region had witnessed spectacular development in crop yields which even surpassed the population growth rate in the past decade. However, pockets of hunger remain when landless or small farm rural population lack economic access to food because of a lack of remunerative non-farm employment in rural areas, where 80 per cent of Asia-Pacific's 400 million poor live. It has also been suggested that with the acceleration of crop-diversification programmes and the transformation of agriculture to commercial production levels, women's lot had been even further worsened by the addition of new burdens which they have to shoulder in order to realise profits in farm operations. Rural women who are obliged to attend to all the household chores, children's welfare, nutrition and family cohesion along with farm work, are desperately driven to adopt a survival strategy to save the family food security from total collapse. Rural poverty has increased in the region particularly for farmers as priority has been accorded to the industrial and service sectors: this is both the cause and an effect of rural-urban migration leading to the 'feminisation of farming'. Thus the numbers and the proportion of rural women among the absolutely poor and destitute, currently around 60 per cent , is expected to increase to 65 to 70 per cent by the year 2000. In spite of social, political and economic constraints, women farmers have proved extremely resourceful and hardworking in their attempt to ensure household food security.

Social constraints place barriers around their access to scientific and technological information. Lack of collateral denies them access to agricultural credit. Culture or traditions accord membership of cooperatives only to heads of households - usually a man. Many rural women, even in highly mechanised farming systems such as the Republic of Korea and Japan would have agriculture for work in other sectors if choices were available. After some decades of development, global problems and issues concerning environment, women in development, and poverty have reappeared. All these have emerged in rural communities and threatening their sustainability. Rural communities with norms developed for managing resources are important for the stability of community life. Gender-oriented rural development programmes which focus on role of women to guarantee the stability of life provide a sound basis for integrated development of the quality of life. In progressive economies like Japan, rural women have shown anxieties over several concerns affecting their livelihood.

Conclusion

In the past some efforts have been made through which member-organizations, cooperative and agricultural departments all over Asia and Africa have been requested to make special programmes for rural women and set aside budgets for their implementation. In some cases some good responses have been received. While it is generally agreed that education is central to women's development the participation of girls in the national educational system continues to lag well behind that of boys at every level. Among the factors that are believed to contribute to this gap are women's self-perpetuating negative social status, economic constraints and male-oriented biases in the design and delivery of primary and secondary education. These limitations have meant that millions of women have not received formal education and that millions more are deprived of the opportunity for more than token participation. Women, however, retain a strong orientation to self-help and group cooperation. They look to their own resources and to other women when faced with a problem of opportunity. This perhaps is the key factor on which women's development programme could be developed. This is their greatest asset. They have kept folk art, family bonds, religious traditions, cultural heritage alive, thriving and vibrant. They have played significant role in food security efforts and rural and small industrial sectors.

Policy Suggestions

- Special programmes have been instituted to improve their social and economic status through provision of education, employment, healthcare and involvement in social and economic institutions.
- The role of agricultural co-operatives agencies very important which hold enormous potential for the development of women, and more particularly the rural women.

- Rural women are actively involved in the process of food production, processing and marketing. They often lack the legal status which prohibits them to have access to credit, education and technology. Co-operative institutions should come forward to help accelerate the process of development and participation of women in their organizational and business activities.

28

Food Production after Economic Reforms in India

K. Nagendiran
Dr. C. Dhandapani

INTRODUCTION

The century ended with the country's output of food grains crossing 200 million tonnes, a fourfold increase since 1960-61, mainly due to the success of the green revolution since the 1970s. Over years most farmers have shifted to rice and wheat cultivation because of the MSP offered by the Government. The coarse grain production has remained stagnant. Although the area under cultivation with food grains has remained virtually constant since 1970-71, the yield has increased by 65 per cent. India which had to import food grains for some time after independence, but now it has emerged as a marginal exporter of food grains (Ministry of Finance, 2000). Agriculture contributes nearly one-fourth of the GDP (Reserve Bank of India, 1999) and provides a livelihood to about two-thirds of ail workers in the country (Central Statistical Organization, 1999). Although the per cent age of land cultivated with food crops that is irrigated increased from 24 per cent in 1970-71 to 41 per cent in 1996-97, the performance of Indian agriculture still largely depends on monsoon rains. In spite of a fourfold increase in food production since the early fifties, daily per capita net availability of food grains has increased by only 18 per cent, from 395 grams to 467 grams per day (Ministry of Finance,

2000). During the 1990s the growth rate of food grains production declined to 1.9 per cent per annum from 3.5 per cent per annum during 1980s. Similarly the growth rate of productivity in food grains decelerated to 1.3 per cent as compared to 3.3 per cent per annum during the 1980s. In terms of productivity the country lags behind others.

The production of kharif food grains during 2006-07 is estimated at 209.2 million tonnes (second advance estimates), which is higher than 208.6 million tones estimated during 2005-06. The production of rise is estimated at 90.1 million tonnes compared to 91.8 million tonnes during the previous year. The production of wheat is estimated at 72.5 million tonnes, which is higher than the previous year production of 69.3 million tonnes. The production of coarse cereals is estimated at 32 million tonnes, which is lower than the previous year's production of 34 million tonnes. Sugarcane production is estimated to be higher at 315.5 million tonnes (first advance estimates), as against 281.2 million tonnes during the previous year. It is a matter of concern that massive improvement in food grain availability, substantial decline in cost of cereals, improved access to subsidized food grains through Targeted Public Distribution System have not resulted in elimination of hunger or reduction in under-nutrition especially in vulnerable groups.

Uttar Pradesh, Punjab and Haryana are the major producers of food grains in 2004-05. Rajasthan, Madhya Pradesh and Gujarat are oilseeds producing States; major sugarcane producing States are Uttar Pradesh, Maharashtra and Tamil Nadu. Almost all States produce food grains. Punjab and Uttar Pradesh rank highest in production of food grains. Punjab and Haryana top the yield of food grains. It is obvious that there are huge differences not only in area under cultivation but also in yield between states. Agricultural productivity in different states. Improvement in productivity in large states like UP will have a major impact on food grain availability in the country. As there is not such scope in terms of increase in area under cultivation, an effort to increase productivity has to be given priority over the next decade.

The very success of Green Revolution brought about some major problems. Many states have attempted to increase production through subsidies on inputs such as power, water and fertilizers, rather than by building new capital assets in irrigation and power. Unsustainable practices like excessive use of water together with imbalanced use of fertilizers especially in the Green Revolution areas of northern and northwestern parts of the country have adversely affected soil health and environment.

Though the consumption of pesticides seems to have declined, because of the propagation of the Integrated Pest Management (IPM) approach and the increasing awareness about the hazards of pesticides, the availability of quality pesticides and pesticide residues in foodstuffs, remained a matter of concern. Many of the erstwhile high producing states are experiencing Green Revolution fatigue. Very little attention is being paid to achieve integrated fanning systems that will ensure sustainable evergreen revolution essential for appropriate dietary diversification to achieve nutrition security.

To meet all the nutritional needs of the growing population, the country will have to produce an extra five million tonnes of food grains annually and increase the production of livestock, fish and horticultural products. This has to be achieved in the face of shrinking arable land and farm size, low productivity, growing regional disparities in productivity and depletion of the natural resource base. Appropriate steps have to be taken to minimise the potential adverse consequences of globalisation on domestic production, employment and price stability of food commodities. In India the productivity has been quite low. The challenge is to take appropriate steps to improve productivity in all the states. The low productivity can also be viewed as an opportunity, which can readily help the country to increase production without worrying about the country's inability to expand the area under cultivation.

Cereal Production

The country has been producing adequate cereals to meet the needs of the population since mid seventies. Over the last five decades per capita net availability has been showing improvement and by 1991 it was sufficient to meet the RDA for cereals. The production of cereals has increased tremendously in past five decades though the area under the cereal production has not increased much information on production of various cereals in largest cereal producing States. West Bengal, Andhra Pradesh and Uttar Pradesh are the largest rice producing states. Uttar Pradesh, Punjab and Haryana are largest producers of wheat in the country; coarse cereals are mainly produced in Maharashtra, Karnataka and Rajasthan.

Inputs needed to achieve a sustainable increase in food grain production to meet the needs of the growing population have to be provided. Locally produced and procured coarse grains made available through the Targeted Public Distribution System (TPDS) at a subsidized rate may substantially bring down the subsidy cost without any reduction in calories provided. This will also improve targeting as only the neediest are likely to buy these coarse grains. Millets are rich in minerals and micronutrients and hence increased consumption will improve the intake of these vital nutrients by the poor. Some states have taken steps to include coarse grains under the TPDS. This is a welcome step and may result in increased local production and consumption of the coarse grains.

Pulse Production

India is the key player with 25 per cent share in the global pulse basket from an area of about 32 per cent, the annual production being 13.63 million tonnes in latest triennium. The important pulse producing States are Madhya Pradesh, Uttar Pradesh, Maharashtra, Rajasthan, Karnataka and Andhra Pradesh, which together account for 75 per cent production. In the last five decades, there has been a progressive decline in per capita availability of pulses and pulse consumption, especially among the poorer segments of the population. This is due to stagnant production and consequent rising cost of pulses. This trend has to be reversed.

The source of growth varied in different periods. Area expansion was the major factor for growth during 1951-67; the yield improvement has been the key element in the post-All India Coordinated Pulses Improvement Programme (AICPIP) period (1967-2002). National pulse production has increased from 10.6 million tonnes in 1980-82 to 13.4 million tonnes in 2005-06, registering a growth of 1.7 per cent annually. However, the share of pulses in the total food grain production has declined from 15.8 per cent in 1951-55 to 6.3 per cent in 2005-06.

Interstate differences in area, production and yield of pulses in 2005-06 are shown in Madhya Pradesh, Uttar Pradesh and Maharashtra are the largest producers of pulses. The production of gram is highest but has not changed over the years. However, over the years there has been some increase in production of *arhar* and lentil.

In post-Green Revolution period, the per capita availability of pulses has declined sharply in the country, as growth in pulse production did not keep pace with the population growth. The country has experienced progressive decline in per capita availability of pulses from 69 g in 1961 to 32 g in 2005. Because of the shortfall in national production, the country has been importing pulses. During 2001-02, the country imported 21.8 lakh tonnes of pulses valued at Rs. 3155.7 crore.

It is estimated that to meet the needs of the growing population the requirement in pulses will go up to 19.6 million tonnes by 2007, and 21.3 million tonnes by 2012. To make the nation pulse sufficient there is a need to increase the area under pulse cultivation and improve productivity. A proactive strategy from researchers, planners, policy-makers, extension workers, market forces and farmers aiming not only at boosting the per unit productivity of land but also at reduction in the production costs is needed to improve availability and affordability of pulses. Lack of assured market is one factor responsible for the stagnation in pulse production. Due to serious problem of stored grain pest infestation and lack of storage facilities, farmers are compelled to sell their produce to middlemen at low price.

The minimum support price announced by the Government does not benefit farmers in absence of procurement mechanism. Moreover, all pulse crops are not covered under the minimum support price. Therefore, procurement policy for pulses needs to be strengthened immediately and reasonable buffer stock needs to be built up to meet the contingencies. Appropriate market intervention and promotion of post harvest technology are also necessary to encourage farmers to invest more in pulses production. Distribution of pulses through TPDS may improve access to pulses and help in stabilization of cost of pulses.

India has identified horticultural crops as a means of diversification for making agriculture more profitable through efficient land use, optimum utilisation of natural resources (soil, water and environment) and creating skilled employment for rural masses, especially women folk. However, if these efforts are to succeed some of the concerns of the farmers have to be addressed. The shelf life of food grains is over 3 years or more but shelf life fruits and vegetables ranges from a week to 3 months. Currently hardly 1 per cent of over 140 million tonnes of fruits and vegetables produced in the country goes through the processing route. Losses during packaging and transport are estimated to be about 30 per cent and when coupled with poor off-take, it can spell major economic disaster for the farmers. It is therefore imperative that creation of essential infrastructure for preservation, cold storage, refrigerated transportation, rapid transit, grading, processing, packaging and quality control get the necessary investment to enable the horticultural sector to achieve its full economic potential. The Tenth Plan has emphasized the need for Nutrition Security with rapid increase in dietary diversification. With the increasing economic growth and emergence of a large middle class, which is aware of the importance of vegetable and fruit intake in their diet, it is expected that the demand for fruits and vegetables over the next few years will show a steep rise. This must be met through increased production of these in the country.

Efforts are on to encourage private investment in hi-tech horticulture with micro-propagation, protected cultivation, drip irrigation, and integrated nutrient and pest management besides making use of latest post-harvest technology particularly in the case of perishable commodities. As a result, horticulture crop production has begun to move from rural confines to commercial ventures and has attracted young entrepreneurs, since it has proved to be intellectually satisfying and economically rewarding. This will not only help in retaining educated youth in the farm sector but would also enable the micronutrient needs of the population to be met through a sustainable food-based approach. The processing, storage and transportation for horticultural products in a manner that there is no glut and distresssale, will make their production economically attractive to farmers and improve availability to the consumers.

In spite of being a major vegetable and fruit producing country in the world per capita consumption of these in India is very low. Consumption of adequate quantities of vegetables, especially green leafy ones, is essential for meeting the dietary requirement of vital micronutrients. Besides, vegetables also provide several phytochemicals and fibre essential for health. At present, there is insufficient focus on the cultivation and marketing of low-cost, locally-acceptable green leafy vegetables, yellow vegetables and fruits. As a result, these vegetables are not available at affordable cost throughout the year. Health and nutrition education emphasising the importance of consuming these inexpensive but rich sources of micronutrients will not result in any change in food habits unless the horticultural resources in the country are harnessed and managed effectively to meet the growing needs of the people at an affordable cost.

Oilseeds

In India vegetable oils are used mainly for cooking. Groundnut, sesame, coconut and mustard oils are used traditionally in India. Oilseeds production has increased over the last five decades but the increase is not sufficient to meet the demand; the country therefore continues to import oil. National Mission on Oilseeds and Pulses was formed in 1986 to give focused thrust to oilseed production in the country and improve availability of oil. A major effort was to introduce the newer oilseeds/oils in the Indian market. Over the last two decades soybean, sunflower, safflower, corn, rice bran oils have been introduced and have found acceptance.

Review of the edible oil production in the last decades shows that there was not much change in production of groundnut oilseeds. Mustard and rapeseed production has increased in the Past ten years; there has been tremendous increase in production of soybean, which was introduced as the newer oilseed. There was not much change in production of sunflower, safflower and sesame seeds in last ten years. Net availability of rice bran, soy, and mustard oils has increased over the last ten years.

Transfats are a popular component in various food products and widely used by all-from housewives to food product manufacturers. The fast food industries use transfats instead of ghee because it is inexpensive. Transfats are found in margarine, crackers, candies, cookies, snack foods, baked goods, and other processed foods. Lack of time for cooking due to busy lifestyles has resulted in many persons from all income group consuming ready to eat foods from various eateries; many of the products in these eateries are fried in transfat to reduce rancidity and improve shelf life and this results in people inadvertently consuming large quantities of transfatty acids. Currently, in India there are no specific guidelines for regulating use of transfats. Government of India has taken the first step in the regulation of transfatty acid use by making it mandatory from September 2007 to indicate the amount of transfatty acids in the label of all manaufactured food products. The annual production of *vanaspati* (fully or partially hydrogenated vegetable cooking oil) in India is 5 per cent of total edible oil. The consumption of *vanaspati* has declined over the years as a proportion of total edible oils consumption, even though awareness on the dangers of transfats remains very low .There is an urgent need to improve awareness among the consumers and producers. Simultaneously the government may have to impose stringent rules and regulations to reduce or even ban transfats in food products. A combination of both awareness and regulations against usage or production of trans fat would perhaps help rapid in reduction and elimination of use of trans fats.

Conclusion

The Approach Paper for the Eleventh Plan has taken into account all the challenges and will focus on strategies to overcome these and ensure that agriculture plays its critical role in economic growth as well as nutrition security for the population. The Approach Paper to the Eleventh Five-year Plan has emphasized on rapid increase in agriculture growth to 4 per cent. Accelerated agricultural growth will require diversification into horticulture and floriculture which in turn imply structural changes in the relation between agriculture and non-agriculture. Diversification requires effective marketing linkages, supported by modern marketing practices including introduction of grading, post-harvest management, and cold chains.

The National Agriculture Policy (NAP), 2000 and the Eleventh Plan have set a target of a 3.9 per cent growth for agriculture. This is to be achieved through: Growth that is based on efficient use of resources and conservation of soil, water and bio-diversity; growth with equity, *i.e.*, growth which is widespread across regions and covers all farmers; growth that is demand driven and caters to domestic markets as well as maximizes benefits from exports of agricultural products in the face of the challenges arising from economic liberalization and globalization; growth that is sustainable technologically, environmentally and economically. The sector has the opportunity to contribute towards substantial increase in GDP, provide employment in rural areas, improve nutrition security of the population and achieve significant decline in macro and micronutrient under-nutrition.

REFERENCES

Agricultural Statistics at a Glance 2007.

Approach paper to the Eleventh Five-year Plan.

Department of Animal Husbandry, Dairying and Fisheries: http://dahd.nic.in/stat files/BAHS2006%20web%20web.pdf; accessed on 27/09/07

Economic Survey of India 2006-07.

Indian Horticulture Production at a glance, 2004-05.

Tenth Five-year Plan 2002-2007.

29

An Economic Analysis on Food Production and Food Security in India

M. Vadivel

Dr. Ponnarasu

ABSTRACT

In this context, the production of all districts of Tamil Nadu comparatively fully achieved over other states in India. The significant level between quantity levels by tonnes of agriculture production related to receipts in lakhs stored in regulated markets on basis of food security. In India food security system has been much has not concentration over the development level of economic life. Higher government procurement will lead to a lower availability of food grain for the open market, pushing up prices. According to the NSSO consumption expenditure survey 2004-05 the average monthly per capita rural consumption of wheat and rice for the lowest MPCE classes constituting 49.9 per cent of the rural population was 10.11 kg., while the urban consumption for the lowest MPCE classes constituting 30.2 per cent of the urban population was 9.35 kg. This implies that even the priority households which constitute the most vulnerable section of the population will have to procure 25 to 30 per cent of their consumption requirement from the open market. The actual requirement is likely to be higher since people consume wheat and rice in processed forms like bread, biscuits, sooji, maida etc., which are not reflected in the consumption estimates worked out here. In other words the market prices are extremely relevant for the household budgets of both the entitled and other households.

Food security, as defined by FAO, provides a useful goal towards which the world should strive. It can also be useful for monitoring an important aspect of the well-being of households and for the design, implementation, and evaluation of policies, programmes and projects. However, the interaction between household food access and household food acquisition and allocation behaviour means that household food security is of only limited value as an indicator of individual food security. Because of a high prevalence of poor sanitation and unclean water in many developing countries, its value as an indicator of individual health and nutrition is evens less. Food security is a valuable concept if used with a clear understanding of what it means, its limitations, and how it interacts with behaviour and non-food factors. Estimates of household food security, combined with individual anthropometric estimates for children and a thorough understanding of household behaviour provide a powerful input into the design and implementation of policies and programmes to improve nutrition.

Food Grain Requirement *Vs.* Current Production and Procurement

NAC has estimated the entitled food grain requirement (PDS) for phase 1 at 49.36 million tonnes and for the final phase at 55.59 million tonnes. These estimates are based on the assumption of 85 per cent off-take of food grain during phase 1 and 90 per cent off-take of food grain during the final phase. It is understood that NAC has used the population projections of the National Commission on Population for October 2010 for estimating the grain requirement for both the phases.

There was a sharp increase in the procurement of wheat and rice in the year 2007-08 both in terms of absolute quantity and as a percentage of the total production. The procurement peaked at 59.07 million tonnes for the production year 2008-09 reaching almost 33 per cent of the production in that year. In the sub-sequent year, the absolute procurement fell sharply; decreasing to 54 million tonnes, but the fall in the relative procurement was muted because production had also fallen sharply. In the period 2000-01 to 2009-10 the average procurement as a percentage of production was at 26.6 per cent. However, for projections this may be too conservative in the light of higher procurements in the last few years.

Indian agriculture is still highly dependent on rainfall and drought years cause production declines which can take a couple of years to be made up. A case in point is the drought year 2002-03 where the production of wheat and rice fell by 28.53 million tonnes over the previous year. It took 3 years to make up and it was only in 2006-07 that the production at 169.17 million tonnes exceeded the 2001-02 level. Similarly 2009-10 witnessed a production decline of 10 million tonnes (in rice) which was however expected to be made up this year but the current monsoon position has introduced some uncertainty. The implication of this for future projections is that to estimate the total available food grain (wheat and rice) for the first and final phase of the NFSB it is best to be somewhat conservative and use the long-term trend growth rates. According to the projections made by Department of Agriculture, the total projected food grain production (wheat and rice) is expected to be 187.82 million tonnes for 2011-12 and 192.02 million tonnes for 2013-14. As well as agriculture production particularly in spices of India also depicted below the Table 29.1 based on area in acres and production in tonnes to measure food requiring level to the nation.

Table 29.1 mentioned that the Agricultural Production of India during 2002-03 to 2006-07 (area in hectares) (production in tonnes) it has been summarized by categorized lists of spices in Indian Agriculture Production. Cinnamon, Vanilla and Clove were produced little bit of level compare with others in specified periods.

It is important to note that the current issue price for BPL and APL household is higher than the food grain price proposed in the NFSB for priority and general households respectively and in all likelihood at these prices the off-take is likely to be 100 per cent. Based on this we have worked out a Scenario according to which the food grain requirement for

Table 29.1: Agricultural Production of India during 2002-03 to 2006-07 (area in hectares) (production in tonnes)

Name of the Spices	2002-03		2003-04		2004-05		2005-06		2006-07	
	Area	Prodn.	Area	Prodn.	Area	Prodn.	Area	Prodn.	Area	Prodn.
1	2	3	4	5	6	7	8	9	10	11
Pepper	223940	70920	235430	74260	267112	81930	257244	50000	236177	49997
Cardamom(S)	73125	11920	73237	11580	73725	11415	73795	12540	73228	11235
Cardamom(L)	30008	5300	30039	6154	30039	5773	30039	5185	30039	4303
Chilli	827950	906994	824400	1289340	843280	1376580	742200	1023128	809437	1325273
Ginger	103220	422820	107780	545280	114730	647160	125847	810934	129014	721539
Turmeric	149710	526289	153430	587130	164110	751869	173139	867074	183917	856464
Corriander	302450	188950	508990	405390	396310	296050	357040	257068	361767	287647
Cumin	521250	134753	430840	202980	367678	176068	403033	199854	409033	176511
Fennel	22898	27602	43036	51752	39820	51026	40909	61307	61128	92260
Fennugreek	50596	64221	63535	79683	50400	62745	33393	38990	44984	55780
Garlic	114920	459080	164280	747780	163242	739879	162503	624794	169612	833157
Vanilla	2545	92	3543	134	5370	236	5815	188	5129	233

Contd...

1	2	3	4	5	6	7	8	9	10	11
Clove	2076	1369	2397	1755	2231	1469	2144	1194	1941	742
Nutmeg	8668	2208	9979	2593	9996	2723	11270	2914	13709	11564
Cinnamon	398	77	420	30	452	20	500	24	530	27
Tamarind	61958	178974	60629	183871	61624	194032	61084	192186	58624	190073
Dill Seed	10926	6330	12788	8648	14595	10408	9351	5660	11083	9679
Ajwan	10375	1629	10816	10205	15381	9528	24300	8334	31657	15850
Saffron	2880	6.53	2742	5.15	3075	4.83	2989	8.85	2928	4.85
Celery	2800	3000	2800	3000	1197	4577	1154	1492	1799	2350
Tejpat	6140	15961	6140	15961	6140	15961	6140	15961	6140	15961
Sweet Flag	7200	3557	7200	3557	7200	3557	7200	3557	7200	3557

Source: Ministry of Agriculture, GoI.

the two phases works out to 58.76 million tonnes and 63.98 million tonnes. In all the three scenarios to obtain the total food grain requirement, we must add another 8 million tonnes required for the other welfare programmes of the government like Mid Day Meal Scheme, ICDS, Social Welfare Hostels and Natural Calamities. Moreover there is a need for maintaining a buffer stock which is an important tool for food security especially in times of droughts, natural and other calamities. According to some estimates a food security reserve of about six million tonnes is required.

Regulated Markets Function and Food Security in Tamil Nadu

Table 29.2 depicted that Regulated Markets, Rural God owns, Commercial Grading Centre sand Kapas Grading Centres in Tamil Nadu has plays important role in food security in context the of people in future concern. That's belongs to every make demand for all agricultural commodities like food grain, spices and other relates. In the list of districts Villupuram listed as first with 468678 metric tonnes of agriculture goods in regulated markets and Thiruvannamalai and erode districts were placed as a next in the quantity of 254147 and 188434 metric tonnes respectively. In this list The Nilgiri has not availability of agricultural goods in regulated markets. Krishnagiri placed above of the The Nilgiris district that denoted by Tamil Nadu government.

Statistical Analysis for Food Production in Quantity in Tonnes and Values

This analysed about agricultural production and its enrolment in food security but in this world many countries has not sufficient sources in primary sector contribution. But in the Indian context this has been welcome one in leading the economy with secondary and third sectors. In the point of one sample statistics where quantity in tonnes contribute compare with its value based on amounts, further this analysis made the conclusion these conditions fulfilled and discussed in proper manner, mean value and standard deviation results were very accurately analysed.

Table 29.2: Regulated Market, Rural Godowns, Commercial Grading Centres and Kapas Grading Centres in Tamil Nadu 2008-09

Sl. No.	Districts in Tamil Nadu	In Regulated Markets	
		Quantity of Arrivals (MT)	Receipts (Rs. in lakhs)
1	2	3	4
1.	Kancheepuram	16065	42.980
2.	Thiruvallur	22760	101.020
3.	Vellore	84515	234.980
4.	Thiruvannamalai	254147	316.630
5.	Cuddalore	80352	221.930
6.	Villupuram	468678	571.640
7.	Salem	32532	282.340
8.	Namakkal	14380	140.570
9.	Dharmapuri	15878	73.870
10.	Krishnagiri	7418	102.270
11.	Erode	188434	651.540
12.	Coimbatore	44824	605.380
13.	Tiruppur	106709	506.970
14.	The Nilgiris	0	0.00
15.	Tiruchirappalli	28753	124.960
16.	Karur	18008	43.200
17.	Perambalur	2337	18.950
18.	Ariyalur	10213	45.480
19.	Pudukkottai	31007	106.840
20.	Thanjavur	44984	523.780
21.	Nagapattinam	29918	95.260
22.	Thiruvarur	26933	149.360
23.	Madurai	34005	159.910
24.	Theni	26744	73.870

Contd...

1	2	3	4
25.	Dindigul	25627	264.000
26.	Ramanathapuram	19662	209.700
27.	Virudhunagar	30022	157.230
28.	Sivagangai	20779	80.690
29.	Tirunelveli	50738	168.380
30.	Thoothukudi	25210	104.320
31.	Kanyakumari	10978	249.520

Source: Commissioner of Agricultural Marketing and Agricultural Business.

In Tamil Nadu, the scenario of quantity arrivals to markets and it associated with value of receipts in lakhs were measured by some statistical analysis due to it has been critiqued. Tables 29.3 and 29.4 statically analysis explained the trends in how many amount of agricultural products particularly spices, pulses and other food were mentioned on the other hand it expressed the value of amount in basis of tonnes of products held in regulated markets in districts of Tamil Nadu for further compiling usages to equalise the food insecurity in Tamil Nadu. The one sample test and statistics explained the means of both which depicts 5.71 and 2.07 respectively. As well as standard deviation expressed 933 and 181 respectively. Both have complementary and relatively inter measurement in one action in markets in the during the year 2008-09. It always stated that the significant relationship between side as well as weight and amount to measure the production level in Tamil Nadu districts.

Table 29.3: One-Sample Statistics

	N	Mean	Std. Deviation	Std. Error Mean
Quantity in tonnes	31	5.7181	93306.99100	16758.43030
Receipts (Rs.) in lakhs	31	2.0734	181.54206	32.60592

Table 29.4: One-Sample Tests

	Test Value = 0					
	t	df	Sig. (2-tailed)	Mean Difference	95% Confidence Interval of the Difference	
					Lower	Upper
Quantity in tonnes	3.412	30	.002	57180.96774	22955.6871	91406.2484
Receipts (Rs) in lakhs	6.359	30	.000	207.34097	140.7508	273.9311

State-wise Area and Production of Spices

Table 29.5 depicted the production of spices by state-wise in India, in this context Andhra Pradesh had more producing agricultural spices production compare with Himachal Pradesh has low level of producer of India during the period of time 2003-07. In statistical based Correlation analysis is significant at the 0.01 level (2-tailed) has placed from 2004 to 2007 and correlation between productions of every state has significant level over the spices production.

In the paired sample data have been significant level between production and state contribution in production aspects. Increasing the production based on years 722785 tonnes of production and 333446 acres were utilised in Andhra Pradesh in 2002-03 and later in 322356 acres produced 1210667 tonnes during 2006-07. Pondcherry has pointed out in the list by last belongs to area cultivation and production yield in during the period.

Table 29.7 showed that the significant level between state wise production and acres of land were utilised by State-wise Area and production of Spices. During the perion from 2002-03 to 2006-07 the significant level accepted for we have that analysed data nearly correlated with 985 to 987 in forthcoming years. In Table 29.8 depicts significant level of acres of land and production of states in India mention in the manner increasing the significant level. (*See tables on 275 page*)

Table 29.5: State-wise Area and Production of Spices

States	2002-03		2003-04		2004-05		2005-06		2006-07	
	Area (hec)	Prodn (Tons)	Area (hec)	Prodn (Tons)	Area (hec)	Prodn (Tons)	Area (hec)	Prodn (Tons)	Area (hec)	Prodn (Tons)
1	2	3	4	5	6	7	8	9	10	11
Andaman and Nicobar	1420	1846	1792	2453	2009	3621	1797	3395	1652	3259
Andhra Pradesh	333446	722785	365236	1152425	326423	1209271	287947	1108039	322356	1210667
Arunachal Pradesh	6570	36620	6780	41140	6610	37310	7410	37610	8000	45300
Assam	71520	171900	71650	172270	71080	1 82700	71400	183130	72290	183660
Bihar	11550	12110	10950	10540	11000	11010	12530	13450	11071	19088
Chhatisgarh	9330	5410	13320	9960	13530	8880	13780	7560	13542	8608
Gujarat	256137	194513	329005	358626	327837	395300	400804	486978	414629	599256
Himachal Pradesh	0	0	5830	17970	7580	21340	6060	1 8420	6277	23369
Jammu and Kashmir	4310	1377	4142	1405	4615	1505	4569	1509	4052	10703
Karnataka	240259	273830	191457	413087	255387	589263	228637	519208	244848	591821
Kerala	293042	158322	301492	159961	325216	173333	328826	141341	308117	137255
Madhya Pradesh	134390	126750	212770	230180	231660	280590	188160	213680	212662	281195
Maharashtra	112540	105970	104420	98800	116620	95380	114060	105810	112472	99568

Contd...

1	2	3	4	5	6	7	8	9	10	11
Manipur	11740	8410	11740	8490	14870	11560	8930	7730	13580	12670
Meghalaya	17450	71491	18390	75011	18880	73881	19450	81351	19560	88971
Mizoram	6840	35310	6100	34200	6170	40960	6421	53254	5720	42720
Nagaland	2940	26083	3100	12420	3744	27068	2147	13263	2222	13443
Orissa	143530	191150	144160	192940	137360	184710	145050	195480	146030	199260
Pondicherry	20	41	10	31	10	40	8	20	10	19
Punjab	13020	32290	13200	32840	12107	35797	12394	33812	13299	36930
Rajastan	543942	347847	602129	652353	427622	430038	360433	307978	393303	361449
Sikkim	32114	29560	33714	4063 1	33774	41430	33994	42027	33994	41383
Tamil Nadu	144313	191686	152139	193726	141134	255287	129012	271027	141398	309431
Tripura	4290	16920	3390	9480	3980	22800	4410	9560	4400	9635
Uttar Pradesh	49345	132026	55783	160637	55527	161455	60520	176700	56302	167075
Uttaranchal	5901	33426	5948	39739	5948	39699	6305	48510	6816	52186
West Bengal	86074	104380	85805	109773	77015	108783	74795	100438	79035	114196

Source: Commissioner of Agricultural Marketing and Agricultural Business, Chennai-32

Table 29.6: State-wise Area and Production of Spices

Correlations							
		State	**2002-03**	**2003-04**	**2004-05**	**2005-06**	**2006-07**
State	Pearson Correlation	1	-.078	-.086	-.090	-.092	-.091
	Sig. (2-tailed)		.699	.670	.655	.649	.651
	N	27	27	27	27	27	27
2002-03	Pearson Correlation	-.078	1	.999**	.999**	.998**	.998**
	Sig. (2-tailed)	.699		.000	.000	.000	.000
	N	27	27	27	27	27	27
2003-04	Pearson Correlation	-.086	.999**	1	.999**	.998**	.998"
	Sig. (2-tailed)	.670	.000		.000	.000	.000
	N	27	27	27	27	27	27
2004-05	Pearson Correlation	-.090	.999**	.999**	1	1.000**	.999**
	Sig. (2-tailed)	.655	.000	.000		.000	.000
	N	27	27	27	27	27	27
2005-06	Pearson Correlation	-.092	.998**	.998**	1.000**	1	1.000**
	Sig. (2-tailed)	.649	.000	.000	.000		.000
	N	27	27	27	27	27	27
2006-07	Pearson Correlation	-.091	.998**	.998**	.999**	1.000**	1
	Sig. (2-tailed)	.651	.000	.000	.000	.000	
	N	27	27	27	27	27	27

** Correlation is significant at the 0.01 level (2-tailed).

Table 29.7: State-wise Area and Production of Spices

Paired Samples Statistics					
Pair 1	2002-2003	2.7581E5	27	5.03065E5	96814.92813
	2002-2003	4.3038E5	27	8.20541E5	1.57913E5
Pair 2	2003-2004	3.0289E5	27	5.56957E5	1.07186E5
	2003-2004	6.3354E5	27	1.22941E6	2.36601E5
Pair 3	2004-2005	2.9806E5	27	5.60423E5	1.07853E5
	2004-2005	6.8665E5	27	1.35137E6	2.60071E5
Pair 4	2005-2006	2.8466E5	27	5.35733E5	1.03102E5
	2005-2006	6.4848E5	27	1.27628E6	2.45621E5
Pair 5	2006-2007	3.0439E5	27	5.74202E5	1.10505E5
	2006-2007	7.260 1E5	27	1.43122E6	2.75439E5

Table 29.8: State-wise Area and Production of Spices

Paired Samples Correlations				
		N	Correlation	Sig.
Pair 1	2002-03 and 2002-03	27	.985	.000
Pair 2	2003-04 and 2003-04	27	.985	.000
Pair 3	2004-05 and 2004-05	27	.985	.000
Pair 4	2005-06 and 2005-06	27	.985	.000
Pair 5	2006-07 and 2006-07	27	.987	.000

Accordingly, we have assumed that it will be possible to procure 30 per cent of the total production which translates to 56.35 million tonnes in 2011-12 and 57.61 million tonnes in 2013-14. In view of the cycles in agricultural procurement, it may be imprudent to assume an average procurement level of more than 30 per cent. It has been estimated by the Department of Agriculture that the marketable surplus of wheat and rice in 2010-11 was about 106.5 million tonnes. The expected procurement of 53.22 million tonnes in 2010-11 works out to about 50 per cent of the marketable surplus. A larger procurement has the danger of distorting the food prices in

Table 29.9: State-wise Area and Production of Spices

Paired Samples Test									
		Paired Differences					t	df	Sig- (2-tailed)
		Mean	Std. Deviation	Std. Error Mean	95 % Confidence Interval of the Difference				
					Lower	Upper			
Pair 1	2002-03	1.54565E5	3.36042E5	64671.24 721	-2.87499E5	-21631.34753	2.390	26	.024
Pair 2	2003-04	3.30651E5	6.87716E5	1.32351E5	-6.02702E5	-58599.46541	2.498	26	.019
Pair 3	2004-05	3.88590E5	8.05109E5	1.54943E5	-7.07080E5	-70099.23622	2.508	26	.019
Pair 4	2005-06	3.63820E5	7.54387E5	1.45182E 5	-6.62245E5	-65393.91825	2.506	26	.019
Pair 5	2006-07	4.21620E5	8.69207E5	1.67279E5	-7.65467E5	-77773.28466	2.520	26	.018

the open markets. This is an important consideration, since the proposed entitlement of 7 kgs per capita per month for the priority category, does not cover their total consumption requirement, necessitating the purchase of the balance food grain from the open market.

Conclusion

The World Food Summit of 1996 defined food security as existing "when all people at all times have access to sufficient, safe, nutritious food to maintain a healthy and active life". Commonly, the concept of food security is defined as including both physical and economic access to food that meets people's dietary needs as well as their food preferences. In many countries, health problems related to dietary excess are an ever increasing threat, In fact, malnutrition and food borne diarrhoea are become double burden. Food security is one convenient for agricultural and economic development of the every country. Because every agricultural products have more demand for living things. In the context of production basis the Indian economy have some sufficient growth to maintain the food security level in the nation as whole. In the above statically analysis we knew the both production in acres of lands and yielding have significant level and it analyzed for food condition and security aspects for future needs of the people in the country.

REFERENCES

FAO (1996) *Declaration on World Food Security*. World Food Summit, Rome.

Government of India (2010) "State-wise area and Production of Spices", Ministry of Agriculture.

Government of India , Commissioner of Agricultural Marketing and Agricultural Business, Chennai-32.

Spice Board of India in Various Versions.

WHO (2007), *Diplomacy and Health Foreign Policy*, Trade.

Index